"Stories I Haven't Told"
(From Barefoot Farm-Girl to CEO in America)

Memoirs of a Depression Baby

Dorothy May Mercer
(1932-   )

©Mercer Publications & Ministries, Inc.
Stanwood, Michigan
USA

"Stories I Haven't Told"

ABOUT THIS BOOK;

Born and raised on a Michigan farm during the Great Depression, Dorothy tells stories about her remarkable life with insight and wit. She brings the scenes to life with repartee and colorful descriptions so real that you will easily imagine yourself in the scene. Details of farm life during the 1930s are fascinating for the uninitiated and quite real for those few who remember those days. Her life has had its share of love, romance, adventure, close-calls, success, failure, faith, joy and tragedy. She makes it real in a way that will bring nods, smiles and a tear or two. You will get to know her as a real person and friend. You can read this book all at once, or one scene a day, without getting lost. Each scene is written to stand alone as well as being part of the overall plot. Are you one that likes to read the last chapter first? There is no penalty for skipping. Just enjoy it any way you like.

Praise for "Stories I Haven't Told"

"Mercer's book is a heartwarming story of love and life during the Great Depression. True-to-life details make the narrative vivid and suspenseful. If you lived then, you'll smile in reflection. If you didn't, you'll enjoy seeing what life was like during a simpler time that now seems otherworldly."

–Margaret Maunder, Peabody Award journalist,
Author of "Those Darn Lawyers"

"Loved your book! It's fascinating! Couldn't put it down."
–D.N.M.
"What a great legacy you have written. Thank you, thank you."
–A.E.C.
"Keep on telling those stories…"   –T.L.W.

ISBN 13: 978-0-9827189-1-9

© Copyright 2010 by Mercer Publications & Ministries, Inc.
8651 Mohawk Ct.; Stanwood, Michigan USA 49346-9644

Visit us at www.mercerpublications.com

To Miss Amy Lynn Watkins, my indefatigable editor and granddaughter, who inspired in me an interest in family history.

To my husband, Mr. David Neal Mercer, who insisted my life story was very interesting.

For my grandchildren, Amy, Emily, Kendal, Alden, Byron, Grant, and their children yet to come.

Table of Contents

May, 2009

Acknowledgements:

By definition, an autobiography is a story about one's life. However, by nature, I am disinclined to talk much, especially about myself. Nevertheless, it may be instructive, perhaps even useful, for my descendants, in their own struggles through life, to know some of my strengths, weaknesses, pitfalls and pratfalls. I shall attempt to keep the story about *my* life as it relates to the people around me and not get lost in telling someone else's story. (That should be their book.) I shall disclose some of my own dark secrets while trying to refrain from divulging the secrets of others, unless it is vital to the story and the party has either passed on to a better life or is too old to care.

I would be remiss not to give credit to my granddaughters who have shown an interest in me, and who have prodded me with questions about my childhood, *or was it simply a school assignment?* In them, I see much better versions of what I once was. Also, to my husband of fifty-eight years, who, having read a first draft of the first experimental chapters, embarrassed me by raving to all and sundry about how wonderful my book is going to be.

This book was greatly improved by the excellent editing by my eldest granddaughter Amy Lynn Watkins, who is an experienced writer and editor. Amy perused more than one hundred thousand words with an eagle eye. No extra space or misplaced comma escaped her attention. She found more than eight hundred misspellings, errors and typos. If any were missed it is my fault entirely. No doubt I sneaked them in after Amy had finished her work. She made herself available to me for patient answers to endless questions. Also, she offered several suggestions of deletions and additions that improved the manuscript. Thank you, Amy. Watch that girl. Someday she will be a famous writer.

Finally, I'd like to leave something worthwhile behind, when I vanish into dust.

Dorothy Mercer

Chapter One

March 17, 1951
Concord, Michigan, USA

It was a beautiful spring day, unseasonably warm for Lower Michigan, sunny with a high of 70 degrees. My 18-year-old bridegroom, Neal Mercer, waited at the altar, flanked by his best man and two groomsmen, opposite two of my best friends as bridesmaids and my 11-year-old sister, Anna, as maid of honor. Some had suggested she was too young and would serve better as a junior bridesmaid. But I loved her, wanted her and have never regretted my choice. Bless my mother, she never objected either. She was married at eighteen, herself.

The only suggestion my parents made was that it might be better to wait a while to get married, perhaps until Neal and I had finished at least one year of college. But he and I had pledged to wait until marriage to have sexual relations and we were unable to wait any longer. Now, from the perspective of 58 years of marriage, that seems awfully young, but at the time we didn't think so.

Small town tradition called for the groom's friends to meet after the ceremony and decorate the get-away vehicle. Conversely, the groom took pains to hide it in a secret place so that no monkey business could take place. The groom needed a trusted friend to guard the vehicle and bring it around just in time for the couple to escape on their honeymoon, hoping to lose any pursuers. Woe unto any newly married couple whose hiding place was discovered. Not only would the car be covered with "Just Married" signs, paper streamers and tin cans to rattle behind, but sometimes "friends" took fiendish delight in soaping the car with suggestive slogans and even rummaging through the bride's suitcase to tie her underwear in knots, or worse. When the bride and groom took off in their freshly decorated car, gleeful friends would follow, tooting horns, laughing and generally cutting up.

Our reception was held in the basement of the Methodist church, directly after the ceremony, therefore the reception was "dry" and relatively short. There was no big dinner as is customary in the 21st century, just punch, coffee and wedding cakes served by the church ladies. I kept careful track of expenses. Our wedding cost about $250, including my gown[1], the attendants' gowns, engraved invitations, photographer, flowers, food and music.

Fortunately, Neal had done a good job of hiding the car, so we were spared any vandalism and my trousseau was intact. However, there was no escaping the entourage of friends following us around the small town in a raucous parade. We happened to be riding in my folks' rusty old 1940 Ford sedan with holes in the floor boards that one could see right through.

We left town by a circuitous route, hoping to loose our followers by tearing up and down some of the gravel roads. An especially hilly one was a teenagers' favorite known as "Monkey-Run" because of the sharp and tight roller-coaster hills and deep ruts. It was springtime and the road had turned to mud. As such it was nearly impassable. As we slogged through the mire, we lost most of our followers, but the muddy water came splashing up through the floor boards and nearly ruined the white satin train of my wedding gown.

We stopped at my farm home long enough for me to change into my honeymoon outfit, kiss my parents goodbye and change to our own car that we had bought for $50. It was a Chrysler HydroDrive, one of the first automatic transmissions. Neal had found a great motel near Kalamazoo that had a restaurant and an attached and enclosed garage with each of the units. Thus, we could hide the car from view, sparing us any concern about being discovered by any scouting parties bent on interrupting our first night of love-making together.

We were worried about another tradition of small towns known as a "belling". This would take place either during the honeymoon or as soon as possible after the couple returned. Friends would get together after dark carrying every known device for making noise, from bells to pots and pans and crosscut saws. They would quietly creep up on the sweetly snoozing honeymoon cottage and begin making a huge clatter, the point being to

---

[1] See wedding photos at the end of the book.

interrupt the loving turtledoves, if possible. Nothing would do except for the couple to rise from bed and invite everyone in for refreshments. We kept a supply of soft drinks ready, but when we survived the first three months without any "belling" we relaxed and decided that our friends had moved on to other things.

*   *   *

Chapter Two

"Grief-Stricken"

It was early morning. Five and one half years later, I awoke to the gray November drizzle outside as it dripped off the barren limbs of the trees scraping outside my window. As awareness gradually entered my consciousness, I realized something was different. Dave had left for the office. I called him by his first name now. Ever since he entered the Army he went by his first name, David, instead of his middle name, Neal.

"What was so different?" I asked myself, as I hauled out of bed and drifted toward the bathroom. Fortunately, Dave had left the coffee pot on warm. As I sat in the back room taking my first sip and vacantly staring off into the backyards of the closest neighbor's houses, it suddenly dawned on me. Last night was the first time in more than a year when I hadn't cried myself to sleep. November seemed to be the turning point in my long year of grief over the loss of our baby son, Jeffrey David Mercer, November 2, 1955. Dave was still a young man, only 24. Perhaps he was puzzled by my endless tears, but he always supported me and did the best he could. Other friends and family members had no idea of my lonely nights quietly crying myself to sleep. They wouldn't have understood. Beyond the first spate of sympathy, it was expected that life should go on. "Dave and Dorothy are young," they said. "They could have more children, so what was the problem?"

Looking back, years later, I realize I should have had grief counseling, possibly a support group. But we were too young to know better, so we muddled through. Besides, counseling had a stigma against it back then. One didn't turn easily in that direction. And so, when we drove home from a gathering of friends or family, Dave comforted me as best he could whenever I burst into tears over some comment made over someone's babies or children. "I'm sorry, Honey," I would plead, "but, I just can't bear to be around people when they talk about their children. I can't understand how they can be so callous. Don't they know I'm hurting?" *Didn't they know that I had failed to conceive again?*

I finally began to claw out of my deep hole only after Dave let me get a job. At first he didn't want his wife to work. "After all, a man's place is to support his wife," he said. *And her place is at home.* That sounds so quaint today – chauvinistic, too. But back then it was the norm. Perhaps he understood that I needed to get out of the house in order to heal; perhaps he was just desperate to have me happy again. I started working at Polachek's fabric store in Jackson. It wasn't long before I knew all the fabrics so well I could tell by feel just what the content was and what percentage of each fiber. I also had the prices and widths memorized, knew just how much yardage it took for each size and garment, could cut a straight line across the fabric and swiftly fold it into a neat package. I discovered I was a pretty good salesman, too.

*   *   *

Eighteen months after our baby, Jeffrey's, death, I confirmed I was pregnant again. I was of two minds over this news: naturally I was relieved of the worry over my inability to conceive a second time, but, at the same time, there was no avoiding the fear of repeating the outcome of my first pregnancy.

This time I was sick, but not as sick as a dog, the way I had been with Jeffrey. His pregnancy had made me so sick that I couldn't keep anything down for months. Dave had to send me back to the farm to stay with my mom and dad, because I required full-time care. Fortunately, back then we had effective nausea drugs that helped. Nowadays, they have all been taken off the market because of nuisance lawsuits. Without nausea drugs, I don't think I could have lived through a pregnancy. Seriously.

Even with the drugs, I needed to learn all the tricks for coping with nausea. Before retiring I lined up my supplies close by. Upon first awakening in the morning, I swallowed my pink and blue nausea pill. Without moving a muscle or raising my head, I lay perfectly still, breathing shallowly for 15 minutes. Next, I would swallow a tiny nibble of a soda cracker and wait another 15 minutes, then another and another in the same fashion, until the whole cracker was down. It might take me an hour to get my stomach settled enough to get out of bed.

* * *

1939

Anna Marie (Unk)   Dorothy May (Dort)

Chapter Three

"Sister 'Unk'"

March 18, 1939

C ousin Hilda, puleeeeeeze, can I go home now?" I whined for the umpteenth time. Too young to know better, I was expert at wheedling my way from one of my favorite people.

"Not yet, darlin'. How about another cookie?" Hilda Eggleston was my adult cousin.

Whining hasn't worked with Hilda, I'll try her mother. "Aunt Minnie, I want to go home, now, please."

"Here, honey, I'll look for some colored funny papers that you haven't seen."

I shook my head, vigorously turning down one of my favorite activities: Mom couldn't afford to buy newspapers.

"Ok, let me see, how about another puzzle?" (Another favorite)

(It was only years later that I wondered why Aunt Minnie had no husband. On this day, it hadn't yet occurred to me to think that a bit odd. I had no idea where babies came from.)

"We could do another puzzle, one we haven't done too many times already," she said.

"No, thank you, Aunt Minnie".

"Would you like to come upstairs with me to my room. I'll let you play with my jewelry."

A stray tear began to form in my eye. "I just want to go home."

At six and a half years old and bright as a new penny, I wasn't so easily fooled. *Something was wrong at home.* It had been a long morning. We had a great time feeding the bunnies, running up the hill and down, playing Rummy and Old Maid, baking cookies and getting my straight hair curled with the curling irons that were heated on the wood stove. It was important to get them hot enough to curl without getting them so hot that they burned the hair. The iron must sizzle just so when a wet finger tapped on it.

Aunt Minnie and Cousin Hilda had outdone themselves entertaining Esther's little girl from across and down a ways. They had rolled out all their tricks to keep me busy, acting like everything was normal. I loved to go over to Eggleston's. This was one of my favorite entertainments so it hadn't been hard at all fooling me – for the first few hours.

At long last Hilda relented. "All right, child, I'll ring up your folks and see if it is OK for you to come home."

Fear clutched at my heart. It was strange indeed that Mama wouldn't want me to come home. *What could be wrong?* The whole delaying tactic was a new experience for me. *Usually they were more than happy for me to go home.* Hilda picked up the receiver from the wooden telephone hanging on the dining room wall, listening carefully to make sure there wasn't anyone else on the eight-party line, grasped the crank and gave it the familiar two shorts and a long.

"Aloh...aloh, Leon?... (pause)....ayah.....ayah....ayah....," Hilda nodded.

I could make out my father's voice on the other end of the line, but I couldn't hear what he was saying. A smile lit up her face. She looked at me, "I guess you can go home now, Dorothy, but your dad says to be careful crossing the road. Your mother has a surprise for you. "Look both ways," she shouted at my retreating back as I skipped happily out the door.

I dashed into the farm kitchen door and skidded to a halt at the figures gathered around the dining room table. There was Daddy and Dr. Keefer huddled over something wiggling on the table. Bug-eyed and frozen in place I gazed in wonderment at the tiny figure lying on a cloth under the bright chandelier. Dr. Keefer seemed to be fussing over it, doing something. Daddy smiled at me, "Hello, Dorothy, glad you finally came home. Say hello to your new baby sister."

This was the happiest surprise of my lonely life; so far, a life not exactly full of surprises. My fondest wish had come true. "Ooh, can I see?" I stretched up as tall as I could and gazed in wonder. How I had longed for a baby sister and teased my parents unmercifully to get me a sister to love, someone to play with. I was mesmerized. She was the most beautiful thing I had ever laid eyes on.

I loved my baby sister, as did everyone. She was the sweetest thing. As Anna Marie grew into a toddler, she was so cute and plump we dubbed her "Dumplin'" and "Punkin" which eventually got shortened to "Punkie" and then "Unk". Poor dear, she was known to us as "Unk" until she grew into a lovely, slim young lady, too smart and beautiful for that nickname.

Anna was to be my dearest and only sister, playing flute to my piano, treasurer to my president, and mother to my two nieces.

*   *   *

Chapter Four

"Earliest Memories"

It is Summer 1992.

We sit sipping coffee at my sister, Anna's, kitchen table on Reynolds Road, overlooking her bird feeder hanging from a tree in her spacious back yard. "There's a letter here I want you to see." Anna hefts a box onto her lap and leafs through a stack of old letters. As executor of Mother's estate, Anna has the unenviable task of going through Mother's things. Having survived the Great Depression and a long married life, Mother was a poor farmer's wife. She raised four kids. Struggling to make ends meet. Mother knew how to "make do". She never threw anything useful away.

"Ah, here's the letter I'm looking for," Anna says. Curious, I open the envelope and read from the yellowed lines, "Dear Esther,". The date is 1932, the depths of the Great Depression. A woman's hand continues, "Congratulations to you and Leon on the birth of your new daughter, Dorothy May. I'm sure she's very sweet and precious, indeed, after two sons. However, I must say, you are both very brave to be taking on another child during these times. I wish you the best. How are Leon and the boys? Is Leon going to be able to hang on to the farm?"

It was a big productive farm, as farms went in those days: over 200 acres in Southern Michigan. Dad was proud of it. Already in his forties, he had worked long and hard to achieve his dream farm. But he would keep it less than another three years. The economic depression was sucking up every cent. The bank was bleeding him dry. By 1935, he was forced to give up and move his growing family to a much smaller farm of only 60 acres that would never be a farming success. Dad avoided the humiliation of foreclosure by trading the farm for a rented house in the nearby city of Jackson that never amounted to anything and was eventually lost too. Dad was not cut out to be a landlord.

Although I was only two and a half when we moved, I remember many things from those times. Too young to realize the ramifications of a worsening economy, I had been successfully sheltered in our little world. The farthest away I wandered was to visit our neighbors, Valla and Jesse Gardner, and Bob and Ruth Rowlison, who had the nearest telephone. I could talk and run fast as the wind. On more than one occasion Mother sent me flying to their house to have Mrs. Rowlison phone the fire department because the boys had set fire to the straw stack across the road and behind our barn. First, Mother would have sent one of the boys out to the field to summon Dad. Together they would fight the fire with buckets of water from the well until the volunteer firemen arrived.

There was a splendid and fascinating water well right outside our kitchen door. Sometimes Daddy would lift me up high so I could peer over the circular stone wall protecting it and call down the deep cavern that could easily swallow up a little girl. At these times, he always held me tight and warned me never to touch or go near the apparatus. A wooden windmill was positioned high up over the hole, wildly spinning away in a most wondrous whirling cacophony. Even though I wasn't really thirsty I would beg for a drink merely to watch in fascination as Dad loosened the chain that held it, engaging a system of noisy gears and long poles. A bucket of cool fresh water at the end of a long rope would slowly rise to the top. Dad would dip a long handled tin cup into the water and offer me a drink. Nothing will ever again equal that marvelous slightly rusty taste or that feeling of love and security in my father's arms.

Most of the time, Dad had to work, dawn to dusk. But there are other memories of him during those early times. Dad was the one who rocked me to sleep at night in a squeaky wooden rocking chair. It never took long to go to sleep, listening to the monotonous rhythmic squeak-squawk. I would have had a busy day of playing outside in the fresh air or "helping" mom in the kitchen, plying her with endless questions.

"What makes that sound, Mommy?"

"That's a train whistle, Dorothy."

"What's a train?"

"Well, it's a big strong engine that pulls a long line of train cars. The cars carry things all over the country, like corn and pigs and automobiles for rich people. You must never go back in the field near the train."

"Why?"

"Because tramps sneak rides on the trains. You must never go near a tramp."

"Why?"

"Because a tramp is a man who might grab you and hurt you. Promise me you will never go near the train tracks or talk to a tramp."

Mother regularly warned me to stay away from tramps. Thus, I was truly frightened of them, and so was she, although her country rules of strict hospitality forbade her to ever turn one away. Sometimes a raggedy, dirty, bearded man would come to our back door and beg Mama for food. I would cling to her skirts and she would whisper to me, "Hide and be still", while she hastily prepared a plate of food. She cautiously handed it out the door, then quickly closed and latched it tight. At those times, she, no doubt, wished that Leon wasn't working far out in the fields. Her only protection was a big friendly collie dog named Maggie. Mother was only sixty-one inches tall and weighed maybe 100 pounds or so.

By then, my elder brother was probably taller than she and well on his way to 6 feet 2. My only memory of my brothers at that age was of mother begging them to fetch some wood for the kitchen cook stove. Mother wasn't much on discipline, so they rarely complied with alacrity. The wood bin had openings on two sides. A person could lift the hand hewn cover and fill the bin from outside the house. Another cover from inside the house allowed a person to reach in and retrieve logs for the kitchen or the sitting room stoves.

Now and then we would go together to a meeting held at

the corner country one-room school house. The atmosphere would be stuffy and overheated from the pot-bellied stove and the perspiration of the bodies of all our neighbors clad in clean overalls and heavy coats. The ladies wore their best dresses and go-to-meeting hats and gloves. I sat on Mother's or Daddy's lap. The purpose of these meetings wasn't important to a child of two.

Once, we had a visit from relatives: Dad's sister and her family. They were well dressed and brought gifts. They gave me an incredibly beautiful velvet dress with a white lace collar, such as my wondering eyes had never seen. I tried it on and stood still for them as they took my picture with the other fancy device they brought along: a camera. It was the only picture ever made of me as a small child. (I know because I saw it in their album, sixty years later, when I visited my West Coast cousins.) Everyone conversed far into the night. Our relatives waxed eloquent over the wonders of their hometown, a place called Seattle. I listened for as long as I could stay awake, tucked under my quilts on my canvas cot in the dark corner of the sitting room.

Except for those times, farmers' families retired early, me to my cot and my parents and brothers upstairs to their bedrooms. Being the youngest and still a tiny tot, I was allowed to sleep near the only source of heat. There were a few nights when my parents remained, quietly whispering to each other from the far side of the darkened room. From time to time one of them would tiptoe to my cot, feel my brow and urge me to drink, or take a spoon full of foul tasting liquid. I wasn't feeling too perky, but their strange behavior worried me more than that. Fortunately it never lasted more than a few days and nights and I was soon up and running around as usual.

It is amazing how much freedom a little girl was allowed in those days. So long as there were no tramps around, which was most of the time, I could wander at will in the house, yard and barns. I must inform Mother if I went back to the fields to find Daddy, or if I skipped down the gravel road to visit Ruth Rowlison. Pedophilia was neither feared nor understood. Our house was never locked. There were no vandals or thieves. After all, there was nothing of value to steal.

Mother enjoyed wash days. We journeyed to the house of my grandmother Dodes. They seemed to have a fine time laughing and talking as they moved about the kitchen amid the wash tubs. The only thing I remember about my grandmother is her legs and her skirt billowing about them as she took charge of the scrubbing and rinsing. Occasionally they would allow me to try to turn the crank on the wringer. They had to hold me up with one hand and assist my feeble cranking efforts with the other. It was even more fun to feed the sopping wet clothes into the wringer as they disappeared into the rollers on one side and came out flattened and half dry on the other.

Next we proceeded out into the back yard of what would one day in the future be my childhood home. Chickens pecked around in the grass. A thin rope would be strung from pole to pole. Mother shook the clothes out, one by one, and hung them up to dry. I was allowed to hand her the clothes pins until I became bored with that and turned to chasing the chickens or frolicking among the sheets as they snapped in the wind.

*   *   *

"Mother, Mother, why are you crying?" *Something must be terribly wrong. Mother never cries.*

"Sh," she hushed me and sniffed as tears rolled down her cheeks.

It was 1934. A small crowd of friends and neighbors were standing amid carved oblong stones in a grove of trees. Off to one side a man dressed in somber black read from a book in low tones. Eyes wide, I hid behind Mother's skirt and held on tight in mystified alarm. It was the end of those happy times in grandmother's kitchen and the beginning of our families' move to the sixty acres on Pulaski Road.

*   *   *

Years later the mystery was solved when I was old enough to understand death. Grandmother Dodes and Doris Railer, mother and daughter, were killed in a horrible auto accident. It happened just a hundred yards from their destination driveway. Somehow, the Model T or Model A Ford auto had stalled as they paused in front of the neighbor's house. The driver, Doris's eldest son, Clair, heard a distant car engine whining down the hills from the South, seemingly at a high rate of speed. In a panic, he leaped out and began to turn the crank to restart the engine. Realizing their peril, Doris began to push her mother out the door just as the speeding vehicle plowed into the rear of their stalled deathtrap, with a sickening crash. Clair had leaped to safety just in time, but Grandmother was thrown wide and died instantly. Sadly Doris was critically injured as well and lived only a few days. Thus, what remained of my Mother's family of origin was wiped out in one swift blow. The awful day of the funeral would remain indelibly imprinted on my mind.

*   *   *

Chapter Five

"Pre-School Years 1935-1939"

I was too young to understand the dire economic situation the country was suffering, and knowing nothing else, life seemed perfectly normal for me. Since Grandma's death, we now had a home and farm to sustain us. Mother had inherited half the 60 acre farm. She and Dad bought the remaining half from the other heir, Doris's widowed husband. Uncle Bill had a good farm of his own about five miles away on which he could raise my five cousins. The youngest was my only playmate my own age.

My two older brothers hung around with neighbor boys their own age. I alternated between being a pest and a plaything for them. With little else to do, I tagged along after them when they hiked in the woods or played in the barns. We went swimming at the County Park on Swains Lake, adjoining our property. The park also had swings, a slide, teeter-totter and merry-go-round. We played Hide and Seek, Anti-I-Over, Mother-May-I, Hop-Scotch and Jump rope with one of mother's clothes line ropes. Another favorite was to climb out on the lower barn's shiny tin roof, run and slide down it and fly off into the straw stack below.

My misfortune was that one of the boys' favorite games was to tease and torment their little sister. There were four years between each of us, so I was outnumbered, outclassed and outmaneuvered. The elder was the ringleader, and the rest more or less went along. A favorite tease was acorn war. When the giant oak tree in our yard shed its acorns the boys would use me for target practice. When acorns weren't available they shot me with a B-B gun. You will notice that none of the games required toys, tools, or props, except for the B-B gun. I don't know where they got that as we had no money to buy it. Must have belonged to the neighbor. I was gullible, young and eager to please. I would bend over for them so they could shoot me in the fanny.

In the fall, we liked to rake leaves into rows and circles and play a game of chase called Fox and Geese. Sometimes we raked them into a huge pile and jumped into it. One time I jumped into the pile and stirred up a swarm of angry bumble bees. My agonizing screams from the burning hot stings must have aroused latent sympathy. My brothers actually carried me inside to mother with tender concern. We also played Fox and Geese in the winter by stamping out a maze in the snow. Snow provided other sport, such as snowball fights, making snowmen, igloos, tunneling into snow banks and sliding downhill.

I never learned many card games, because Dad's religion prohibited playing cards as well as smoking, dancing and drinking. But we had a radio and loved listening to the popular shows, such as The Lone Ranger, The Green Hornet, Amos and Andy, Jack Benny Show, Your Hit Parade, Fred and Gracie Allen, Inner Sanctum Mystery Theater and singers such as Dinah Shore, Bing Crosby and Frank Sinatra.

*   *   *

Speaking of religion, we never missed a Sunday. What social life we had centered on the church. Dad was a pillar of the church, one of the trustees and taught the adult Sunday school class all of his life. Mother was in the Ladies Aid Society. She helped put on money-raising bazaars, church suppers and wedding and funeral luncheons. The Sunday school picnic, held once a year at the Swains Lake County Park, was a highlight. I loved the organized games, such as the penny scramble and the three-legged-race and the homemade ice cream for dessert. But my all-time favorite was the Christmas Eve program. I was mesmerized by the grand finale – the arrival of Santa Claus amid much, "Ho-Ho-Ho, Merry Christmas," and jingling of bells. Every child received a small cardboard box with circus animals decorating it. A white string served as a handle. Inside the box was filled with hard candy treats. My favorites were the long pale yellow ones with the peanut butter filling. We also got a candy cane. As each child's name was called we were allowed to go up to the front and receive our gifts directly from Santa's hand. You see, there was no problem with so-called separation of church and state. Whoever heard of such nonsense? The whole town was made up of white, Protestant Christians, 605 of them to be exact.

The Christmas Eve program consisted of various singing of carols, vignettes on the Christmas story and recitations. While still very young, I gave a recitation from memory of the poem, "T'was the Night Before Christmas". I can still recite that poem to this day, seventy-one years later. At an earlier occasion, at the age of three, my father actually made me get up in front of the whole Sunday school and sing "Jesus Loves Me" right on key. I was so terribly shy that he had to force me to do it. But after I received my first taste of real applause, I was hooked.

* * *

The Depression was a terrible burden on the adults, but I was too young to appreciate any different kind of life. We had plenty of food from the farm. So what if we only had meat once a week? We had rich home-churned butter, real whipped cream and milk from the cows and eggs from the chickens. Eggs were our cash crop as well, so we only ate a chicken if she stopped laying. Those chickens were nothing like the fryers we buy today. Rather, they were lean and tough. But mother knew how to make them delicious, by long and slow cooking. Once a year in the wintertime, Dad butchered a steer or pig. We kept the meat out on the front porch to keep it from spoiling as we had no refrigeration. For a while then, we ate lots of meat, until it had to be preserved. At that point, Mother would can the rest. Mother did not own a pressure canner. She used the water-bath method for everything except tomatoes. For those she used the open kettle method. We never got sick from her canned food. It was delicious and nutritious. I count my slim strong body to that upbringing, lots of fresh air, exercise and food from the farm. Junk food was unknown.

Mother also canned everything from her huge summer garden, enough to last the winter. Dad grew several acres of potatoes. They were kept in a bin in our unheated basement. Throughout the year we ate potatoes at every supper. Many times, scalloped potatoes were our only main dish. Mother would make a huge round enameled deep pan of scalloped potatoes, with flour, milk and butter. The growing boys could eat the whole thing at one meal. Mother knew lots of different ways to serve potatoes and I loved them all, but my favorite was potato chips deep-fried in lard. We also had a lot of apples, carrots and other root vegetables because they could be kept fresh in the root cellar. Parsnips were a favorite, because they were left in the ground to freeze and dug up in the Spring. Freezing made them very sweet. We also had canned peaches and pears and other canned vegetables such as green beans, corn, tomatoes and peas. Some of our food was dried as well, such as sweet corn, beans and popcorn.

Popcorn grown on the farm is similar in appearance to sweet corn, except the ears and kernels are smaller. After harvesting, we peeled back the husks exposing the ears. Several would be grasped together by the husks, tied with twine and hung up to dry. When dried the kernels could be removed from the cobs by hand and stored in quart mason jars where they would keep indefinitely. When heat is applied, the tiny bit of moisture remaining in the kernel turns to steam, thus expanding and causing the kernel to explode. After many months, if the kernels become too dry to pop, a few drops of water added to the mason jar solved the problem. We popped the corn in lard, melted in a cooking pot shaken over a hot fire in the cook stove. Butter and salt were added later.

Every Sunday night we had popped corn and apples. Sometimes, homemade chocolate fudge was added to the treat. At Christmastime we strung popcorn for decoration and made popcorn balls.

The only food Mother bought in the store was salt, pepper, a few spices, oatmeal, flour and sugar. Sometimes she had flour ground at the mill from our own wheat

.

*   *   *

Trips to the mill in Concord were wonderful fun. I can still smell the odors of ground wheat, mingled with corn and oats. The sounds of the grinding machinery made a great racket too. While Dad did his business, I could peruse the notices tacked on the walls for Auctions.

On Saturdays, we might all pile onto the wagon and go to a farm auction. Mother would pack a picnic to supplement the free coffee and lemonade. It was a social occasion where we might meet old friends and make new ones among the farm families in attendance. This was the best way to acquire used equipment for the farm as we certainly couldn't afford to buy new.

Mother seldom bid on anything. For one thing, she was shy, for another she was short. But Mother had a particular hankering for an ice box. Now that we had a lake we had a source of free ice. An ice box would be an improvement to Mother's kitchen. One day we were all together at an auction. Mother spotted the perfect ice box made of oak with a tight fitting door and several shelves. It had a compartment lined with tin on top for the ice. This had a drain hole with a rubber hose attached for the melt water to escape. The ice box would fit nicely into our pantry, on the wall away from the window. Mother teased Dad to bid on it for her. "Well, all right, Esther, I'll try. Maybe it will go cheap," he said. "But I have my eye on that cultivator too, so we'll see."

When the cultivator came up, Dad put in a beginning bid. The bidding was furious and soon it was too high for us, so Dad dropped out. He managed to get a box of miscellaneous hand tools for fifty cents. So far, so good. I saw a pair of ice skates go for a quarter, but I didn't expect anything for myself. I kept my fingers crossed for Mom. As the auctioneer moved over to the kitchen things, many of the other people left. After all, the men had come for the farm tools and implements. Dad whispered to Mom, "I have just three dollars left." The auctioneer didn't want to lose all his audience, so he moved quickly through the kitchen things, pots, pans, miscellaneous dishes, beds, and cupboards. At last he came to the ice box. "We'll begin the bidding on this beautiful item, ladies and gentleman at five dollars, do I hear five dollars?" Silence. "Surely, someone will take this for four dollars, do I hear four dollars?" Silence. "Don't tell me you all have ice boxes in your kitchens, ladies? What'll it be…do I hear three dollars? Two dollars?"

Mother poked Dad in the ribs. He shook his head, "Wait, Esther," he said.

"But, Leon, what if…?" Mother was worried.

"Fifty cents," Dad shouted, "I'll bid fifty cents."

"I have fifty cents, do I hear one dollar?" sang the

auctioneer. Silence. "One dollar, do I hear one dollar for this excellent ice box?" Silence. "Do I hear seventy five cents?" Silence. "Going. Going. Gone! To the gentleman in the back." Down came his gavel.

Mother got her new used ice box for fifty cents. Jubilation reigned on the way home.

Dad spent his spare time during the fall, building an ice house in the back yard and stocking it with saw dust from sawing operations. The ice house was solidly built of boards from the farm, and lined with tar paper for insulation.

The following February after the lake was frozen solid and the ice was plenty thick, Dad and the boys hitched up the horses to the wagon and drove onto Swains Lake to cut blocks of ice for the ice house. Using ice tongs to load the blocks onto the wagon, they transported their cargo up the lane to the ice house and unloaded it, carefully packing sawdust all around each block. The following summer, we had plenty of ice for Mom's ice box, as well as all we needed to make homemade ice cream.

*   *   *

Say all you want about modern ice cream that is "to die for", but nothing will ever compare with homemade ice cream made on the farm with non-pasteurized real cream from a Jersey cow, known for its high fat content. Within minutes of milking the cows, Dad brought the milk in to cool. Enough whole milk was saved for Mother's use in the kitchen. The rest was poured into a machine called a milk separator. You turned a crank on the separator which whirled the milk until the cream was separated. This was sold to a commercial "creamery" that turned it into butter. The leftover skim milk was fed to the hogs.

1917 Esther at age sixteen.

Sometimes mother used some cream to make butter for the kitchen, using a wooden churn. That was a good chore for little kids, like me. Other times she whipped the cream with an eggbeater, adding sugar and real vanilla, to serve on top of desserts such as fruit pies or jello.

During the summer we made ice cream on two special occasions, the Ruff and the Dodes family reunions. Both were Mother's relatives. Dozens of descendents of the founders of each family gathered around long rows of tables set up under the maple trees on our front lawn. Tables and chairs were borrowed from the Methodist church in Concord. Each family brought their own table service and dishes to pass. Those ladies could cook! The tables would soon be covered with colorful cloths and groaning with food. After the meal, as the tables were being cleared, it was time to start making ice cream.

Our ice cream freezer had two main parts. The outer part was a tall waterproof bucket, made of heavy wooden slats held tightly together with iron straps. The smaller inner piece was a tall, two gallon cylindrical tin container for the cream. A ladle was made to fit inside that would stir the ingredients. A device fitted to that was attached to a hand crank by a system of gears. When the handle was cranked it caused the ladle to turn, keeping the ingredients constantly stirred just enough to make the ice cream smooth and lump free. The filled container was placed in the wooden bucket, crushed ice and salt were layered around it and the cranking device attached to the top. All was in readiness for the cranking ceremony. Traditionally, the little kids took the first turns while the cranking was still easy, moving up to the older kids as the cranking became more difficult. As the salt melted the ice, its chilling properties would pass into the cream. From time to time the ice would be pushed down with a wooden spoon and more ice and salt added. It was important to keep the drain hole unplugged, so no salt water rose high enough to contaminate the ice cream. At the end, the strongest older youths took the final turns until the ice cream became too hard for stirring.

At that point, Dad would be summoned for the final step. After removing the cranking mechanism, he carefully cleared the ice and salt from the top of the container, lifted the lid and pulled out the ladle with a large pair of pliers. We watched eagerly as he scraped the excess off the ladle and placed it back into the cylinder. Then the ladle would be deposited into a waiting dish pan, where the youngest kids waited, ready to attack it with spoons and tongues. This was a mere taste of coming delights for the remaining ice cream had to "cure" for what seemed like an eternity. The cover was replaced on the container. More salt and ice was placed around and the whole thing covered with burlap, while the adults proceeded with the business meeting.

Minutes were duly read from last years' reunion. Oftentimes, a bit of history of the family was read. Marriages, births and deaths were solemnly noted. I liked to stick around for the roll call as each member's name was called. It gave me a special sense of pride to respond with "Here" as my name was called. It felt good to belong to something important.

At last the meeting was over and we could line up with our bowls and spoons as the ice cream was dished out. Mm, it tasted so good and melted just right on our tongues. No embellishments were needed. We took care not to be pigs, lest the extreme cold "go to our heads". Many's the time I fell victim to that mistake. The pain spread from the roof of your mouth up through your facial bones and forehead. The only cure was to open your mouth and rapidly suck air in and out until warmth took the pain away.

*   *   *

I never wore shoes in the summertime. When I started school I had one good dress and one pair of Buster Brown shoes for school and for church. Shoes were made entirely of leather, except for the heels which could be of hard rubber or leather. When the heels wore down and the soles became thin, Dad would get out his "last" and shoe repair kit. The "last" was an iron device shaped like a foot and fastened to a sturdy wooden post about knee high. Dad would fit the shoe over the last, carefully remove the heel and tack a new heel in place with a small hammer. Next he would carve a piece of leather about the right size for the sole with a sharp jackknife, then carefully glue and tack it into place. The tacks were placed around the edges so as not to work up into the foot later on. After the glue set, Dad would smooth and fit the edges and apply dye and polish for a fresh shine. The next day we were allowed to try them on… mm, good as new!

The boys went through a phase of wearing partial heel plates made of metal, similar to those worn on tap dancing shoes. Supposedly this added protection and kept the heels from wearing off so fast. An added benefit was to add a certain swagger to the walk as the boy would click-clack through the halls at school.

Cash was extremely scarce. We could only afford the bare

necessities. Mother and Dad darned, remodeled, patched and "made do" with what we had. I did not have toys, except for one small naked doll that an aunt gave me. We couldn't afford an automobile.

I can remember driving to church with my dad in a horse and buggy. In the winter our laps and legs would be covered in a cozy horse blanket, not a cloth blanket that goes on a horse, but a blanket made out of a horsehide, with the hair still attached. It never occurred to me to wonder what the horse pulling the buggy thought of that state of affairs.

At other times, I rode to town with Dad in the wagon to take care of some farm business. It might be to visit the hardware or the blacksmith shop. Whenever Dad needed a repair part, he either fashioned it himself, or he took it in to the smithy to make a new one. The smithy would fire up his forge until it roared and glowed red hot. He wore a thick leather apron that completely covered his front, long canvas gloves and a heavy hat with a glass visor that pulled down over his face and neck. After selecting a piece of iron, he grasped it with iron tongs and shoved one end into the forge. Soon the iron part would glow a fierce red, too hot to gaze at with the naked eye. When it was just right, the smithy would pull it out, lay it on a sturdy iron pedestal called an anvil and whack it with a heavy iron mallet, reheating and shaping parts as needed and joining them together until the part was formed.

The smithy also sold horseshoes in various sizes and shapes. Dad let me watch, but I had to stand back when he shod the horses. In school, Dad had been taught to write right-handed, but he hammered with his left hand. He could accurately hammer in those horse shoe nails with a few swift blows.

*   *   *

In our new home on the farm on Pulaski Road, we had a few amenities that weren't available in our previous home. Our eight party line telephone must have pleased mother to no end, for now she could talk with Hilda anytime. Mother grew up in this house, after all, so this was coming home for her. Hilda was her childhood pal, a cousin who lived across the road and down a piece. They "chewed the fat" on the phone nearly every day.

Doors were never locked in the country. No one came to the front door and only strangers bothered to knock. Friends came to the back door, unannounced, opened it and hollered, "Hallo, is anybody home?" Visitors were frequent and always welcome. Traveling salesmen were a frequent treat, too, breaking the monotony. It might be Harold Andrews, the insurance man, who sold Dad my first $1,000 policy, or the Watkins man who was a regular.

The telephone was an oblong wooden box that hung on the wall in our dining room. When in use, one lifted an ear piece, which was called a receiver, off a hook on the side of the box in much the same manner as one would lift a nozzle off a gas pump nowadays. When the hook raised up it automatically engaged the receiver. One held that to the ear and spoke into the mouthpiece jutting out from the front of the box. All eight customers were hooked together so that all eight phones would ring and all eight could speak and hear at the same time. Thus it was necessary for each party to have a different sounding ring for incoming calls. Our ring was two shorts and a long. A single long ring was for the operator, and meant that someone was making an outgoing call. The "Operator" sat at a switchboard at the main office in every small town. She answered the call by plugging in a jack and asking "Number, please?" The caller might say, "Hello, operator" and speak the number, if known. However, just the person's name was sufficient as the operator knew everyone's number. If she didn't she would look it up. She would connect the other end of the cord by means of another jack, then ring the desired combination of rings.

Parties on the line were honor bound to ignore calls meant for someone else on the party line. This prohibition was not strictly observed, however. "Listening in" was a stealthy practice and common pastime, relieving the boredom. One had to lift the receiver very gently so as not to make a "click" and give away one's presence on the line. Also, it was important to cover the mouthpiece so that no sounds from the room would be heard. For the legitimate user prudence dictated that one did not disclose any family secrets on a party line lest they be broadcast to the neighborhood. It wasn't unusual to hear several clicks after one answered the phone. My prankster brothers loved to speak an insult about Hilda after which they might hear a loud crashing noise in their ear as she hung up in disgust.

In our family it was understood that Hilda listened in most of the time. Nothing escaped Hilda's notice. She was the town's source of news. Once a day she would enter our house as was customary without bothering to knock, plop her bulky self down on a kitchen chair and regale Mother with all the latest tidbits of gossip while Mother busied herself in the kitchen. Mother didn't believe in gossip and taught me the same, but she would never offend Hilda. So she listened with polite detachment and cautioned me later not to repeat what I heard.

*   *   *

Another luxury we enjoyed in our new house was a basement with a coal or wood burning furnace. Atop the furnace a metal jacket directed the heat upward through a three foot square iron grate called a register. This, along with the kitchen cook-stove was the sole source of heat in the house. Naturally the further away one was from that heat source, the colder one became. Thus, it was customary to gather around the register in the evenings and listen while Dad or Mother read aloud by lantern-light. A staple for Dad was a well worn Bible story book. I learned the traditional stories at an early age and thus became indoctrinated into Christianity without realizing anything else existed. Other favorite books, borrowed from the town library, were Gulliver's Travels, Swiss Family Robinson, Tom Sawyer, Robinson Crusoe and short stories by Edgar Allen Poe. I learned to read at an early age and have always loved books.

Houses had no insulation in those days, nor did they have storm windows. During the cold winter nights, frost would form on the windows in myriad crystal patterns. It was especially beautiful when the sun shined through. While stirring oatmeal, flipping pancakes and setting out the pure farm butter and maple syrup, Mother would comment, "Looks like ole' Jack Frost came to visit last night. He sure painted up the windows." I loved to stand at the window, licking it with my tongue or drawing patterns in the frost with my fingernail.

Dad and the boys, with the help of a neighbor, harvested plenty of wood off the farm with which to fire the furnace. It was only years later that we were able to afford coal. Trees were felled with a long, thin "cross-cut" saw with handles on both ends. Two men would grasp the saw by the handles and expertly pull it back and forth across the tree trunk in perfect synchronized tandem.

The night before a tree harvest, Dad would sit in the kitchen and gently sharpen the saw-teeth to a razor sharp edge using a fine file about a foot long. There was no escape from the raucous grating sounds from that filing: they set your teeth on edge. The saw would be held in a brace attached to a large, round piece of a log brought in from outside. This was no small task, because the saw had dozens of teeth that had to be precisely filed, just so. Otherwise the saw might catch and buck dangerously as the two men pulled it back and forth through the tree. Felling a huge tree was not for the faint of heart. One of our town's oral histories included the tale of "Charlie" and how he was killed when a tree fell on him. When the tree started to fall with a distinctive crack and crash, the workers ran for their lives.

Once the tree was felled there was plenty of work for everyone, even the smallest family member. The tree had to be trimmed of small branches. Those were dragged away and put into a brush-pile for the wildlife or for later bonfires. The trunk and large limbs were sawed into manageable lengths small enough to fit inside the stove or furnace. These were tossed onto a wagon for hauling up to the house, then tossed onto a wood pile in the backyard for drying and later splitting with a sharp ax. The split logs were neatly stacked into woodpiles where they would remain for several months to dry before they were thrown down the chute into the furnace room. Dad had a sense of humor. He joked that firewood warmed you twice, once when you burned it and once when you split it up.

* * *

Another luxury was indoor water (not indoor plumbing. That came years later). The water well was under the kitchen sink area. A hand pump was positioned directly over the well, attached to a counter next to the sink. This sink was used for all kinds of washing, from dishes and hand laundry to "washing" up before dinner. Full-body baths were held Saturday nights in a wash tub behind the kitchen stove where it was nice and warm. Water was heated in a reservoir permanently attached to the side of the cook-stove or in a large copper kettle set atop the stove. The children took turns in the bath. It felt so good to climb into a clean nightgown and crawl beneath a fresh, air-dried sheet. Notice I said sheet, not sheets. Mother usually changed the sheet on Saturday. She would remove the bottom sheet for Monday's wash and place the relatively clean top sheet on the bottom. A clean sheet became the new top sheet. The covers consisted of three or four hand-made quilts. No one bought blankets in those days, only the cotton or wool batting to fill the quilts. Sometimes the batting was made from wool from our own sheep.

In modern times, quilting has become a highly acclaimed, skilled craft and hobby. But in those days it was a necessity. There is no need here to describe a quilting bee, as much has been made in romanticized folk lore of the social nature of such events. However, in my mind's eye I remember the murmur of ladies' voices as they hummed above the quilt and the filtered light that came through the many colored squares of cloth. I was allowed to play among the forest of legs underneath the quilt. Mother took me everywhere. Her mother and sister were gone. She had no other baby-sitter than my school-age brothers. Told to stay put under the quilt I avoided the heights lest I be stabbed by the sharp needles that were precisely poked through the squares with one hand, grasped and pulled through with the other, and just as swiftly passed back up. The quilts were tied every few inches with strands of woolen yarn. The ladies were skilled at multi-tasking even before the word was invented.

*   *   *

I didn't have cuddly animal toys the way children do today. Who needed them? I had the real thing: kittens, puppies, piglets, calves, colts and lambs. Lambing and sheep shearing were two of the most exciting events of springtime. The morning after lambs were born, Dad allowed me into the pen to pet the oh-so-cuddly newborns. Although I begged to watch, Dad never let me observe animals being born. Thus, I was not introduced to sex education the way one might expect for a farm girl.

Not long after this event, the weather would turn warm and the adult sheep had to be divested of their thick wool coats. Sheep shearing was one of the few tasks that a farmer hired out. "Sheep-shearers" were highly skilled workers who traveled from farm to farm in the springtime. Battings of wool were marketed for that scarce commodity — cash — and they had to be perfectly cut and packaged. Contests were sometimes held to determine the best and most efficient sheep-shearer. Judging was based on time and skill. Timing started when the worker approached the fat, gray, miserably hot flock and ended when the newly naked sheep was released to run away looking shockingly white, having been mercifully relieved of its hot winter coat. The spectacle was similar to the modern day rodeo, except that no horses were involved. First a sheep was grabbed out of the flock, subdued by grasping it firmly around the head and flopping it down on its back with its feet flailing the air amid much bleating and protesting. Eventually the sheep quieted enough to allow the shearer to go to work. He had to carefully trim around the eyes and ears, the tail, and then each hoof and leg. Only then could he attack the belly, quickly finishing up with the back before the stupid sheep realized it was on its feet again. The wool must be sheared as close as possible, none left behind, without nipping the skin and drawing blood. Points were subtracted for blood and other errors and the whole exercise disqualified if the pelt didn't come off in one piece.

While the shearer worked, a trio of helpers prepared a device for baling the fleeces. The baling device consisted of a specially constructed wooden pallet made of five equally sized square boards. One square made up the center. The remaining four squares were hinged to the four sides of the center square. The outside edges were notched at even intervals. The helpers prepared the baler by laying it flat and threading binder twine through the notches in a certain pattern. The fleece, sans its owner, would be placed on the baler, the four sides drawn up and the twine tied off to compress the bale into a neat little square bundle. The baling table was then laid flat again and the new bale removed to make ready for the next woolen fleece.

If a farmer didn't have enough sons of his own to serve as helpers, he asked a neighboring farmer for help. There was no charge for this service, but a strict code of behavior involved proper payback. Once a favor was owed it must be paid back in order to avoid the humiliation of charity. Pride did not allow for charity. Only under the direst of circumstances did a grown man accept charity either for himself or his family members. Exceptions to that would be in the case of severe illness, incapacitation or death, in which case, people from miles around were obliged to help.

Neither my mother nor I were permitted to do heavy work in the fields. We took care of the garden, gathered eggs and fed the chickens. One of the few times we helped with men's work was if a cow escaped a fence and went up and down the road. In that case, it was an emergency and all hands were on deck. Sometimes a passing motorist alerted us. Other times a simple cry went up. "COWS ARE OUT, COWS ARE OUT".

This didn't mean that I wasn't permitted to follow Dad around in the fields. Before the age of tractors and motor driven planters and harvesters, Dad had two work horses named "Prince" and "Queen". I never quite figured out their relationship, but I knew one was a boy and one a girl from their underneath parts. I loved to ride with Dad while he was working with the horses. I either road bareback on one of the horses, sat on Dad's knee, road beside him on the planter, reaper, or cultivator, or walked behind him behind the plow. A favorite game was to run ahead, place my feet just so, and allow Dad to plow them under with the rich brown soil. He must have been very skilled because he always covered my feet just right and never took off a toe. Some of the other tools were too dangerous for those types of games. Many a farmer lost fingers or a hand in a mower, or an entire arm in a threshing machine.

Another exciting occasion when everyone helped was the annual burning of the hedgerows. It was important to burn off the dry grass and weeds to prevent it from accumulating over the years and burning out of control. Each family member would have a shovel or a rake. We would spread out along the fire line and keep it contained.

*   *   *

Threshing (pronounced thrashing) was the only other time when farmers hired outside entrepreneurs. Threshing machines were ugly tin monsters that were pulled down the roads, reminding one of a dinosaur. They moved from farm to farm with a small crew of operators following the wheat harvest in mid-summer. Their purpose was to separate the wheat from the straw. The machine would be powered by a separate gasoline engine similar to the generators we have today. The engine turned a wheel. A long continuous leather belt ran from the wheel to the threshing machine. Harvested wheat was fed into the maw of the threshing machine. Straw was blown out the other end in a long arc, similar to water out of a fire engine. Midway the kernels of wheat were beaten away and fed into a pipe that had a clamping device on the end. One worker would fasten an empty gunny sack onto the pipe while another removed the previously filled sack and moved it away. A third worker efficiently tied the sack closed and loaded it onto a wagon to be carried away to storage. [2]Sometimes the wheat would be poured loosely into a wagon and drawn to a wheat storage bin, called a granary, for later feeding to chickens or geese, or ground into mash for the cattle and horses. What fun we had rolling and jumping in the granary, sinking into the fresh warm kernels up to our hips and sliding down the hills of grain! Sometimes the wheat would be taken to a buying cooperative, then sold for cereal manufacturing and various other uses.

Arranging the straw into a proper stack was another exacting, strenuous and very dirty job, requiring a strong man. Sometimes the farmer hired someone for this. These men might be paid the handsome wage of five or ten dollars a day, equivalent to a month's wages for other work. The end of the blower nozzle could be manipulated in and out, back and forth. A second man did this task. It was important to arrange the straw stack in the best fashion for shedding rain water. Round and tall was best, with a nicely rounded top. As the second man manipulated the nozzle, the first man, stripped to the waist, muscles rippling and slick with sweat, tromped around the stack arranging the straw with a pitchfork, sometimes disappearing from view in the cloud of

---

[2] Thanks to my friend, Mara Maunder for suggesting this memory.

blowing straw and billowing chaff.

For the rest of the year the straw was used for bedding in the horse stalls, birthing pens, milking parlors, etc. After the animals had dirtied the straw sufficiently with their excrement, the farmer would clean out the stalls and make a fresh bed.

It is easy to see that threshing was a neighborhood project requiring many hands. Each farmer helped his neighbors and was helped in return. As the work moved from farm to farm, so did the noontime diners. Mother had to prepare enough food to serve "thrashers", thus introducing a new term into the language, and all the daughters and wives helped. Feeding threshers could go on from two to four days at each farm. All the food was hand-grown and hand-prepared, from bread, rolls, pies and cakes to cold tea, lemonade and coffee, huge pans of scalloped corn and mashed potatoes, platters of meat and chicken, dumplings or biscuits and gravy... hungry man's food. There were relishes and several kinds of homemade pickles and coleslaw. There must have been something very satisfying about preparing and serving such a meal.

Traditionally, the men washed outside in the clothesline yard with plenty of soap, water and towels to toss over the line. They ate around a huge long table stretched out in our dining room, covered with a white linen cloth. Dad said the blessing, food was passed family style, and the women hovered nearby ready to jump and run whenever something was needed. The men ate quickly with much relish and lavished appreciation on the hostess. After all were stuffed, they groaned away from the table and quickly went about their work. The ladies were left to clear things up and heave huge sighs of relief and satisfaction over a job well done. Only then did the wives and children serve themselves from the leftovers and settle down for a more leisurely afternoon of washing dishes and chatting over the latest news.

*   *   *

No telling of early times would be complete without describing the little house out back; that is, the outhouse, the can, Mrs. Jones' or the privy, to name a few of its euphemisms. Seldom was it a mere one-holer, more often a two-holer and rarely, in the case of really large families, a three. The hole was just that, a hole cut into a board, hopefully filed and sanded for smoothness. In the winter, it was freezing cold; in the summer, buzzing with the hated houseflies that probably traveled back and forth between here and the manure pile behind the barn. A Sears and Roebuck catalog hung by a string from a nail. This was handy for reading purposes and also for use as toilet paper. The best pages were those made of thin tissue-like paper. These were the first to go. Toward the end of the season all those that remained were the thick shiny pages. They didn't work so well and weren't too comfortable. The very last to go were not only thick and shiny, but also colored. The most anticipated mail was the new season's catalog with a supply of fresh clean tissue paper pages. At night the men of the family could "take a leak" outside, but we ladies had an indoor arrangement. This was a white enamel pot with a carrying handle and cover. This chamber pot had an opening just the right size for sitting, with a smooth, rounded and flange lip. In the morning, the pot must be emptied in the outhouse. Generally, my Dad did this for us, bless him – after he got the fire started in the furnace and put the coffee on to perk. What a guy!

*   *   *

Chapter Six

"Innocent or Not, You Decide"
XXXX

Mothers, if you allow your innocent small daughters to run free and unsupervised in the company of males, be they trusted brothers, cousins, or friends of the family, all I can say is, "Shame on you." Same goes for Dads. Whether it is intentional or whether it is instinctive, there will likely be "inappropriate touching".

I've already mentioned that my older brothers played with me, out-of-doors. They played with me indoors as well. Having no toys other than my small dolly, we had to improvise. My beloved dolly made a wonderful prop for a good game (for them) I'll call "Keep-away". This was a simple game, perfect for two boys and one small girl. One of the boys grabbed the doll, making sure that I saw the snatch. Just as I reached for it, he tossed it to the other brother. As I turned and ran for it, the second brother tossed it back and so on. A variation on this game for one participant was one boy simply taunting little sister by keeping the doll just beyond reach. The object of the game was to see little sister jump, run, scream, beg and cry.

We had double-hung windows in the dining room. The worst variation of "Keep-away" was when the doll would be placed high up on the window sill and left there out of my reach.

Another category of game I will call "Torture Little Sister". It bears a striking resemblance to some of the torture techniques the C.I.A. is accused of using on terrorist prisoners. Sub-titles of games in the Torture category would be such activities as "Floor Wrestling", "Pillow Smother", "Tickle" and "Going-too-far".

Pillow Smother simply involved covering little sister's head with a feather pillow, listening to her muffled screams. Tickle involved tickling her under the arms and on the bottoms of her feet to make her laugh uncontrollably until she cries, "Uncle". At the cry of Uncle, the tickler was supposed to stop. "Going-too-far" meant tickling until little sister wet her pants, then calling "Mom,

Dorothy wet her pants. Naanh naanh n'naanh naanh". Floor wrestling could easily evolve into Tickle and Going-too-far, although, to be fair, generally the brothers would stop before that happened. They never left the pillow over my head long enough to actually kill me. Otherwise, would I be here to tell the story?

Speaking of "telling", I was not encouraged to be a tattletale. Believe me I tried. But I learned early-on that running to Mother to tell on the boys was not productive. She didn't take sides between us. It seemed to me that she was too busy or too weak to bother, but maybe I have a warped view on that and she is no longer here to defend herself. I was left to my own meager defenses.

* * *

In their own way, I think my brothers were "just being boys". Although the behavior was risky by certain standards, they watched over me enough to keep me from serious harm. Moreover, they defended me from outsiders.

The swimming area at the County Park had a boardwalk extended out into the lake until the water was perhaps three or four feet deep. Swimmers could then proceed out farther into the deep water to a floating dock. During the summer, my brothers took me with them to the County Park every day. I learned to swim at a very early age. Consequently, I must have been really little when the elder brother saved my life, because I was not yet able to swim. The risky part of this incident was that he shouldn't have carried me out to the dock on his shoulders in the first place. No doubt, I begged to go out on the dock with them, as I had no fear. He told me to "Sit right there and dangle your feet in the water, but don't jump in, understand?" Then he left me to watch as he performed amazing dives off the diving board. His body was tanned, beautiful and strong, and I loved to watch him. It wasn't long until rowdies arrived from Concord and began having a wonderful time alternately pushing and shoving each other off the dock and into the water or simply running up the diving board, doing a "cannonball" into the water and making a huge splash. This was all great fun and wonderful to watch. But soon the group split up into two teams on opposite sides of the dock pumping their legs to make the floating dock rock and roll. The goal was to cause the opposite team to fall off the dock backwards into the water. This was all perfectly harmless, so long as you could swim. I held on to the wet-slick dock enjoying the ride until...

Suddenly, I disappeared underwater, rapidly sinking. I opened my eyes and looked around at emerald green depths. I knew enough to hold my breath. Eternity passed as I considered my options. *Which way was up? How does one swim? Like a fish or like a frog? Up must be in that direction, toward the strongest light. One must move arms and legs.* And so I moved my arms and legs and looked toward the light. Before I had time to panic, my brother's strong arms were lifting me out of the water. He had a fierce temper and was capable of quite earthy language when aroused. A strange quiet fell over the crowd as he directed that temper toward the outsiders that had nearly drowned his little sister. For once, I felt a kinship with him.

*   *   *

Sometimes my brothers were invited to play with cousin D at his house. D was about the same age as my elder brother, maybe a bit older, and I was the bratty little sister, sometimes tagging along. D was an only child. His dad had a job. D had more toys than we did, so it was novel to play at his house with his toys and games. I wasn't always invited so I'm not sure how it came to be that we were upstairs playing in Aunt M's room on her bed. Maybe I had been sent up there for my afternoon nap. At any rate, the three boys had joined me. They had an unfair advantage. It was three against one. They were laughing and having a ball, while I was screaming. The nature of the game was different this time with D. He boldly moved his hands and fingers around under my dress in places that my brothers never touched. They slapped his hands away from those places from time to time and began to withdraw from the game. *What was he thinking? Was this, perhaps, "Going-too-far"?* I was too young to understand the implications when Aunt M burst open the door, ordered no more of this nonsense was to take place in her house and the bedroom was off-limits.

*   *   *

There was never any sex education in our home. Still, there must be an instinctual protective nature that warns little girls when they are in danger.

One of the amenities of the County Park was a camp ground where one could pitch a tent. One day when I was returning alone from swimming, D saw me and suggested. "Come this way, Dorothy, I'll walk home with you", as he took a shortcut through the campground. I followed along, but stopped short when D ducked into a darkened canvas tent. "Come on inside", he coaxed, "I want to show you something." Suddenly I felt shy and discomfited.

"Come on, Dorothy, it's really fun in here."

I hesitated.

"It's Ok, come on in and play for a while. It's fun," he wheezed.

Still as a mouse I took one small step and peeked inside. There he sat over in the darkest corner of the tent, his bathing suit pulled down.

"You can change clothes in here," he said.

"No, thank you. I gotta go home," I said, clutching my towel closer.

"Come here, Dorothy," he said in firmer tones, "I want to show you something. Don't you want to see this?" he asked, as he moved his hand down and waggled his *thing* at me.

I gasped and froze in horror for an instant before I took off for home, running as fast as I could. After that I hated D and cringed in his presence. But he never came near me again and I never *told*. Somehow, without having been "educated" I had known it was very wrong. I just didn't know, until years later, that he was the one in the wrong and not me for having peeked.

*   *   *

Chapter Seven

"Narrow Escapes"

One might actually compare my early life to that of a cat with nine lives, because growing up on a farm in the thirties and early forties was a dangerous existence. I can actually count at least eight narrow escapes. In addition to the time when the town "rowdies" pushed me off the swimming dock and my brother saved me from drowning in the watery depths, there was at least one other close call having to do with that dock.

This one happened after I had developed into a very good swimmer, quite able to join in the pranks and water play with the rest of the gang. We dreamed up all sorts of games, from racing across to the other side of the lake to competing to see who could make the splashiest cannonball, jump the highest off the diving board, or hold one's breath and swim the farthest underwater. Another game was to toss a white glass disk into the water and race to retrieve it before it hit bottom. The perfect disks were obtained from the inside of Mother's zinc mason jar lids. I loved to swim underwater, open my eyes and look around. A wooden ladder was attached to the side of the dock. A favorite trick was to swim between the rungs of the ladder and out the other side. If one could hold his or her breath long enough, one could swim back through again, perhaps a third time as well. Also, it was a challenge to see how low you could go. The ladder itself extended all the way to the bottom of the lake, as many as five or six steps in all.

One day I became bored with swimming through the upper rungs. I decided to try and swim farther and farther down until I tried the very bottom rung. There was just enough room to squeeze underneath it. Taking a huge breath, I opened my eyes and descended farther and farther down until I could squeeze below the bottom rung. At half way through, I became stuck and could go neither forward nor back. Quick thinking told me I had just a few seconds to get out before it was too late. There was no way to call or signal for help. Feet went by above me as other folks using the ladder started out on a much higher rung. Trying not to panic, I hurriedly began to dig under my body in the loose sand. A cloud of bottom sand soon filled the water around me. At last, I freed my midsection and managed to squeeze my hips through the rest of the way. There still remained several feet of water to swim through to get to the surface. I could see the surface shimmering a long way off as I clawed my way toward the light, burst through and commenced gulping in air. All around me life was going on normally, as if nothing earth-shattering had happened. This was not the sort of thing one confessed to one's parent. I tell it here for the first time.

*   *   *

On two occasions, I was knocked unconscious. The first time, I was crossing the road to board the school bus. Just as I dashed into the road, a big high school boy on a bicycle ran into me. He was coming down Lippert's hill, lickity-split, with no thought of little girls in traffic. I suppose that in those days, no laws prohibited folks from passing a school bus. Of course, I didn't remember a thing. My brothers said I was knocked twenty feet and hit my head. They gathered me up. I was taken into town to Dr. Keefer's office where he examined me. I didn't wake up until much later, after I was taken home. It was several more hours before I remembered anything about the day. My brothers delighted in asking me questions in order to hear me acting goofy.

Some years later, after my elder brother could drive, he had his own car, a two-seater known as a coupe. There were no such things as safety restraints and child-proof doors. In fact, the doors were engineered such that they opened from the front to the back, rather than back to front. He had picked me up from school and was driving me home. The door hadn't completely latched when I first closed it. We were still speeding out of town, near the cemetery, when my brother mentioned the door needed to be closed. The last thing I remembered was reaching for that door handle. As the story was reconstructed, when I opened the door, the wind caught it and wrenched it open along with my small body. I was thrown into the ditch and against a curb. This time I was unconscious for several hours.

No thought was given to keeping me in the hospital. No one went to the hospital, except to die. There were no fancy MRI's or Cat Scans. We only had aspirin; rest and home remedies, such as milk toast and Castoria for stomach ache, Vicks Vapo-Rub; onion poultices and Smith Brothers cough drops for colds and flu. We used cool water for burns, unless it was really bad and then Mother might kiss it and put some butter on it. For itches and stings, we applied a paste made of soda and water and tried not to wiggle too much or it would fall off. We didn't even have band aids. Bleeding fingers and scraped knees were wrapped with clean strips of old worn white sheets, the only color anyone had. No home was without a box of Epson salts, useful as a laxative and for a rare case of infection. A good soak in a hot solution of "salts" took care of that. There was iodine for disinfecting a wound and Vicks Vapo-Rub for almost anything. Common childhood diseases were considered normal. Nearly everyone caught mumps, measles and chicken pox. Tonsillitis and whooping cough were common. Diphtheria and polio, though less common, were greatly feared. Outbreaks of polio seemed to come in the summer-time. Parents were urged to keep their children home and away from crowds, to lessen the chances of catching polio.

*   *   *

Serious illness can account for lives number four and five. When I was little, I had "Quincy Sore Throat". I'm telling you, this is the sorest throat you can imagine: Really, really sore and swollen. Impossible to swallow, eat, drink or talk. I lay in bed, weak and suffering for days. Dr. Keefer made house calls to check on me. Eventually he decided that my throat must be "lanced." That was a new word for me, so I dutifully opened my mouth while he stuck a tongue depressor into it, followed by a long shiny instrument of some sort. Next thing I knew, he had cut my swollen throat open, allowing blood and puss to gush out. Nothing has ever hurt so much before or since. Fortunately, he was quick, as I would never have let him into my mouth for a second try. Truthfully, I must admit, the treatment worked. Relief and recovery were rapid.

Years later, another house call was required when I was laid up in bed for three days with fever and terrible pain in my abdomen. It was thought quite all right for him to examine me upstairs in my bed. In no time, he diagnosed appendicitis. Mother was instructed to treat it with ice packs and watch me. If the appendix should rupture, he would have to operate. In a few days the pain was gone. I was up and around, and never had another such attack. Another narrow escape.

*   *   *

There were two barns on our farm with hay mows above. Lives number six and seven occurred when I fell down the "chute", at different times, in both barns. No broken bones resulted – only the usual cuts and bruises – but I could easily have suffocated to death the second time, if Dad hadn't noticed I was missing. He and the men were forking newly mown hay into the loft. What fun I was having, leaping and jumping around in the fresh hay, no doubt being a pest to my brothers and others who were working and sweating in the suffocating environment. The old chute in this barn was no longer in use, so the men filled it and covered it with the new harvest. Unknowingly, all at once I stepped onto the spot and quickly vanished out of sight down the old chute, totally buried several feet deep in Alfalfa. My screams and struggles went unheard and unnoticed as chaff filled my nostrils and darkness descended around me. More hay was gradually building up on top, making matters worse.

At some point, Dad began to ask where Dorothy had gone. Everyone looked around. "She must have gone up to the house," someone said. "Let's get this job done." Another added, "It's too damn hot." "She was being a real pest," said another. "Let her bother the women for a while."

"No," said Dad, "Shut off that machine and everyone be quiet."

"Jesus Christ, do we have to?"

Dad only motioned for silence. He hated to hear the boys swear. At that point, I screamed all the louder and tried to wave my hands to no effect. It wasn't long before my dad's strong arms were reaching for me. He pulled and I kicked.

"Give me a hand, here," he instructed the boys. They rushed to assist, and soon sobered when they realized what a close call this had been.

*   *   *

Number eight occurred when I foolishly climbed between the front of the car and a light post. Mother was waiting in the car to drive me home from school. *Why didn't I simply walk around? Was I stupid or just accident prone? No telling.* Anyway, just as I pulled this stunt, mother's foot slipped off the brake and the car rolled forward, pinning my leg against the pole. "Oh my God!", I yelled. "Mom, don't take your foot off the brake. Don't start the car. Don't do anything!" A look of horror crossed Mom's face Just then a favorite teacher, Mr. Rourke, emerged from the lower level. "Help me," I yelled. "I'm stuck here."

Mr. Rourke took charge. Quickly, he recruited two more strong men and they positioned themselves at the front of the car. "Altogether men, now heave."

They easily pushed the car back a safe distance. I wasted no time in leaping away, effusing thanks, and walking to the car with as much dignity as I could muster.

*   *   *

During the spring of my senior year in high school, I came down with a strep infection. The new wonder drug, Penicillin, had just come out. Dr. Keefer gave me a shot of Penicillin. Within hours, I felt wonderful. One can hardly say that my life was saved, but surely my senior year was saved from certain calamity.

As I am not counting the many times I fell out of a tree, I believe I have one more life to use up. After all, cats never get hurt when falling from heights. Mayhap I should hang on to that one remaining life.

*   *   *

Chapter Eight

"Elementary School Years, 1938-1950"

The birth of my sister, Anna Marie, in March of 1939, ushered in a new era in my life and a new family dynamic. My elder brother was already noticing girls, engaging in a life outside the family circle and, thank God, losing interest in making my existence wormlike. I was no longer the baby of the family, but faded now into a distant "third child" position. Dad was always working and never took an active part in our discipline or in women's work. Mother was much too busy to do everything for Anna or discipline the rest of us. I became the little mother. I led Anna around by the hand, played with her, held her, fussed over her, took care of her and even spanked her a few times if absolutely necessary. This happened when she ran away, or when she chewed up razor blades that Mother had carelessly left out in the open on the sewing machine. Once I cut her hair, when I thought she would look much cuter in bangs and pig tails (braids). Mother gave me a severe "talking to" for that. I never did it again, but now it was too late. She had bangs and they couldn't be pasted back on.

*   *   *

Mother thought it best to hold me back from starting school until age six even though I begged to go and was truly more than ready. The problem was lack of transportation. It was necessary for me to walk to school two miles away. I would be walking with my brothers, but that didn't provide enough assurance for my parents at that time. It wasn't until 1938 that I was sent to morning Kindergarten. My teacher taught Kindergarten in the morning and first grade class in the afternoon. Mother had made special arrangements for me to stay late while I waited for my brothers to walk me home. I hung around in the school room watching the first grade class and taking it all in. At the end of the school year, I was promoted to second grade. Actually, I didn't skip first grade. I merely took both grades together in one year.

School was a much needed social outlet for me after six sheltered years of relative isolation on the farm. It was good for me to make friends with people my own age with whom I could relate as equals. It was good to learn that I could excel at something, that I was not as inferior as I had been led to believe. In fact, there were some things at which I was rather superior to the average.

I had a driving need to excel and inborn ambition to succeed that lasted well into my seventies. School provided the perfect opportunity for that. There was no need for my parents to push me to get my school work done. They were ahead of the times in that respect, because they didn't believe in pushing their children to overachieve. Rather, they accepted them as they were. My personal goal was to get all A's in school and I did just that, all the way through grade school, junior high, high school and college, not receiving my first lower marks until grad school.

A kindly old gentleman by the name of Dr. Armstrong lived in Concord, where I attended school. He was known by everyone and was affectionately called "Doc". Doc was the closest person to a real live Santa Claus that I ever knew, complete with the right body shape. He owned and ran the drug store on Main Street, was a veterinarian and Justice of the Peace, and gave out candy on Halloween. Clearly, he loved kids. The drug store had a soda fountain. Most days, Doc could be found holding forth behind the counter. I heard that Doc had a practice of rewarding any elementary school child who received a perfect report card with an ice cream cone. In those days all ages received letter grades, A through E in academics. In addition, secondary students also received a plus or minus in various aspects of deportment, such as listens well, pays attention, participates in discussions, cleanliness, hygiene, obedience etc. In addition, the teacher wrote a brief written critique.

Now, I dearly loved ice cream and seldom had it. So the first time I got my perfect report card, I went into Doc's drug store and stood there clutching it in my little hand, too shy to ask, but hoping he would see me. Mother had remonstrated with me over the idea of accepting charity, but that couldn't hold me back. I stood there feeling scared while Doc waited on a progression of customers. I would have to leave soon because lunch hour was almost over, and I had to be back to class. At last, all the customers were cleared out and I was alone with Doc, shaking in my shoes.

He was an imposing man, big and round with a hearty laugh. He peered at me over his glasses. "Well now, little girl, what can I do for you?" I merely grinned a shy half-smile and pointed at the list of ice cream flavors listed over the mirror. "Do you want an ice cream cone?"

I nodded.

"And what flavor would that be, vanilla, chocolate, strawberry, butter pecan?"

I stared.

"Vanilla?"

I nodded again.

"Double dip?"

I shook my head "No."

"Single dip?"

I nodded.

"Cat got your tongue?"

I nodded.

"Ok, now let's see, you would like a single dip, vanilla. Is that right?"

I nodded.

"That will be five cents."

I blanched and shyly held up my report card.

"Well, now, what have we here? Let me see that." Doc examined the card. "So you are Miss Dorothy Douglas, Yes, indeed, I know your Mother and Dad. Fine people, those

Douglases. What's this I see? Will you look at that? Spelling, A. Arithmetic A. Writing A. Deportment, A. Study habits, A. Let me see what the teacher says here... Dorothy is a fine student, well behaved and works hard. I enjoy teaching her. Now, doesn't that teacher say some nice things about you, Miss Dorothy? I believe that definitely calls for a free ice cream cone, don't you?"

"Yes, sir, thank you sir," I say, beaming from ear to ear. Doc made me a triple-decker with one of each color and I floated out of the store at least six inches taller.

Doc has been gone for many years, but I'll never forget him and my free ice cream every month.

*   *   *

Every school child's favorite class is, of course, recess. Our playground had the standard swings, slide and merry-go-round. This was supplemented by organized sports, such as softball, races, and soccer. I loved to play soccer, but my favorite was racing, because I could run faster than anyone in my class, even the boys, until midway through our fourth grade, when a disaster put an end to recess on the playground.

It happened in the middle of the night. Word went out over the party lines, "The school is on fire!" Dad and the boys threw on their clothes and rushed into town. Mother stayed home with Anna and me. As hours passed, trying to sleep was useless. By morning, it was clear: the destruction was complete. The school had burned to the ground. It was said that the blaze was so hot, no one could get near to save anything. The brick walls, glass windows and chimney had collapsed in a pile of rubble. The sad story was told that as the bell tower collapsed, the bell rang all the way down in a mournful farewell. There was jubilation from some students, but I was devastated. By and large, the townspeople and surrounding farm families were in shock. The school board met in emergency session with overflowing attendance. What to do? A survey of available rooms was made.

It took months of work, but eventually school resumed, with classes meeting in empty rooms up over the stores in the block-long commercial section of Main Street. Third, fourth, fifth and sixth grades met in two rooms over the town tavern. Special high school classes were held in the church basement. Seventh through twelfth met in the old opera house, its basement and rooms over the adjoining drug store. The main auditorium of the opera house served as a gym, locker room and study hall. The stage was a classroom during the school day and a stage at other times. I danced the Junior/Senior prom on that opera house floor, acted in plays, performed in school concerts and gave my valedictory on the opera house stage.

Mrs. Lemoine Bogue was teacher for the third and fourth grades. Next door, Mrs. Hoxie was a teacher for the fifth and sixth grades. Looking back, I can see that we kids were such brats! Our secret name for Mrs. Bogue was "Lemonade Bogue". We thought that was hilarious. The poor things had no personal break and no privacy. Mrs. Hoxie had to groom herself at her desk. We tittered behind our hands as she smoothed on lipstick and peered into a tiny mirror as she checked out her nose and applied powder. Our special name for her was "Old Lady Hoxie".

There simply was no possible way the poverty stricken School District could raise money for a new building. For eight more years, through World War Two and beyond, they struggled, trying to find help from the government, foundations, the State of Michigan and from every possible source. Finally, as the War ended and the populace was beginning to climb out of the depths of the Great Depression, plans were drawn up for a beautiful new campus on the edge of town. The father of one of my best friends, an architect named Carl Kressbach, volunteered to draw the plans and head up the building committee. Unfortunately, his daughter and I were members of the last class to graduate from the old opera house. The new school opened the following fall, in Sep. 1950.

* * *

Chapter Nine

"The Piano"

Most kids would tease for a bicycle, a horse, a doll, skates...whatever. I wanted a piano. Dad tucked that idea away, until one day opportunity struck. One of his tenants was willing to sell him an old upright for ten dollars. It was awesome; tall and black with shiny white and black keys. They felt so smooth and beautiful under my hands as I caressed them. I sat on the bench and earnestly prayed that I could play like the ladies did in church. Then with the pure faith that only a child could have, I positioned my hands and pressed the keys, believing beautiful music would come forth. It did not. So I prayed and tried again. Same result. This was my first lesson in delayed answer to prayer.

Mrs. Ota Nowlin was the only piano teacher in town. She was also the pianist at church and a member of the Ladies Aid Society. Dad approached her about giving me lessons. Mrs. Nowlin said, "I'm sorry, but Dorothy is too young. I don't take students less than seven years old". This was a crushing blow, but I had no choice in the matter. At last, June 1939 arrived and I was seven years old. Piano lessons were fifty cents apiece and were generally held after school or on Saturdays. I whizzed through John Thompson's Level One and on to Levels Two through Five. Soon I was the Sunday school accompanist. By age twelve, I was the church accompanist, the school accompanist and the whole town's accompanist.

The day Mrs. Flower came to town was a lucky day for me. She started a K-12 vocal music program in the schools. Naturally, in my humble opinion, every vocal music teacher lives and dies by her accompanist. Mrs. Flower turned me into an expert. She took me out of class with her when she visited the elementary grades. She installed me as chief accompanist for the High School Glee Club. I accompanied all her rehearsals and concerts for the remainder of my years at Concord Schools. Together with the Glee Club, we attended many State Festivals where we sang in a huge auditorium with a thousand kids from all over the State of Michigan, under the direction of the very best professors at the

State Universities. Mrs. Flower started a community choir, as well. I accompanied my first Messiah as a seventh grader. As a high school student, I was introduced to the director of the Jackson Choral Society in the nearest city. That year I accompanied Handel's Messiah for them.

One problem that all accompanists face is page turning: when to do it and how to do it smoothly and efficiently. After all, your hands are pretty busy. The question always arises, "Is it better to have someone else serve as page turner, or do it yourself?" Personally, most times, I would rather do it myself. It takes a rare and gifted person to turn pages correctly for someone else. They either turn it too soon, so as to cause you to miss the last few notes on the page, or they turn it too late and you miss the first few notes on the next page, or they get their arm in the way of your face, or they don't read music at all and become completely lost. To further complicate matters, publishers seem to have no sympathy or regard for the beleaguered accompanist. They seem to arrange the pages to suit the singers, giving them ample time to turn their pages while the pianist is playing the interlude. In this respect I suppose they are wise because, as every music student knows so well, instrumental majors are much smarter than vocal majors. After all, vocal majors can't count!

My most embarrassing musical moment came while working for dear Mrs. Flower. I attempted to solve the page turning problem. This happened after Scotch tape had been invented, but before the days of copy machines. Thinking I would outsmart the page-turn gremlins, I scrounged up enough copies of a particularly tricky seven page choir number to tape them together in one wide string. Placing this long piece on the piano worked quite well during rehearsal, but I had not allowed for the hot stuffy evening of the Concert, held in the Presbyterian church. The piano was placed close to the side of the room, and all the windows were opened wide. The room was packed with parents and friends. A hush fell over the crowd as Mrs. Flower raised her baton and gave me the signal to begin. The music began and lovely young female voices floated over the evening air. I was totally focused on making music when a gust of air blew through the nearby window and raised the edge of my music. Every musician who has ever played outdoors knows what happened next. I continued playing with one hand and frantically grabbed for the music with the other. Too late, it sailed away and floated to the floor landing in a tangled mess.

In some languages there must be a better word to describe utter and complete chagrin, embarrassment beyond words. Of course, dear Mrs. Flower was all sympathy and understanding to her young accompanist. Someone from the audience who understood all too well hastened to help. After I stopped shaking, we were able to start over and the concert continued. But I learned an important lesson that evening that never needed to be repeated. I have since developed a nearly foolproof method of organizing my music for a long concert that I've taught to every one of my students. As every instrumental musician worth his salt knows, the best protection against flying music sheets is "Clothespins".

By this time, I was studying piano with Miss Nellie Field, who taught at Albion College, and was the organist at the First Methodist Church there. Miss Field held recitals twice a year where I got to play on the big stage on a real Steinway grand piano. Miss Field introduced me to all the classics: Bach, Mozart, Beethovan, Chopin and more. Eventually, Miss Field suggested that I should study even farther away from home with Mr. Wray Lindquist at Hillsdale College. So, during my last two years living at home, I drove to Hillsdale every week for my one hour lesson with Mr. Lindquist. His studio was at the college and he taught on two grand pianos. It was wonderful to play two piano duets with him.

After graduation from High School, I was accepted into the University of Michigan School of Music as a piano education major. It was here that I began to study voice, music theory, music literature, ear training, conducting and choir. It was a thrill to sing in huge choir concerts under the direction of Maestro Maynard Klein in the acoustically perfect Hill Auditorium.

But I never finished college at U of M. The United States, by now, was embroiled in the Korean War. Moreover, I had met a handsome redheaded eligible bachelor. It seems that he interrupted my musical career.

*   *   *

Chapter Ten

"What Were They Thinking?"

Somehow, I learned what it was all about from my girlfriends. We were having a pajama party, whispering and giggling far into the night. One of the girls was so much worldlier than the rest of us. We reacted with considerable doubt.

"Eeeuuu, how appalling!"

"You can't be serious."

"I've seen my brother."

"Me too. No way can a boy put that floppy thing in there!"

"Yuck!"

"Yes, they do. Really. You've seen dogs get hung up haven't you?" she insisted.

"Oh my goodness, not like that!"

This was ghastly news. I wasn't sure I wanted to grow up.

*   *   *

Looking back on it, I sometimes wonder what my parents were thinking, to let me grow like a weed, without supervision so much of the time. It wasn't as if they didn't care. They were saintly, good, honest and generous people, working terribly hard and sacrificing everything for their kids during the toughest economic times in that century. It had to be just the way it was done; that is, what seemed right to them. My dad seemed to think that the way to bring up kids was to read the Bible, pray at every meal and take them to church. That is all well and good, but shouldn't there be more?

Remember, there was no television in those days, and movies were strictly censored. The only movies were for general consumption. There was no such thing as porno shops. Everything was G-rated: advertising, radio, commercials. It wasn't necessary to protect your children from such things, because they simply didn't exist. The only sex education available was in the Bible, and there is plenty there if you understood what it meant to "covet" your neighbor's wife or have an abomination with animals. If there were any explicit books, they were kept in a locked room in the library. Even the dictionaries were censored.

I'm not suggesting that sex didn't exist – just that it was under the covers (pun intended).

My mother was so embarrassed to talk about it that she allowed me to start my periods unprepared. It happened one Sunday while we were in church. I felt this wet sticky stuff between my legs and knew without looking what was happening to me. I was thirteen years old and entering eighth grade. I stuck it out until we got home, worrying all the time that blood might be showing through on my dress. As soon as we got home I said to Mom, "I've started menstruating, Mom, and I need some pads."

"Oh, uh, well, I don't have any pads, but I'll find something", she said, and left to rummage around in the depths of her closet for five or ten minutes. She came out with some old rags and some safety pins. "We'll just tie this one around your waist and pin the other one between your legs," she said. "Tomorrow you can go to the store."

Alas, that was the last time Mother and I discussed anything related to the reproductive function of humans. Somehow I managed to figure it out for myself.

*   *   *

Chapter Eleven

"High School Heart Throbs"

It would be fair to say that I always liked boys; more accurately, other peoples' boys. My brothers and male cousins fell into a different category. There was no doubt in my mind that I would fall in love, marry and have children, in that order. In those days, people often married right out of high school, so high school was prime time for looking over the possibilities. This was done by "dating". A girl saw someone she liked, flirted with him and hoped that he asked her for a date. It might begin by informal chance meetings over lunch, in the library, at a school event or going out in a group, making sure that there were smiles, laughs and occasional brief touches. Girls never directly asked boys for dates, except perhaps through a friend or intermediary, dropping a hint that one might be interested. This could work both ways. A boy might enlist the aid of an intermediary to inquire whether the object of his interest would welcome an invitation out.

The first real date might be a double date; that is, two couples going out together. It might begin with a subterfuge, such as a "study date" where Boy A feigns a need for help in a certain area of study. In this case, they agree to meet at the library or at her house when her parents were there. Eventually the boy either drops her or moves on to the next serious step. The process might go as follows: Boy A telephones Girl A. After some idle chit-chat, boy mentions a movie (or other) event coming up and asks the girl if she has seen the movie. Depending on her response, if encouraged, he will then ask if she would like to go. If she says yes, he proceeds to the next step of inviting her to go on a specific evening. If Boy A was too young to drive, or had no older friend with a car, he might inquire whether she would like to sit together at a school event. In that case, she would provide her own transportation and they would meet at the event. There were all sorts of ways to get together.

During the "date", said boy and girl would probably hold hands. Upon parting, boy would be expected to initiate a fairly chaste kiss. Based on this first encounter, both parties would decide whether or not they cared to proceed with the relationship.

Either one could stop it. The boy could avoid the girl altogether and never call again. The girl could be "busy", politely declining next time he asked; or again, the services of an intermediary might be used in order to save face.

Assuming they both decide to progress, the relationship could proceed with meetings during and after school and more "dates". As time went on, the couple could proceed to parking and "necking". Parking meant simply sitting together in a parked car. In any town, there would be favorite spots for teenagers to go parking. An ideal place would be dark, safe and fairly romantic, such as a drive-in movie, the girl's driveway, or a nearby park. Necking involved sitting upright with clothes on, kissing and hugging with all hands kept strictly above the waist. Nice girls never allowed more than that. Everyone knew who "nice girls" were and who weren't.

After several successful dates, a boy might ask a girl to "go steady". This meant that they each agreed to date each other exclusively. The boy would present a token to the girl such as a class ring which she would wear on a ribbon or chain around her neck. This signified to everyone in school that she was going steady, thus not "available" for dating other guys. When a couple decided to go steady, or later on, to "break up", the ring being returned to its owner, news traveled with the speed of sound.

One of my first real dates was with "Donnie". I was a Sophomore and Donnie was a Senior, thus having the distinct advantage of being able to drive. Donnie was my boyfriend. We dated for a month or two, mostly double dates, either just driving around or going to a movie and out for a hamburger afterward. Donnie was a tall, fun-loving, handsome debonair kind of guy with nice white teeth and a little mustache. After a few dates he asked me to go steady, but I declined, saying I was too young to go steady. Donnie was nice, but his weakness, for me, was that he wasn't exactly, shall we say, an honor student. Donnie was a year older than his fellow classmates. I soon tired of Donnie and we agreed to break up.

I had other friends who were boys, that being a different category from boyfriends. I spent time with Dale and with Bert, but we were just pals and the relationship was strictly platonic. Either Dale or Bert might drive me home, sit and talk, have fun together when not otherwise "dating", or even engage in light "flirting," but it didn't go beyond that.

In my Junior year, I became quite serious with Bill, who was a Senior. Again, I refused to go steady, but no one else would ask me out as I was considered his "girlfriend". So we might as well have been going steady for all the good it did me. Bill's mother was divorced. She lived alone and had to work to support her children. For this reason alone, I suspected, my Dad never quite approved of Bill as divorce was against Dad's set of beliefs. Bill was nice looking and tall enough for my standards. Mostly, I liked him because he was closer to being my intellectual equal than any of my other dates. I didn't mind that he didn't have a car. Bill managed to get out to my house in the country by hitchhiking. We spent a lot of time together at my house and at school events. After Mom and Dad went to bed, we sat on the sofa and necked. Now and then, Dad would call out from the bedroom, "Dorothy....."

"Yes, Dad"

"Dorothy, it's time for you to go to bed. Tell Billy to go home."

"Ok, Dad, I will pretty soon, Dad," after which we would go on necking and laughing and talking. After two or three such calls, Bill and I would break it up and he would walk home. Our timing was exquisite. We knew just how long we could stall before Dad would come out of the bedroom in his comical nightshirt and confront us.

Sometimes in nice weather, Bill and I would stroll down to the County Park, but never "up in the pines", that place where naughty girls went with their beaus. Rarely, if we overstayed at the park, Dad might come after us and insist, to my embarrassment, that I come home. Dad never quite trusted us together. I greatly resented that and did not understand Dad's feelings until I became the parent of a seventeen-year-old girl, myself. After all, I was a somewhat foolishly naïve little virgin, planned to stay that way until married, and expected my parents to trust me.

Sometimes Bill and I would borrow my parent's car or double date with friends. Bill was motivated and resourceful and transportation wasn't a problem. The only problem in our relationship, one that I didn't realize at the time, was that Bill was somewhat domineering. Actually, I was accustomed to that kind of treatment from the other men in my life: my brothers. I guess I thought that was normal.

Bill graduated one year ahead of me. He got a job in Jackson and we continued dating until he joined the Navy for a four-year stint. When he left, I was still refusing to go steady, because I thought it unwise to be promised to him all that time. We continued to write and talk on the phone and Bill got an occasional pass or leave to come home.

The summer following my graduation from high school, Bill decided to bring the issue of our relationship to a head. Dressed in his finest sparkling white uniform and with a diamond ring in his pocket, Bill formally asked me to marry him. We talked, but with tears of regret, I declined as gently as possible. There would be no remaining "just friends". We bid a fond and emotional farewell, and I never saw Bill again.

I had met someone else.

*   *   *

Chapter Twelve

"David Neal"

Who is to say what fates can do? Do you believe in serendipity? Love at first sight? I do, and here's the reason why.

Normally, I don't have a good memory for faces; but to my dying day I shall never forget the first time I laid eyes on David Neal Mercer. It was a Saturday in the late winter of 1950. I had driven myself in to Jackson High School for my scholarship interview. I was to meet a member of the University of Michigan Regent's Alumni committee. It was customary for the Regents to award a tuition-free scholarship to every Valedictorian and Salutatorian of a Michigan public school, providing they applied to U of M., met the criteria and passed the interview process.

When I entered the classroom that served as a waiting room, another candidate was waiting there alone. He was seated in a typical one-arm student desk, leaning on his elbow and gazing directly at me with riveting blue eyes. His face was becomingly freckled, his curly red hair carefully combed. He was dressed in sharply pressed pants, white shirt, tie and blue varsity sweater with a large letter "S" on the side.

"Hi," he smiled at me with a devilish grin.

"Hi," I demurred as I shrugged off my coat and carefully set it aside. I took a seat opposite him.

"Are you here for the interview?" he offered, though it was quite obvious why we were here.

"Oh, yes, and you?"

"Uh-huh," he nodded, "Where are you from?"

"I'm from Concord. And you?"

"That's great. I'm from Springport".

"Oh, really? Then, we play against you in football. You beat us up really bad, too. I see you have a letter. Do you play?"

He nodded, "Matter of fact I play basketball, too. I believe we are meeting your team in a few weeks."

"Um, well, take pity on us, will you? Are you next in line here?"

"Yes, I believe I am, but they seem to be running behind. You can go first if you need to get going," he offered gallantly.

"No, no, that's all right. I'll wait my turn." I adjusted my skirt, primly.

And so it went as we continued grinning at each other rather stupidly and the next half hour seemed to fly by.

Upon my arrival home, as was customary, Mother sat down with me and waited to hear me talk about my day.

"Oh, Mom, I met the nicest boy!" I began, and then proceeded to tell her all about it as she patiently listened, murmuring acknowledgements and encouragement from time to time. Mother was a great listener. Perhaps that is where I got it.

Two weeks later, I shamelessly inveigled Bert into driving me to the "away" game at Springport. Poor Bert had no idea I was using him. He didn't go out for sports, but he allowed himself to be easily duped. A bit late arriving at the game, we took seats in the bleachers. I had eyes for only one player. I could tell that he saw me too, and then proceeded to play as if no audience existed.

I learned that Neal was the star of the team, the point guard and highest scorer of the game. I watched him with starry eyes, not minding at all that Springport badly "whupped" Concord's team. An announcement was made, a kind invitation for all guests to remain for refreshments and a short dance after the game. Bert was ready to go home, but agreed to stay only because I asked.

After the crowd had left, students and chaperones remained

seated in the bleachers. The lights dimmed to a soft but respectable glow and recorded music began, slow and romantic. Soon a freshly showered line of Springport men emerged from the locker room amid triumphant cheers and whistles. The defeated Concord team had already left on their bus. My eyes were trained on the door, hoping *he* would emerge. Suddenly he was heading straight for my seat in the bleachers. I held my breath and my heart speeded up. He climbed up to stand towering over me, gazed down, grinned at me and smiled, "Hi, there, Dorothy!"

"Hi," I returned

"You know this guy?" Bert observed in some astonishment.

I introduced them and waited, expectantly.

At last, to my vast relief, Neal asked, "Would you care to dance, that is, if your escort doesn't mind," he added without turning his head.

"No, go ahead," grumbled Bert to my retreating back.

We danced. Oh, how we danced! I remember the feel of his varsity sweater against my silk blouse, his arms around me, a bit too close, his large warm hand holding mine, his chin brushing the top of my hair. It felt so good. We were a perfect fit. I was in heaven.

"I'm so glad you came," he breathed. "I set up this dance afterward, just for you."

"Thank you," I gazed into his eyes, "How did you manage that?"

"It wasn't too hard."

"Yeah, right," I scoffed, "Come on".

"It's true. Really. It just so happens that I'm the President of the Senior Class and President of the Student Council," he offered with feigned modesty.

"Wow!" I was impressed. We danced some more.

"Who is that little guy you are with?" he twirled me around.

"Just a friend."

"That's all, just a friend?" he teased.

"Yes".

"You're sure? Nothing more? Just a friend?" A smile touched his lips.

"Yes, uh, well, I asked him to bring me tonight. I was hoping…" I blushed and glanced away.

"Hoping what? Tell me," he coaxed.

"Um… I was… sort of… hoping I might see you again," I confessed.

We danced quietly and snuggled just a bit closer.

"Is there anyone else?" he drew breath and looked at me, as I hesitated.

"Well, there is someone," I answered, "But we aren't going steady," I hastened to add.

"Uh, can I see you again?" he continued.

"Yes, you can see me… if you want to."

"Where do you live?"

I told him.

"May I have your telephone number?"

I waited for four days, dying for his call. At last, it finally came. We agreed on a first date, the first of many.

*   *   *

Chapter Thirteen

"Courtship"

To this day, David Neal maintains that I was his first and only girlfriend. His mother corroborated this, claiming that men in their family fall once and fall hard. I found it difficult to believe that some other girl hadn't snapped up this perfect man. I believe now that they tried and failed. He simply doesn't notice anyone else.

Our courtship proceeded rapidly. Neal had his own car, a vintage Model B Ford with red, wooden-spoked wheels and a rumble seat. Sometimes he drove his parents' nice new Ford as well. He came over several times a week and, once, skipped school and surprised me on the school lunch hour. In turn, I daringly took the rest of the afternoon off. It wasn't like me to disobey the rules. We drove to my house for lunch. Mother lovingly chided us both but took it in good humor.

I had a regular Saturday night baby-sitting job for Clair and Pat Railer's kids. Neither Clair nor my mom minded if I had my boyfriend visit, after I got the kids in bed, of course. One April evening, Neal shocked my heart into standing still. We were baby-sitting, just sitting quietly in their living room, opposite each other, visiting while time passed. I don't remember for sure what we were discussing, or why he said it, but I will never forget his words or the stricken look on his face. Perhaps he had asked me to go steady.

"I love you," he blurted out. It was a defining moment that forever changed us.

I stared at him in silent astonishment. I liked Neal, liked him a lot, but I couldn't honestly reply in kind. It was too soon.

"But, how can you be sure?" I stammered, "We've only known each other for two months." I felt really sorry for the poor boy. "I like you too, Neal, but I'm sorry if I misled you into thinking it was more than that." He looked miserable, maybe even a bit defeated.

"Well, I guess it may seem a bit sudden to you," he offered, "It's Ok if you don't feel the same way yet. Even if you don't want to go steady, can we go on seeing each other?"

"Sure we can," I replied with some relief, "but, let's not get too serious, Ok?"

At this, Neal brightened and readily agreed, "No more serious stuff," whereupon he bent himself to pursuing his intended goal with all the charm at his disposal.

Letters, visits, flowers, gifts and phone calls every day – sometimes twice a day – followed in rapid order. Neal charmed my friends, charmed my family and charmed me. I learned that not all men were bossy, domineering and fond of belittling the weaker sex. I basked and glowed in his attention. He was an expert dancer. He neither smoked nor drank. He was a popular fellow, Salutatorian of his class, and an excellent student without half trying. Had he worked at it he could have been Valedictorian twice over, but he didn't really care all that much. He played the clarinet. He attended my concerts and recitals. I attended his band concerts and basketball games. We exchanged hugs and kissed, but he never asked for sex or stepped out of line. He squired me to the Concord Senior Prom and I was his date at the Springport Senior Prom and banquet. He took me to church, on picnics to the park, introduced me to fishing and hunting and treated me with gentlemanly courtesy and unfailing kindness. I met his family and attended their family dinners as he did mine.

I didn't hide my relationship with Bill, but Neal made sure that he alone was the one by my side. In a matter of weeks, my fondness for Bill faded and I began to realize that Neal was the man of my dreams, a man equal with me in intelligence, a man who would go places, I was certain, and a man my father and mother approved. I realized I had fallen in love with him.

One balmy August evening, Neal picked me up in his folk's car. He was dressed in his best and seemed just a bit nervous. I had on a spring dress with a fitted bodice and full softly gathered skirt. There were tiny little pink flowers on a white background. I sat up close to him. Neal handled the car with quiet confidence, one arm about my shoulders. He drove us to a lovely grassy parking spot beside the rippling waters of the little Grand River. He found some soft music on the radio and opened the windows to a gentle breeze. I held my breath and looked down at my hands primly folded in my lap. I had an idea what was coming.

Neal drew me closer, gently kissed my cheek and whispered, "I love you, Dorothy," not for the first time.

I turned to face him. "I love you too." We smiled into each other's eyes.

"Darling, I love you so much." he repeated, "Please, will you marry me?"

My heart flipped, a lump grew in my throat. "Yes, I will," I nodded almost imperceptibly.

Neal gathered me in his arms, sighed with satisfaction, carefully slipped a diamond ring on the third finger of my left hand and kissed me as if I belonged to him.

* * *

Chapter Fourteen

"Engagement"

Next day I asked my parents if I could have their permission to get married. Dad's first question was, "Which man do you want to marry?" Perhaps I shouldn't have been so surprised at his question.

"Neal Mercer."

"Oh," a look of relief passed over his eyes.

Mother wasn't shocked. She had it figured out. "What are your plans?"

"We will go together to the University in the fall."

"Well, is there married housing on campus?"

"I don't think so. We will have to wait."

There were no questions about how Neal planned to support me. In those days, there were plenty of jobs for non-skilled workers and cheap cars and apartments. It was not uncommon for couples to go to work and marry right out of high school. Neal and I were both working full-time. Neal had worked half of his life, starting with a paper route at age ten. This was my first job. Mother and Dad were firm in their belief that I should concentrate on my schooling. I had asked to be allowed to get a job before graduation, mostly because I wanted to escape; but they saw right through that ploy. Neal's folks took the opposite view with him and expected their sons (not their daughter) to work from the "git-go." Girls were more sheltered in those days.

Keeping up a hot romance and a job, too, put a strain on our sleeping hours. Neal and I saw each other every evening and talked on the phone when we were apart. It was not unusual to stay together until midnight or one o'clock, rising again at six in the morning. I was definitely suffering from sleep deprivation and found myself sneaking a quick nap in the ladies room at work.

Fortunately, I was young and strong and never got caught.

Now that we were engaged, there was no more rule about keeping hands above the waist. We were free to explore our bodies with passion, so long as we stopped short of consummation. Every evening we either sat on the front porch or sofa in the living room, necking and talking in low tones, or we sat outside in the driveway in the car. We were tempted to go further, but had pledged to wait until marriage. That worked out well for us and I would definitely recommend it to young couples, if possible. However, it does necessitate a shorter engagement. Nowadays, that isn't always possible, because of today's social practices and economic times. Many of today's couples marry later in life, living together before marriage, both parties concentrating on careers and the accumulation of wealth. All too often, to the consternation of the older generation, they wait until they have a furnished house, two cars and the first child is born, to marry.

Our restraint before marriage added to the sweetness of our honeymoon. Also, we proved to each other that we each had the necessary self-control to remain faithful to each other during those times in the future when circumstances would dictate that we remain celibate for a while.

Things were different at college. We could only meet at the library, the coffee shop or around campus, ducking into a corner to steal a hug and kiss. Girls' dorms were strictly segregated from the men, and there were confining rules. Young college people now would be appalled at such restrictions. Men were allowed to call on women, but they were not permitted above the first floor lounge. The house mother was a stern older woman who sat at a desk in the lounge during visiting hours and ruled with an iron hand. Men had to leave and girls had to be in by curfew, ten o'clock on week nights, eleven on Fridays and Saturdays. After that, the doors were locked and you couldn't get in, unless in an emergency and you had prior written permission from the house mother.

From the start, the house mother disapproved of our engagement and looked askance at my diamond ring. More than once she walked the length of the room to where Neal and I huddled together and admonished us for holding hands and sitting too close. For that reason, we stayed outside a lot. Also, we took the bus home from Ann Arbor as many weekends as possible so we could be together.

Accustomed to much more freedom and independence, Neal hated the confinement of school. Also, he was supporting himself now, and money was tight. He needed to go to work.
Together we "made do," sharing the five dollars Mother sent me when she could. That was a lot for her to spare, bless her heart, but my parents wanted to see me educated. Mother was always faithful in writing to me and that meant a lot too.

Winter had arrived on campus. In order to warm up, Neal and I would spend time in the little restaurant just off campus. It was always jammed with students, so the rule was you couldn't have a seat unless you ordered something. The cheapest thing on the menu was coffee at five cents a cup. We would use some of Mom's five dollars to buy two cups and nurse them as long as we could.

It wasn't long until Neal began arguing for dropping out of school and getting married. My parents preferred we wait until we had finished at least one full year of college. I agreed with them. I argued that Neal could be drafted if he dropped out. There was a war on, but students and married men with children were deferred from the draft. I loved school, but I loved him more. So, we set a wedding date for Saturday, March 17, 1951 and left school in December at the end of the first semester. We would be married in three more months. Neal went back to work and I began planning our wedding.

*   *   *

Chapter Fifteen

"Honeymoon"

Seven billion people in this world, more or less. Think about it. Most all of them must be having sex. Otherwise, how would we be here? Amazing, isn't it, how little we talk about our personal sex lives? You're darned right, it's private! But, ah well, how can I tell you about my life without admitting the truth, (this is a first)…Yes, we had sex on our wedding night. Three times at least. After knowing each other and waiting for a year, we eagerly set out making up for lost time. Then we proceeded to have sex every night for the first year, except when I was …ahem… shall we say…indisposed. So, I guess it would be fair to say our honeymoon lasted a year.

After our wedding night in that motel near Kalamazoo, we drove to Chicago and stayed in the Edgewater Beach Hotel. It made no difference where we were. We could have stayed anywhere because we didn't emerge from the room until our last day there. I said to Neal, "We've got to do something besides have sex while we are here so I can tell my parents what we did." Yikes! I can't just say we stayed in our room and made love for five days. Isn't it funny how each generation thinks they were the ones to discover love? (It's true, kids. Your folks *did it* and probably still *do*! I know, it's so embarrassing! Too much information.)

So, the last day we got dressed and went downtown to look around. Mistake. We hadn't allowed for the fact that I was too sore to walk very far in high heels on the cement sidewalks. After we looked around a bit, Neal ended up carrying me the last three blocks back to our parked car. But when we got home we were able to honestly tell our folks what a wonderful time we had looking around in Chicago.

Our first apartment was in Albion, a two room walk-up with a shared bath. Neal worked in a factory and I played at being an eager little housewife. I didn't know beans about cooking, but was so eager to please and nervous as a cat the first time we had Neal's folks over for Sunday dinner. I tried to bake a yellow cake, carefully following the directions on the package of cake mix and pouring it into an eight inch square pan. I didn't know how to turn it out of the pan or that you had to let it cool first. When I tried to flip it a big hunk broke off. I was mortified, near tears and his mother was due any minute.

Neal tried to calm his little wife down, "Now, now, Honey, it's OK. We can fix it," he said. I moaned louder. "But, what can we do?" I wailed.

"There, there, Sweetheart. We'll just fix it with toothpicks."

"Ya' think?"

"Sure, we can do this. Mom and Pop will never know the difference," he said as he picked up the piece and brushed it off. So, I found some toothpicks and we went to work sticking the cake together and disguising it with frosting, careful to make a note which side was broken so we didn't serve that to our guests.

*   *   *

We had to operate on a strict budget. Neal earned $200 a month and we lived on it too. Our rent was $50 a month. Weekly expenses were food $10, gas $5, entertainment $5, clothes $5, misc. $5, emergency fund $5, gifts $2.50.

Our bed was called a "Murphy bed," one of those that folded up into the wall of our tiny living room. When the bed was down, it just barely fit into the room between the sofa and chair. Being honeymooners, sometimes on the weekends, we decided to avail ourselves of the use of the bed during the day. There were no locks and no doorbell on the outside door. One Saturday afternoon, while Neal and I were enjoying ourselves in the bed his folks decided to pay a surprise visit. They banged on the outside door once or twice. Hearing nothing they proceeded up the stairs to our apartment.

Holy Cow! Red alert! We flew around that room at warp speed, hastily throwing on our clothes. Together we threw the blankets back on the bed, slammed it up into the wall without a sound, pulled out the sofa, plopped down and picked up a magazine.

"Mom, Pop, what a nice surprise!' we chorused, "Come in, come in. Make yourselves at home."
I always believed that they never knew.

* * *

By the time New Year's Eve rolled around, we had moved up to a bigger, better apartment with large rooms, a private entrance and a private bath. It was big enough that Neal could chase me around the apartment, just laughing and having fun. Also, I learned for the first time that he walked in his sleep. That was scary, but he outgrew it after a few years.

We decided to throw a New Year's Eve party for our friends, complete with noisemakers, funny hats, hors d'oeuvres, Whiskey Sours and Manhattans. (Tsk-tsk. We were still only nineteen years of age.) That was the only time I ever got drunk. With my strict upbringing, I hadn't learned to pace myself. That was a lesson I never wanted to repeat.

* * *

The following year, we moved into Jackson and found a furnished house we could rent. Neal got a better job working for a dairy, selling and delivering bottled milk and other dairy products door-to-door. We bought our first dog, a darling red dachshund puppy named "Slim." I got a job working at Michigan Bell Tel. We were so happy, no worries, no complaints, madly in love and moving up. Well, that isn't altogether true. There was one worry we didn't talk about ...

I dreaded the day we got that official letter that started out: Greetings...

* * *

Chapter Sixteen

"Introduction to Camping"

When he was a kid, Neal's family camped a lot. On the other hand, mine went just one time when I was very small.[3] So in our first year of marriage, Neal set out to introduce me to the joys of the great out-of-doors in a borrowed canvas tent. We went with Neal's brother, Alfred and his wife Charlotte. Our destination was a rustic Michigan state campground on a trout stream. The idea was that the boys would catch the fish and Charlotte and I would cook. Fortunately, I didn't know how to clean fish and never planned to learn. Cooking was Ok, but I had to be shown how. Neal was patient with his instructions and we got along fairly well until later. After all, we were still practically honeymooners.

It came time to pitch the tent. Neal took pains to choose a site far enough removed from his brother for the needed privacy. He demonstrated how to dig a shallow trench around the tent spot, lay down a plastic ground cloth and pitch the tent on that. The ground cloth was necessary because this tent had no floor in it. We would lay our blankets on the cloth, which would give us some protection from sticks and stones and any creeping things lurking in the grass. Next, we drove stakes in the ground to fasten down the four corners, sides and door of the tent. More stakes were placed further out for attaching the ropes that would hold up the sides. Finally, Neal and I crawled under the tent and simultaneously raised the wooden tent poles, inserting them in the roof. This took a certain degree of cooperation and I'm sure our muffled hilarity could be heard near and far. Finally, we tightened up the ropes and beheld our "home-sweet-home" for the night.

The sun was quite low in the sky and clouds were moving in by the time we accomplished all this, fixed supper, heated water and cleaned up. "I'm learning that this camping business takes time," I whispered to Charlotte.

---

[3] I don't think Mother was too keen on camping. Besides, Dad had a farm and animals to care for.

"Oh yes," she replied. "You don't know the half of it".

Having brushed our teeth out in the woods and washed up as best we could, we spread out our blankets in the tent. By now, it was pitch dark. All we had for light was a flashlight and lantern.

"Are you ready?" asked Neal. "If you're ready, I'm going to turn out the light."

"I'm ready."

It was dark, I mean, really dark. No worries. Settle down. You'll be asleep in no time. Right? Wrong.

I stared at the ceiling and strained to listen to the strange night sounds. A rumbling sounded in the distance. "What's that?" I wondered aloud.

"Oh just a little thunder. No problem. Just go to sleep," said my big strong protector.

"Are you sure?" I asked. "It sounds like it's coming closer".

"Will you quit worrying?! I'm trying to sleep here," grumbled my better-half as he shifted his body, poking one elbow into my side.

I tried, again, wiggling my body around to try and fit it into the bumps in the ground. Pretty soon I began to notice flashes of light shining through the tent, followed by more rumbling. "Uh, Neal, what are we going to do if it rains?"

"We aren't going to do anything. This tent is waterproof. We're snug as two bugs in a rug. Now, go to sleep, will you?" he rolled over pulling the covers off me.

Big plops of water began dropping on the tent. At first, they sounded soothing. *Now, I can go to sleep, just listening to the raindrops.* No way was I going to sleep. Neal began to snore softly under the blankets. The wind came up and our tent began flapping.

Soon the heavens opened up. It was a downpour. *Oh my goodness, what's this?*

"Neal! Wake up! It's getting wet in here!"

"Hmm, what… what you talking about, Dorothy?"

"It's raining! I'm getting wet."

"No way."

"Yes, it is. It's coming right in the tent."

"OK, give me the d____ed light, will you'?"

"Here it is."

Neal stood up, bumping his head. He pulled on his jeans. Grabbed the light and the shovel. By now a big puddle was forming on our floor. He unzipped the tent door and stumbled out into the night. Diagnosing the problem in one glance, he realized that the water was running off the tent onto our ground cloth and right under the sides into our bedroom. Also, it had filled up the trench. With no place to go, it had simply run over. Our ship was sinking.

Captain Mercer took control, calling out orders to his First Mate. "Pick up the blankets and clothes, Dorothy. Stuff them in that big plastic bag. Get them away from the puddle. Pull up the ground cloth and drain it outside while I hold up the side of the tent. Ok. Good. Now, we're going to tuck the ground cloth inside, all the way around. You work on that while I dig a bypass to drain out this trench." Soaked to the skin, he left his clothes outside. "See if you can find me a dry towel, Ok?"

The ground cloth was hopelessly soaked, but it had kept the ground dry underneath. We shoved the plastic to one side, sorted out the driest of our blankets and rolled ourselves up together for warmth on the grass for the rest of the night.

৵

The next day was spent drying everything out. Neal strung up a clothesline between two trees. Together, we draped everything over it. Alfred howled with laughter at us greenhorns. Determined to "show" him, I flounced off to go fishing. Not having mastered the art of fly-fishing, I worked with a spinning rod and worms. After the rain, the fish weren't biting, having already gorged themselves on the food washed into the river. Besides, the water was high and roiled from the rain. But the sun was out and it was a pretty day, so who cared?

Neal and Alfred had waders that come up over their chests, so they were able to work upstream like professionals. I was confined to areas I could reach from the near bank. Undaunted, I worked slowly up and down, trying to think like a fish, until I found a promising deep hole defined by a fallen log and slight bend in the river. *Hmmm, I thought, that looked like a nice place for a big trout to hang out.* I maneuvered ever so cautiously upstream past the hole, eased my bait into the water and slowly let out line, allowing the bait to tumble along the bottom, natural-like. I could see it as it bumped along over the smooth rocks and right into the middle of the hole. Now I slowed down and jigged my line just enough to cause the worm to wiggle. Gradually, it came out the other side of the hole and swept into the current. I reeled in and tried again. This time it got caught up on a rock. I reeled in. Once more, I worked my worm toward the hole. This time it missed and sailed on by in the current. *All right, Mr. Fish! This time I'm coming to get ya'. Now, concentration. Throw it out just right, into that certain spot. Ah. I hit it. Ok, now, smoothly, give it just a little more slack, but not too much slack. Let it drift, slowly, slowly. Just under the edge of the log. Down into the hole. Easy does it. Be ready.*

BINGO! Slam, splash. Fish on! A huge trout leapt out of the water, fell back in and took off downstream. *Keep a tight line. Don't let him head for the branches. He'll get off.* Out he came again. Another leap, then another. My rod was bent double, the reel zinging as he stripped off line. "Neal," I yelled, "Neal, bring me the net!" I could tell Mr. Trout was starting to tire, slowing down some. I reeled in a bit of line. He felt it and took off again, this time with less strength. Next time I tried, I could feel him turning. *I've got him coming my way.* "Neal", I yelled, as loud as I could, "Bring the net!"

"I'm coming!" I heard a faint reply. "Hold on, I'm coming." Soon, I heard his boots slogging through the quick running water. By now, I was steadily reeling the exhausted trout in.

"Get the net ready, OK?' I said "I'll bring him to you."

"Gotcha!" Neal moved into position. He knew what to do. He wouldn't lunge for the fish and risk spooking him. "Just bring him in to me. Get him headed into the net," Neal instructed. "Oh my gosh! What a beautiful fish!"

I had reeled in enough line and began backing toward Neal, carefully coaxing the fish closer and closer. We didn't want any mistakes now. We wouldn't net him until he was ready."OK, Neal, here he comes," I said as I pulled my fish over the submerged net. Neal scooped him up in one swift and sure movement and lifted him up like a newborn babe for all to see.

By now, Charlotte and Alfred had come to see what was causing all the excitement. They gasped, "Oh my gosh! Look at what you caught, Dorothy. Beginner's luck, that's what it was, just beginner's luck." *Yeah right, I guess I showed you, Mister. What did you catch, huh?*

That evening we dined on my fine trout, the largest for the week and the only one caught that day. After a cozy campfire, Neal and I snuggled in our warm and dry tent. *Camping wasn't so bad after all,* I thought as I drifted off to sleep. I had my first taste of trout fishing and I was the one who was hooked.

*   *   *

Chapter Seventeen

"You're In the Army Now"

The postman delivered it one Saturday while I was home and Neal was at work.
Oh no! THE LETTER.

I knew immediately when I saw it. It felt like a snake in my hand going *hssssss!* Shaking so badly I could not open it, I sat down in a chair and glared at the thing for the longest time. Finally, I had to know, so I opened the envelope and read the summons that I had dreaded. "Greetings: You are ordered to report for duty etc. etc." I had hoped against hope that he would escape the military draft; I even suggested we have a baby so he could get a deferment. But Neal would have none of that. He would do his duty.

Slim and I moved back to my parents' home. Neal left for Camp Custer in Battle Creek where generations of green recruits had been mustered in. Neal had his beautiful red hair shaved and received his physical exam, clothes and equipment. From that time forward he went by his first name, David, or Dave[4] to his friends.

Wives were allowed one overnight visit before the men left for boot camp. Our so-called private room was no bigger than the width of a single army cot with just enough room to stand beside it. Spouses were sandwiched together all night, but no one seemed to mind, even though the walls were paper thin. Need I say more?

Parting was hard. We had never been separated. David Neal shipped out to Camp Gordon, Georgia, where he would be held incommunicado, confined to base for ten interminable weeks. He could receive mail, but phone calls or visits were prohibited.

My days passed in a blur of work and sleep. Spare time was spent writing to Neal, playing the piano, helping Mom and

---

[4] Dave had never liked being called by his middle name, Neal, so this was his chance to rid himself of it forever. His Mom could never agree and called him Neal to her dying day.

worrying about the war. My only comfort was my little dog, Slim, and Neal's occasional letters. Although I wrote daily, he reported that my letters came in batches, several in one day, and then none at all. He kept them in his foot locker and read them over and over. I treasured his letters to me and kept them close. He wrote of the hell of basic training and longing for me. I missed him terribly, but tried to keep my letters to him cheerful, newsy and loving. If only we could have talked on the phone, it would have eased the pain. Then something happened that made it possible.

One day I came home from work to be greeted at the door by Mother's tear-stained face. "Sit down", she said. Gripped in alarm, I searched her face, "What is it, Mom, what's wrong?"

She started to cry, "Oh, Dorothy, I'm so sorry."

"Mom, is it Neal? Is it Dad?"

She shook her head. "No, they're all right. It's… it's your baby," she blurted out.

Oh my God, "Slim?"

She slowly nodded, with fresh tears, "It's my fault, honey. I'm so sorry."

Stricken, I sat down. "Tell me what happened."

Mom began, "She wanted to go outside. Usually she squats right near the door and runs back inside. But I don't know why – she got away from me and ran into the road. I chased her and called, 'Here Slim!'" Mom took a deep sigh, and continued, "You know how fast those darned cars speed by our house. I couldn't get to her in time. The car slammed on the brakes, but it was too late. Those awful people didn't even stop. They just stepped on it and sped out of here." Mom felt in her apron pocket for her handkerchief.

"Don't cry," I said as I blinked back tears. "It's Ok, Mom, it wasn't your fault."

"I feel so terrible." Mom raised her handkerchief and had a big blow.

"Of course you do. I know you didn't mean for it to happen," I offered. "Where is Slim, now?" I asked, as a tear escaped.

Mom sniffed again. "Well, your dad buried her in a nice place in the garden. We can show you later. Why don't you get a snack and something to drink and go lie down for a while? I'll have supper on in about an hour."

"Ok, Mom, I'll just rest a while. I'm not hungry." With that I left for my room to contemplate my sorrow.

"I'll let you know when supper's ready," she called after me.

Perhaps this was God's way of preparing me for worse things to come, but for the present, this blow was severe enough. Mom was right about one thing: Slim had, indeed, been my baby. She had taken the place of a real baby in our lives. I thought how excited she was to see me. Her body seemed to wiggle all over as her tail became a blur. She would leap up until I took her in my arms so she could cover my face with doggy kisses. I remembered how sleek her coat felt and her warm body in my bed when she curled up at my feet. Heartbroken, I missed Neal more acutely than ever. I needed his warm comforting arms around me, his sweet breath on my cheek. If only we could talk.

How am I going to break the news to him, I thought. *He is going to feel so bad. He's lonely enough as it is. Should I not tell him? No, that wouldn't be fair. I can't withhold this from him.* Overcome with anguish myself, I had a sudden idea. *What if I sent him a telegram? If I word it just right, wouldn't they have to deliver it? Sure, they would.*

And so, I composed the ten words maximum that would break the news to my darling husband. "Slim killed in road. Stop. Please call home. Love, Dorothy." It worked. David Neal Mercer was called out of the ranks and summoned to headquarters for the grim news of a death in the family. He saluted and stood at attention. An officer handed him the telegram. "At ease, Private Mercer. You have some sad news."

Dave braced himself for the worst: that one of us had died. Relieved that it was only our pet dog, Dave kept his face carefully composed. It wouldn't do to let the officer know he had been duped. "Private Mercer, would you care to use the telephone in my office? You can have privacy in there."

"Yes, sir, thank you, sir," Dave saluted smartly and proceeded to the office.

"Oh, Private Mercer, take all the time you need to call. You won't be allowed leave."

"Yes, sir, I know. You're very kind, sir."

Of all the thousands of times Dave and I had talked on the phone, that call was the sweetest balm.

*   *   *

Life went on. Basic training completed, Dave was given Christmas leave, after which he was to report to Fort Monmouth, New Jersey, for induction into the Signal Corps. For once, the Army got one thing right. Only the brighter soldiers were given that training. Thank God, he didn't have to go into the infantry to be shipped overseas immediately. The grim reality was that Signal Corps training was only a temporary reprieve from combat. But there was no need to worry about that now.

Mom and I met Dave in the dining room. Smartly dressed in his uniform, with a grin a mile wide, he burst in and swept me into his strong arms. The transformation was astonishing. The skinny recruit that had left two and one half months ago was now a soldier, a fit twenty pounds heavier, all of it muscle. He lifted me and twirled around as if I was light as a feather. Our hearts were bursting. Together felt so good. We kissed and held on tight, while Mom looked on in approval.

The time sped away. Soon it was time for Dave to leave for New Jersey. Parting was less difficult this time. I knew that I would give two weeks' notice on my job and join him as soon as arrangements could be made. Dave found us an upstairs apartment in Long Branch, New Jersey. He got a weekend pass to come home and get me. By now, we had traded in our old clunker of a car for a spanking new Studebaker that cost $1,700. We were making payments on it. Golly, it was sleek and beautiful. Too bad we didn't keep it until now. It would be a "classic".

We could make good time in that car, much of the way on the Pennsylvania Turnpike, one of the earliest limited-access modern roadways. Driving straight through to save money, we could make it from Concord to Long Branch in seventeen hours. If exhaustion set in we would stop at a roadside park, lie down in the grass and sleep for an hour or two.

Unable to live on Dave's meager pay and my $75 a month allotment, I had to get a job. Fortunately, I was able to transfer to New Jersey Bell Telephone and resume my position as a Service Representative, with no further training necessary.

Our apartment was in a drafty old frame house, converted into two apartments for military couples. We had three rooms and a bath. Some of the furniture was rather creaky. I remember one evening when we were making love. The bed was rocking. Suddenly, the frame gave way and the whole thing collapsed on the floor with a resounding crash. What could you do but dissolve into hysterical laughter? This was a war story we wouldn't tell our grandchildren.

The downstairs tenants changed often, as men came into Fort Monmouth, were trained and shipped out again. One of the new tenants, a couple from Texas, moved in, unloaded boxes and threw them out the front door for later pick-up. A few days later, I began to notice strange brown bugs in the kitchen sink. They evaded capture. The instant I turned on the light, they would disappear with blinding speed. Thus, I was introduced to Texas cockroaches. They had come into the house hidden in the cracks of packing boxes. From that time forward, we were at war with the infernal pests. Our landlord wasted no money on exterminators.

*   *   *

Dave trained in fixed station radio repair. In those days, radios were bulky things with lots of wiring and glass vacuum tubes. These tubes resembled light bulbs. In small radios they ranged in size from finger length to hand length. Fixed station radios were the largest ones that the Army used to broadcast around the world. They could fill a whole room. When you walked in you saw a forest of vacuum tubes, some as tall as a man. Years later, they were replaced by tiny transistors. You can imagine that it took several months to complete this training. You had to be able to take any radio apart, fix it, and put it back together. After that time, he was assigned to stay right there in Fort Monmouth and do testing on radios as they came off the assembly line. It was necessary to check them out before they were sent off to be used in the field. This was a "cushy" assignment. Dave and three of his buddies drove around New Jersey in Army jeeps. They stopped every hour for five minutes to test the radios. The rest of the time they played bridge. Meantime, I worked nine to five at the telephone business office, walking distance from home.

We made friends among his army buddies and fellow workers at the phone company. We played bridge with the Haywards or the Harlows, partied with friends, swam in the ocean and went for drives. We even drove into New York City a couple of times to dodge taxis and see a show. Whenever Dave had leave, we drove home to Michigan to visit our folks. It was about this time that Dave's maternal grandfather, George McDonald, died suddenly of an aneurism of the aorta. He had been told by a doctor that he had such an aneurism and that it was always fatal. Grandpa was walking down to his garden one day when the aorta ruptured and he died before he could make it back to the house. Nowadays, such an aneurism would be repaired surgically. Even though it was an expense we didn't need, I insisted Dave fly home for his mother's sake, and he did.

All the people who worked at my office were women, except for the head boss. He decided that I could double as a substitute cashier to relieve the head cashier, Greta, when she went on break. At times when the foot traffic was particularly heavy, I could open up another window. At those times, I would close my desk and slip into the cashier's cage. After some weeks, I began to notice that the boss had a practice of cashing checks far more often than seemed necessary. He seemed to use Greta and I as a convenient banking system, coming into the cashier's cage once or twice a day with his personal check made out to cash for various amounts, maybe $200 or $300, depending on how much cash we had in the till at the time. Whenever he did this he had an annoying habit of fidgeting, humming and tapping his fingers on my counter as I counted out the cash, stamped and initialed the back of his check. He also had a disgusting addiction to cigars, smoking them within the confines of his small office. His clothing reeked of it. After getting his money, he would retire to his office. A short time later he would don his hat and coat, emerge from the office and disappear down the street.

I puzzled over this peculiar behavior for some weeks, discussing it with no one but Dave. In those days, before the advent of electronic transfer, it could take several days, or as long as a week for checks to clear from one bank to another. Finally, I could come to no other conclusion but that he was kiting checks.[5] He was overdrawing his checking account and covering it with the cash from our office, knowing that his checks would not clear right away. Of course, he had to cash another check to cover the first one. Thus, he was caught in a vicious circle. No other possibility could explain his behavior. *Could he be caught up in gambling at the horse racetrack in Redbank, NJ?* At length, I decided I had to turn him in. So I wrote a letter to the headquarters of New Jersey Bell, laying out the facts and suggesting they check it out. They didn't answer my letter. I thought *that just goes to show what happens when you blow the whistle.* I never heard a thing about it until months after Dave and I had moved back to Michigan. For a time, I kept up a correspondence with my Long Branch friends. A letter came from Greta, "You won't believe what happened to Mr. X. One morning investigators from headquarters came into the office and arrested him. They put him in handcuffs and took him out of here. We never learned any more about it, but I sure wondered what happened. We have a new boss now. One of the women got promoted. Isn't that great?"

---

[5] a fake financial transaction, somewhat similar to today's Ponzi scheme

∽

Dave and I were counting down the hours and minutes until he passed that magic number, twenty-one months of service on his two year obligation. The Army rule was that whenever you got within three months of your discharge, you could no longer be sent overseas. From time to time, requisitions would come down for so many men with certain training. One never knew when you might get orders to go to Korea, or anywhere the Army needed you. The Korean War was bitter and brutal. Winter fighting was grueling in the mountains. Over 50,000 Americans were killed and many thousands more were wounded. Dave narrowly escaped being sent over when a half dozen men from his unit were called. Of those six, only four returned alive. Dave credits his lieutenant for choosing the ones who had to go and for not choosing him. Not daring to question why, Dave waited until he received his honorable discharge papers. As he bade the lieutenant his last farewell Dave inquired, "By the way, sir, I've always wanted to ask you something."

"Permission granted, Corporal Mercer."

"I've always wondered, sir, why you didn't choose me to go to Korea with the group, sir."

"That's simple, Corporal," he said, "You were the hardest working man in my unit. I didn't want to lose you."

Oh my God! Thank you, Jesus.

We had known the chances were excellent that Dave would be sent over. Escaping simply did not happen, but fate smiled on us. Somehow, when it got down to that critical time when Dave's twenty-one month deadline approached, there were no more calls for men of his training. We escaped the almost certain death sentence. Dave never left the States. Hallelujah!

*   *   *

Chapter Eighteen

"On the Move Again"

Our little Studebaker was packed to the gunnels as we sped down the Pennsylvania turnpike toward home. We would stay on the farm while Dave looked for work. I applied for unemployment compensation and received a blunt turn down.

We could afford to take our time finding just the right job for Dave. It had to be something that exploited his talent and allowed opportunity for advancement. We wanted to be able to live on one income as we started our family. We talked it over. I knew that with his energy and outgoing personality that he would be a great salesman. I asked, "Who was the best salesman you ever met?"

"Al Ware," Dave answered without hesitation.

"Tell me about this Al Ware," I said. "What was special about him?"

"Well, Al would come into the meat market when I worked there. He was a rep for Swift and Company, the meat people. Mostly, it was his smile. He was just so darned friendly. He remembered your name and always asked how you were doing."

"Anything else you remember about Al?" I prompted.

"He never seemed to be in a hurry himself, but he didn't talk too long if you were busy. He was a nice enough looking guy, but it was more than that. I don't know. Al left Swift and Co, and went to work selling insurance. Remember, he was the guy that sold us our first insurance policy?"

"Oh yeah, maybe you could talk to Al and get some advice," I suggested.

"Good idea. I'll do that tomorrow," Dave agreed.

Next day, Dave found Al's number in the Monroe,

Michigan phone book. Al invited us both over to his house to talk and meet his wife Margie. Al was working as a life insurance salesman for the Lloyd "Lud" Lynch Agency out of Detroit. Leaving the Ware's, Dave felt optimistic about a career in life insurance. He set about to interview with several insurance companies. The more he learned, the better it seemed. It boiled down to two companies, Sun Life of Canada and John Hancock Insurance of Boston.

Dave came away from his interview with Lud Lynch, impressed with John Hancock and the Lynch Agency. Moreover, he would be working for Al Ware as his Unit Manager and immediate supervisor. We made preparations to move to Monroe where Dave set out to be the hardest-working, best damned salesman the Hancock had ever seen, and I set out to become a pregnant little housewife.

We had a walk-up apartment south of town. It was fairly new wooden construction. Nice neighbors. The only drawback was something that couldn't be helped. The well water had a distinctly sulfurous odor, i.e. it smelled like rotten eggs. Management had installed the very best water purification available. That lessened the problem for a few days. Then it would intensify again. Neighbors advised us, "In time, you will get used to it." Never happened.

In short order, I met my first objective: I got pregnant. No sooner had I missed my first period than my olfactory nerves began working overtime. *Oh m'god, that smell!* In just a matter of days, I was spending more time on the floor leaning over the john. Soon, I got so weak, I didn't bother with the john anymore. I merely lay in bed with a dishpan on the floor at the ready. Dave would see to me as best he could before he left for work, come home and tend to me at noontime and again at suppertime before he went out for his evening calls. I use the term suppertime loosely. All I could choke down were tiny bites of soda crackers and cracked ice. I spent most of the days lying in our darkened bedroom, dozing off and on between bouts of nausea. Dust, dirty dishes and laundry piled up. Dave was worried. Al noticed this and suggested his wife might be of some help. "Margie is pretty knowledgeable about these things," he said. "Her dad is a medical doctor and her sister is a nurse. Besides, we have two kids of our own."

Margie suggested we see her obstetrician as soon as possible. In the meantime, I should try taking sips of coke syrup along with the crackers and ice chips. This would help calm the stomach and give me calories. Coke syrup was available from a pharmacist without prescription. This helped some, but I was getting weaker by the day. Between starting a new business, taking care of me and keeping house, Dave was overwhelmed. I needed better care and Dave needed relief. So, we decided it was time for me to go home to Mother.

Thus, I spent the next two months on the farm, moving between the sofa by day and the bed by night, accompanied with my paraphernalia close by and consisting of dishpan, ice chips, soda crackers, coke syrup and pink and blue nausea pills. I learned that the term "morning sickness" was a misnomer as it wasn't confined to mornings. The nausea lasted for 24 hours a day. I could fight it by keeping my head perfectly still and not talking.

My two brothers, now married with children of their own, came to keep me company. Well meaning, they tried to cheer me up by telling how well their wives coped with morning sickness. Claude bragged about his wife, Joyce, who simply got dressed, fixed his breakfast, tossed her cookies, then picked up her purse and calmly went to work. It's all in your head, he remarked helpfully. Next, they tried making me laugh. I was overcome immediately with the dry heaves, there being nothing left to toss up. That gave them pause. *Maybe there was more to this than first thought. Must be the Douglas curse.* Feeling rather hopeless, they left soon after.

"Well, Dort[6], we'd better run along," Claude said, "Take care of yourself. Don't take any wooden nickels," he added. "See ya!" as they beat a hasty retreat.

Dave was working hard and spending Sundays driving the two hours to see me. I needed my husband, but I couldn't go back

[6] Dort was their nickname for me.

to that apartment. Just the thought of that odor gave me the heaves. Dave set out to find a better place to live.

It happened that one of his first sales was to a young couple who were to become our best friends. Bob and Edna Kenworthy lived with their baby girl in a single-family home in town. They were kind enough to call Dave when the house next door came up for rent. It was perfect for us: two bedrooms and bath, living room, kitchen, and a garage, all on one floor, with a grassy front yard and a garden in the back. Best of all, it didn't stink. Dave put down a deposit on the house. Bob and Edna helped him get our things moved in and settled. Bless her heart, Edna even washed out the kitchen cupboards and put down clean shelf paper. We were to spend many happy hours visiting and playing bridge with the Kenworthys and Edna taught me all I needed to know about baby care. We also were destined to share two of the worst possible sorrows together.

By the fifth and sixth months of pregnancy, I was into maternity clothes, the baby was a satisfactory bump in my belly and the bouts of nausea had lessened in intensity. I still followed my careful morning routine, but once my stomach settled I could go about a normal afternoon and evening. Dave was working very hard to achieve success. Our spring garden delighted us with surprises as perennial plants popped out of the ground. Dave's parents were avid gardeners and Dave wasted no time in following in their footsteps. Soon we had plenty of lettuce, radishes and a few peas. My brother, Claude, who has a story and joke for every situation, remarked that, "Planting peas is a waste of time. For every handful or seed you plant, you harvest one handful of peas."

My pregnancy was progressing nicely. We busied ourselves painting and preparing the baby's room, choosing furnishings and perusing the book of names, helpfully provided by my doctor's nurse. A boy would be Jeffrey David Mercer. Edna and I were in and out of each other's houses daily. I insisted on baby-sitting with LuAnn. What a good baby! I read "Baby and Child Care" by Dr. Spock and practiced on LuAnn. Margie Ware introduced me to the idea of "natural childbirth". I embraced the concept and avidly devoured the books Margie loaned me.

Freshmen in the life insurance business had to work evenings. During the summer months, daylight lasted far into the evening, so I often rode along with Dave on his calls. I would sit in the car and read while he went through his memorized sales talk three times an evening. Since most couples were both home in the evenings, setting up a rare sales call during the day was just an added bonus. Now and then, Dave would have a "poop out"[7] that gave us a time together just to talk over our day. It would require years of apprenticeship before a seasoned salesman could give up evening calls and work exclusively during the day with business people and professionals.

Fall arrived in Michigan. My due date in early October came and went with no sign of our baby's imminent arrival. My doctor visits increased from monthly to bi-weekly to weekly. My belly expanded and dropped lower, but wasn't making any moves, other than false labor. My doctor was starting to worry. Statistically, it wasn't safe for a first baby to go more than two weeks past term. He began making noises about "induced labor". That raised fears in my mind. It didn't sound "natural" at all. At three weeks past term, my doctor put me in the hospital. I was given a shot of something and told to walk around the corridors. Nothing happened.

Doctor decided to break my water. That should stimulate something. More walking, more exams, more hours passed. Meantime, Dave was busy wearing a path from the office to the hospital, to home, to the hospital and back to the office. Edna and Bob were being as supportive as possible, keeping track of the house, ironing Dave's white shirts and fixing meals. A poignant incident happened when my Dad became so worried about me when no one answered the phone that he drove all the way over to Monroe to find out what was going on. We both tried to reassure him that I was in good hands. Finding that there was nothing he could do, he left for home, feeling more helpless than ever.

Margie visited me. "I agree with your doctor, Dorothy," she said. "It's time you forget about natural childbirth and let him induce labor. You and the baby are both getting worn out. It's the

---

[7] Poop out = the slang for unexpected cancellation of an appointment

safest thing to do," she argued. "It's past time to get that baby out of there." Dave agreed heartily. And so, I was hooked up to monitors and an intravenous drip of a labor inducing drug.

Labor progresses through two stages. During the first stage, the expanded uterus contracts in strong muscle spasms of increasing intensity and duration with rests in between. These so-called "labor pains" are necessary to pull apart and expand the opening so it is large enough to allow the baby to pass through. The normal situation is for the baby's round head to be downward, thus assisting with the process by pressing against the opening.

The second stage of labor commences when the opening becomes large enough for the baby's head to pass through. The attending nurses, having checked the opening periodically, can tell when the baby is ready to deliver. At this point, the doctor is summoned and the patient is whisked into the delivery room and positioned in the stirrups. Meantime, the mother's body spontaneously begins strenuous efforts at pushing lasting a minute or two, interspersed with rests.

After four hours on the intravenous drip, things were progressing well at last. I reached the second stage of labor and moved into the delivery room. Margie and Dave, having been by my bedside the whole time, were banished to the waiting room.

I was ready and bearing down mightily when the pushing sensation came. The nurse said, "Don't bear down yet, Dorothy Just pant like a dog when the pains come." Dr. Middleton told me that the baby wasn't in the correct position. Instead of having his head down, he was in the worst of "breach" positions. He had one foot down and one up. No wonder I had trouble dilating. Dr. told me to prepare myself, because he needed to pull the other foot down, in order to deliver the baby. With this he reached inside, grasped Jeffrey's leg and pulled it down. I screamed in agony. Nothing in my life before or since ever hurt so terribly. It was quick but it wasn't over. I had nightmares about it for years. With each new labor pain, they now encouraged me to push with all my might, on and on, until I collapsed between times in utter exhaustion. "I can't do any more," I gasped. "Yes, you can!" Another wave of pain hit. I screamed. "Come on, Dorothy, now push!" chorused the nurses, one at my head, one at my side, Dr. Middleton at my feet, doing whatever. This went on until I was past exhaustion and could do no more. And then I did more. I had nothing left to give. Doctor prepared a few drops of anesthetic and let me take a few whiffs when the pain was the worst. *Forget about natural childbirth! Just give me the anesthetic!* I sucked eagerly in big gulps.

Once the baby was out, followed immediately by the placenta, they gave me a bigger dose as I sagged back to rest. The fog wasn't complete. I became aware of what was happening. People sprang into action, moving at top speed. Jeffrey was in trouble. Doctor leaned over him doing something to start his breathing, barking rapid orders to the nurses. Professionals ran for the delivery room. I watched my son. He was still and beautiful, tinged with pink. I talked to him, "Come on, honey, breathe! Come on, honey, breathe!" I pleaded. In time, I could do no more. I sucked on the mask covering my face and went to sleep in utter defeat.

Margie had sensed what was happening. She heard my screams followed by unnatural silence coming from the delivery room. She stopped one of the nurses heading for the room. "What's wrong? Is it Dorothy or the baby?"

"It's the baby", the nurse replied as she hurried on.

Margie immediately went to the pay phone and dialed her pediatrician. "Please come up to the third floor delivery room, immediately," she said. "The Mercer's baby is in trouble". Mere minutes later, he arrived in the delivery room, hastily scrubbed and gowned. The baby still had a beating heart, but he was rapidly turning blue. His lungs wouldn't expand. Both doctors did all that they could. Jeffrey David Mercer's short life lasted just twenty minutes until his heart gave out. We never knew what caused it. The autopsy showed no disease or defects. Maybe he was just plain tuckered out.

Jeffrey's tiny body was buried next day in a small white casket in Dave's home town cemetery. Later, a small granite tombstone marked his grave. "Jeffrey David Mercer, November 2,

1955." Dave and our immediate family attended a simple burial service at the gravesite. I couldn't be there.

I awoke that day in my hospital bed, hurting everywhere. The first thing I saw was Margie's angelic face gazing at me, Edna by her side. "It's all right," I said. "You don't have to tell me. I know the baby's dead." The whole thing had replayed in my dreams over and over as my exhausted body began to cope with the shocking truth.

It was a feeling like I had never experienced before or since. I can only describe it as having every sense of one's person or ego or personality stripped away. Nothing of self was left. It was as if all the layers were gone and nothing was left but the core or essence. This core was God. After everything else was taken away, there was only God.

Margie and Edna planned to sit quietly with me while Dave was away burying his son. I stirred myself enough to ask, "Who is taking care of your children?"

"Don't worry about that," they said. "The kids are with a sitter until their fathers get home."

Margie gently inquired whether I would like her to call her pastor to come up and be with me for a time. That concept seemed unnecessary to me. I didn't need an outsider to come and try to bring me God, because God was inside me. The nurse came in. She changed my pads and gave me a pill to help me relax. I drifted back to sleep, too depleted to talk anymore.

My body was wretchedly torn. I needed to stay in the hospital for a few days. During wakeful moments, I couldn't stand hearing the babies being brought to their mothers for feeding. Their cries would cause my breasts to leak and my arms and body to clench in anguish, longing to be filled. I asked to be moved from the maternity floor.

*   *   *

Homecoming day arrived. I hobbled carefully from the car into the house and sat my tender body onto a large "donut" cushion that Margie had thoughtfully provided. I needed that for the first month. Mother stayed with me for two weeks, then Dave's mother, until I was able to begin caring for myself. My breasts became so engorged and feverish that I cried out in pain if touched. Edna gave me tender rubs with a hot medicated oil that relieved the pain and softened some of the lumps. Then she would wrap them tightly to discourage the milk from coming in.

I had expected to be the one to pack away Jeffrey's things. But Bob and Edna had spared me that sad job. When I arrived home, Jeffrey's room had been stripped and even painted a different color. It became a guest room for our mothers.

Sharing such a profound crisis can work one of two ways. Once it is over, it can cause people to come together in closer friendship, or it can become a barrier between them. For Edna and me, our friendship became cemented forever. She stood by me and helped during my worst crisis. Fourteen years later, I was ready and able to return the favor.

*   *   *

Chapter Nineteen

"And Baby Makes Three"

Historically, after a death in the family, people wore black for a year of mourning in respect to the departed one, followed by a year of half mourning when they wore gray. During the time of full mourning, they did not go out or attend dances and parties. In some ways, this may have been overdone. Nevertheless, this practice had its merits. Not only did it honor the departed, but it signified to everyone that the person in mourning deserved a certain kindness as well.

Nowadays, after a tragedy, a person in deep mourning is allowed a much too short "healing time" after which they are expected to "move on". With respect to the death of our son, Jeffrey, Dave and I weren't able to move on until our daughter Shelley was born, twenty five months later. Even then, we remembered our sorrow over Jeffrey for many years, especially on his birthday.

By the time of Shelley Lynn Mercer's birth, Dave had been promoted to Unit Manager for the Lynch agency and moved to Jackson, Michigan, to head up the unit there. We had a rented house in Jackson. Shelley was born right on her due date, December 15, 1957. Her imminent arrival was abruptly announced on the evening before when my water broke during the night. We were taking no chances this time. Dave took me immediately to the hospital and called our private nurse. We had arranged for Margie's nurse sister, Eunice Washbish, who lived in Jackson, to attend my labor. When I stalled along all night without going into serious labor, the question became, "Do I go back home or not?" Taking into account my history, my obstetrician decided to induce labor without delay. He got no argument from Eunice, Dave or I. Once again, I was hooked up to the I.V. drip. This time things went according to the book. Within four or five hours, I was delivered of a beautiful baby girl. Words are inadequate to describe the incredible feeling of joy. There is nothing else like it. At last, you know what your life is meant for. When I saw her for the first time, I exclaimed, "She's alive, she is really alive!" as if I couldn't believe it! I was just so relieved and happy.

Dave was beside himself with pride and joy. We just couldn't quit grinning at each other and gazing at our new baby. Congratulations poured in. Dave called me every two hours to see how we were both doing. Our happiness was complete. The day we brought her home from the hospital was wonderful. We kept her in a little white and pink bassinet on wheels and kept her close by. I didn't want anyone else to even breathe on her, much less pick her up. We didn't take her out in public at all for the first month.

My recovery from childbirth this time was much faster and easier than it had been with Jeffrey. I was able to take care of Shelley Lynn right away. Having her on breast milk saved me from the awful pain of drying up. She was smaller than Jeffrey. The pregnancy and birth were just easier all the way around.

We built our first home on a golf course, the fourth hole, a short par three. It was three bedrooms, dining, kitchen bath and a full basement. Shelley was so cute and good. Edna advised us to put her in her playpen during her wakeful times right from the start, before she could roll over. This was excellent advice. Shelley learned to sit up and play with her toys within view of Mama as I worked in the kitchen, talked on the phone or did my ironing.

The laundry room was in the basement, so when Mama had to run down and move the laundry, it was no problem. Baby was safe in the playpen. Shelley learned to walk by pulling herself up and walking around the playpen.

Likewise, Edna gave us good advice never to rock her to sleep and then put her to bed. Rather, we should let her fall asleep from the start in her own crib. Thus, we were spared a lot of fights later on. She associated the playpen with play time and the crib with sleep times. She was happy and contented both places. This is not to say that we didn't cuddle her, rock her, and play with her a lot. It is just that she was safe and happy in the crib and the play pen, thus I could get my work done while she played or slept, knowing she was safe.

To my discomfort, Shelley was loath to sleep through the night. My child care advisors had plenty of suggestions on how to help the baby learn to do this. After several months of broken sleep, I was tempted to try the last resort: just let her cry. However, this would be difficult to do, living in an apartment house with thin walls. Sucker that I was, I would get up and tend the situation. Shelley had *me* trained.

Summer arrived with no relief from the night feedings. I was ready for drastic action. Shelley and I packed our bags and set out to visit Gram and Grampa Douglas. I warned Mom and Dad that my baby daughter and I were going to have it out and they had better plug their ears. I was ready for the last resort. Sure enough, right on schedule at three o'clock in the morning Daughter Dearest started to tune it up. After five minutes when no mama arrived to pick her up, she really cut loose. This continued for a tortuous twenty minutes that seems like an hour. I was in agony but I plugged my ears and held out. At last she began to run down reduced to a few whimpers and snuffles. Then blessed silence. That was the last time she woke up in the night.

Too many parents wait until it is too late to train their children correctly. Thus, they lose control right from the start and the baby ends up ruling the roost. This is not a healthy or happy relationship.

Another important bit of advice from Edna was to use the correct discipline befitting the age. The child must be taught to obey the words "No-no!" at a very tender age. This is important for the safety and health of the child. Possibly the first important lesson is when the baby starts to creep. She will try to poke her finger into an electric outlet. Edna advised me to slap her little hand and say "No-no!" sharply, then pick her up and move her away from the outlet and distract her with a smile and a toy. Depending on the temperament of the baby, you may have to do this a few times until she catches on. It may seem cruel, but it is far better to teach the child when all it takes is a tiny slap on the hand and a firm voice than to wait until they are older when it will require a much firmer slap elsewhere. If you watch a mother bear with cubs, she will cuff the little things when they do something wrong. The cubs accept it as training. They expect their mother to care enough to teach them right. So it is with children. They depend on the parent to protect them from harm by making the correct decisions and enforcing them. This in no way condones cruelty. Good discipline is necessary if your child is to feel loved.

Do I need to add that the parent must be absolutely consistent? One cannot say "No-no" one time and ignore the child the next. Otherwise the child will test the parent unmercifully in an attempt to learn what she can get away with and what not. Mixed messages are worse than none at all. Consider this; the child is going to learn not to poke her finger in that hole, one way or another.

There is a school of thought that teaching the child to obey "No-no" is not necessary. The better way, they say, is to simply prepare the whole house to be child proof, removing everything that can be harmful to the child. Thus, the entire house becomes a giant playpen. There are several problems with this. First of all, you can never be sure that the entire area is safe. Other people live here and they can drop things on the floor or forget to put something away or leave a cigarette burning or a bottle of medicine open. Also, the child never learns to obey her parent, thus you can't take her anywhere. The child is underfoot and can be harmed by adults doing chores or cooking. Inevitably a stove gets left on, or water left in the tub, or a door is ajar.

I believe that the beginning of self-control starts with parental control. By controlling the tiny child, you are teaching them to control themselves. As they mature, you gradually expand their limits within which they operate under their own self-control, until eventually you cut them loose entirely.

Shelley was a precocious child on the one hand and a mother's girl on the other. She loved to explore the house, walk, climb and get into things. Once she learned to roll over, she was off to the races. She could roll over really fast and get just about anywhere she wanted to go. One peculiarity was that she didn't crawl much because rolling was so much faster. She pretty much skipped crawling and went directly to walking. We liked to joke that she started talking at six months and never stopped. She never "baby talked", but pronounced her words correctly from the start. Before she was two years old she could sing the ABC song right on pitch with perfect diction.

My sister Anna's baby, Cindy, was close in age to Shelley. They were playmates up until the age of two, when we moved away.

I belonged to a ladies bridge club. While Shelley was tiny, I took her along with me to the games in her little carrier. When she woke up I would hold her in my arm and let her nurse, while I went right along playing bridge. Whoever had the dummy hand would change her diaper. The other ladies loved her, of course.

I also belonged to a golf league and had a regular babysitter when I played golf.

*   *   *

Chapter Twenty

"Onward and Upward"

D ave was brought into the Detroit Agency headquarters as an agency supervisor, given a promotion and better salary. We moved to an apartment in Birmingham, a suburb of Detroit, and Dave became a full-time commuter. The offices were in downtown Detroit. That left me alone a lot of the time. It was too far to come home for lunch. Sometimes he missed dinner too, because he had to spend a lot of time training his salesmen.

After a year in the apartment, we bought a house on Buckingham Avenue, right across from a city playground. This made a great place for Shelley and me to play on the swing set, slide and merry-go-round. Shelley was much too little to go there alone. In fact, she wouldn't even play in another room alone, much less in our fenced backyard. She insisted on being with me at all times, except when asleep in her own crib in her bedroom.

Now that we had our own house, we could have another dachshund. Heidi was a registered black miniature. We raised some litters of puppies and sold them. Heidi was a mama's girl too and would not deliver her babies until I sat with her. Heidi lived with us for about nine years until she became arthritic and grouchy.

After working as a supervisor in the Lynch Agency, Dave was promoted to General Agent and given a territory and an agency of his own in Lansing, Michigan. We sold our house in Birmingham and leased two separate houses in Okemos for one year each.

Dave was next promoted to Grand Rapids. He was still a General Agent, but was given the Grand Rapids agency because it was bigger and more prosperous. First, we leased a house in East Grand Rapids for two years, and then we bought a home in Kentwood and stayed there until our girls had finished school.

*   *   *

Chapter Twenty-One

"And Baby Makes Four"
March 16, 1960

It was a horrible night, weather-wise. The Detroit area was in the grip of an early spring ice storm. The sidewalks outside William Beaumont Hospital in Royal Oak were a sheet of ice. As my doctor hurried into the hospital, he slipped and fell, bruising himself and wrenching his back. In the meantime, Dave and I were waiting for him in the labor room, awaiting the birth of our second daughter. For the third time, I would be hooked up to an I.V. to speed up my labor. By the third baby, we had learned that I needed it and I had no objection.

This labor was the easiest of all. After four hours, I reached the second stage and was being prepared for delivery. While I was transported to the delivery room, draped and prepped, I was instructed to hold back by panting like a dog whenever I felt the urge to bear down. Meantime, the doctor was scrubbing and donning a gown and gloves. At last, when all was in readiness, the doc took up his position and instructed me to push with the next "bearing down" pain. And so when I began to feel the sensation, I took a deep breath and pushed hard. Out slid the baby, just as neat as could be. One push was all it took. What a difference! So easy this time!

The entire pregnancy had been easiest of all. There was some morning sickness, but this time it was more like it was supposed to be, confined to the morning. And it only lasted the normal length of time, maybe two or three months. In summary, I was finally getting the hang of it – normal pregnancy, easy birth.

Ann Elizabeth displayed her calm temperament right from the moment she was born. The nurse swaddled her and laid her down as she busied with other things. Ann didn't cry, but quietly lay there on the table next to mine gazing at me with beautiful blue eyes. We were getting acquainted with each other. Because we hadn't named her yet, I said, "Hi, baby," and gave her a welcoming smile.

It is so amazing how different human beings are. As she grew Ann continued to display her even temperament. She was content to play by herself and could concentrate for long periods on an activity or a game she was playing. She was sensitive and self disciplined from a young age. I do not remember ever having to spank her. Usually, a scowl and a cross word was all it took to make her obey. Ann provided the companionship and courage that Shelley had needed in order to let go of Mommy. For the first time, Shelley was able to be in a different room from Mommy or play outside on the swing set or in the sand box, so long as Ann was with her. They were both little blonds, but Ann had blue eyes like her dad and Shelley's were green and brown like her mother.

When the sisters started to play together Shelley tended to boss Ann around. For the first couple years, Ann followed docilely. It was quite amusing to Dave and me to watch their interaction when Ann finally decided that she wasn't going to take that anymore. She had learned to say, "No Sheddy! Mine."

For holidays and family occasions, we loaded up the car with kid's paraphernalia and headed home to visit grandparents, aunts and uncles. In those days, there were no seat belts and car seats for kids. The crib mattress fit nicely across the back seat. We filled the area with blankets and toys, making a regular playpen/crib for the girls. If the baby needed feeding, I simply took her in my lap in the front seat. Usually, we split our time between the two houses: half with my parents, half with Dave's. It was a lot of work, but we were young and strong. By now, all of our siblings had children at home, and our parents were still young enough to be able to put on huge family dinners with all the offspring. Sometimes one of the siblings would host the party.

I remember one special occasion when my side of the family all gathered at my brother's house for a July potluck picnic in their yard. The occasion was my father's eightieth birthday, July 20, 1969. Also, it happened to be the day that the United States landed their first man on the moon. We all gathered around the radio as we listened to Neil Armstrong's awe-inspiring words, "That's one small step for man, one giant leap for mankind." We actually heard and understood the words broadcast from the moon. It was the sort of thing you never forget, right up there with the day

Kennedy was shot, followed by Lee Harvey Oswald being shot, the day the Japanese bombed Pearl Harbor and the day the World Trade Center came down.

Christmases were big occasions requiring three months of preparation. At that time, we still bought presents for everyone in the family: aunts, uncles and cousins. Years later, when the family grew older, we began drawing names. Finally, when we each had grandchildren of our own, we discontinued getting together at Christmas.

Easter was another "biggie". Our immediate family tradition was for us three ladies to get all gussied up in new dresses, hats, gloves and new patent leather shoes to pose for pictures in front of the house, after which we all would attend church. After that, we came home for Easter dinner. Then the girls had to go play in their rooms while Dave and I hid the Easter eggs. When all was ready, they received their little baskets filled with fake green grass and went on their Easter egg hunt. Mommy and Daddy had the camera ready. Sometimes broad hints were required to help the little one. Even so, I often found candy eggs hidden away for weeks later.

*   *   *

Chapter Twenty-Two

"Camping: Phase Two"

W hat could be more fun than taking two preschoolers camping, one of them still in diapers, the other one in night protection? You think I'm kidding, don't you? Not.

I told you I was hooked. Maybe crazy, too. We took our kids camping right from the start. The preparations for a camping trip were awesome indeed. It was necessary to work with a checklist:[8]

> Pay bills
> Stop mail
> Dog sitter
> Water plants
> Clean house
> Clean out fridge
> Take trash out
> Mow lawn
> Notify neighbors
> Laundry
> Plan menus
> Food shopping
> Gas up car
> Check oil, tires, hoses
> Pack clothes for 4 people-
>> Warm clothes
>> Cool clothes
>> Rain clothes
>> Grubby clothes
>> One dressy outfit apiece (never used)
>> Swimsuits
>> Cover-ups
>> Spare shoes
>> Pajamas
>> Underwear
> Towels, linens
> Sleeping bags
> Air mattresses

---

[8] Those of you who have taken little kids camping can skip this.

Laundry bag
Plastic sheet
Clothesline
Clothespins
Laundry & dish soap
Toilet paper, Kleenex
Handi-wipes
Diapers
Toys
Cards
Story books
Tricycle
Bicycles
Beach toys
Favorite blankie
Books
Fishing gear
Bait
Camp stove
Fuel
Ice chest
Ice
Camp cooking pans
Dish pan & drainer
Knives & silverware
Cups
Plates
Hatchet
Plastic table cover
Umbrella
Rug
Matches
Tent
Tent stakes & ropes
Folding chairs
First aid kit
Bug spray
Suntan lotion
Poison ivy itch cream
Tooth brushes & paste
Combs, hair brushes & fasteners

Sun hats
Rain hats
Emergency telephone numbers
Hiking boots
Backpacks and fanny packs
Camera
Binoculars
Sun glasses
Bird book
Canoe and paddles
Extra keys
Licenses
Flashlight
Spare batteries
Camp lantern
Cash

Let's see, did I forget anything? That's why the last item is on the list. We always forgot something. Fortunately, we had one of those old fashioned roomy station wagons. Even so, it was a challenge to get it all in. Dave was up to the challenge. No one was allowed to pack the car but Dave. Oh, we could cart all the stuff out there and hand it to him, but packing the car was a ceremony that only he could perform correctly. There was a certain way to do it and a certain language that was required to make it all happen.

Remember that Girl Scout motto? Be prepared! It is the Boy Scout motto as well. Did I mention that Dave was an Eagle Scout? Maybe that explains it. We were both crazy. Yes, we actually bought ourselves a brand new, waterproof, bug-proof umbrella tent. We were so excited that we practiced putting it up in the living room as soon as we brought it home. The kids had a ball crawling in and out. They would have slept in it too, if there had been a way to stake it down into the carpet.

After the tent was up, the rule was that everyone had to blow up their own air mattress, except the baby. Shelley did quite well with help. Maybe that is how she built up her lungs to become a trumpet player many years later. Imagine us all tucked into our sleeping bags, stretched out four abreast on the tent floor. Actually, air mattresses were a waste for the kids. Once asleep they wiggled off them in short order.

Some of the best times were around the campfire at night, roasting marshmallows, singing camp songs, watching the stars and telling stories. After a busy day of play, and a few pillow fights and giggles, no one had trouble sleeping in the fresh air.

*   *   *

After a few years of tent camping, we started visiting the camper shows that popped up in the malls in late winter or early spring, just when Michiganders were sick of winter and dreaming of their first camping trip. Some of these campers were dreams come true, all right, but their price tags were nightmares. It sure would be nice to have a clean camper, up off the ground, with a heater and a porta-potty, cooking stove, sink and built-in cupboards. We could keep everything in the camper, ready to go. No more loading and unloading the car. And the mattresses... heavenly. Still, the cost was a lot when you consider how few times you could use it in one year.

So, we thought about who we could get to go in with us to share the cost: someone our age with young kids, someone we could trust. The obvious answer was my sister Anna with her husband Duane and two girls, just like our family.

Our partnership with Duane and Anna Coon worked out well for many years, until our kids had left home and had kids of their own. We chose a Steury pop-up tent camper. The beds and top folded neatly into a compact trailer with a hard top, perfect for pulling behind the wagon. When extended, it was 22 feet long with two queen-sized beds, dinette, stove, refrigerator, potty, lights that worked on either battery or electricity, screens, awning, heater... what more could you want? We took turns with our partners, using it and caring for it. It was a perfect arrangement.

Dave and I camped all over Michigan and in the Western States while our kids were very young. We took in the Black Hills, Yellowstone Park, Glacier National Park and more.

*   *   *

Twenty-Three

"Girls, Girls, Girls"

Fortunately for Dave, he didn't mind having two girls and no sons. He felt that he actually did have a son, even though his son was dead. As for me, I was very content with girls. I understood them, whereas sons were a mystery. When Dave and I discussed expanding our family, I said I would like to have more children, but Dave said, "No. I like our family just the way it is." Furthermore, he was "Sick and tired of having my wife either pregnant or recovering from pregnancy half the time," as I had three babies in a row with two years in between. That settled it. We stopped at two girls.

Dave was surrounded by girls, but he seemed to handle it well. My sister had two girls. Our best friends, the Kenworthys, had two girls. We saw each of those families a lot, and often traded babysitting. Then, when our children married, our eldest daughter had two girls. Her children reminded me so much of my own daughters that it often seemed like déjà vu. It wasn't until our younger daughter's first child was a boy that we were shocked to discover the difference.

Kendal Neal was all boy. Knowing only girls, my frame of reference construed Kendal's behavior to seem startling. Instead of the sweet prissy little things to whom I was accustomed, playing with dolls and crayons, his favorite thing was sticks with which he beat up bushes and trees or feigned warfare. If we took the children for a walk, our little granddaughters would follow primly along. Kendal would take off on a dead run into the street, climbing trees or hiding behind houses. Threats were useless. While the girls were "helping get dinner" by setting the table, carefully placing each fork and napkin, Kendal was climbing up on the counters grabbing food. Dave and I joked with friends that this kid was never going to make it to adulthood. Those of our friends who had raised boys told us not to worry, he would settle down.

There were occasions when our grandchildren would visit us, or we would babysit with them at their house. Dave and I would both take off work and devote ourselves to having fun with them. We loved them dearly, but laughingly agreed that it took two of us now to do what one young parent could do. We loved to see them come and didn't mind seeing them go. Only another grandparent will understand that remark. We always needed a rest afterward. In time, our younger daughter had a girl and two more boys. Eventually, Dave and I learned how to handle the boys and did just fine. They learned to fear and obey their grandfather. I don't recall that he ever had to spank them, but he probably threatened to. Also, he had that certain tone of voice that demanded obedience.

No matter where they lived, Ann made a point of bringing the children to Michigan once a year for a visit. Those were precious family occasions. Of course, they grew like weeds, so that each year they would be dramatically changed.

One year, well after Kendal had reached his teens, we couldn't believe the transformation. Here was this charming young man with a deep voice, politely kissing Grama hello, offering to help and saying "Please" and "Thank you". The bratty little kid had morphed into manhood, seemingly overnight. We remarked to Ann, "What happened to Kendal? Who is this well-behaved young man you have with you?" She just laughed with a wise mother's twinkle in her eye. "Honey", we said, "We've got to give you credit. You did it!" I don't mean to pick on Kendal here exclusively. It's just that he was the first boy in two generations. By the time the other two boys came along, he had their grandparents well trained. And so the two little ones' boyish antics were no surprise to us.

* * *

Chapter Twenty-Four

"Deaths in the Family"

Most people have some kind of spiritual experience at one time or another in their lives. It might happen during a crisis, at church or at a Billy Graham crusade; or maybe it is some kind of direct extra-sensory connection with someone close.

An experience common with many people is a connection to someone who has died. In our case, it has happened three times. When Dave's father's time on earth was nearly up, he was recuperating from a simple hernia operation in a community hospital in Eaton Rapids, Michigan. Dave was away at a company convention in Florida. He had no idea that his father's situation was anything other than normal recovery from routine surgery. Dave is a practical-minded, intelligent man, not given to flights of fancy. As Dave tells the story, he was suddenly taken with a strong impulse to go see his father. It happened while he was in an auditorium, listening to a lecture. This feeling was so intense that Dave left the meeting, went to a phone, booked the first flight available to Detroit, packed his bags and left the meeting. Nothing before or since has ever happened to him quite like this.

Upon arrival in Detroit, Dave grabbed a rental car and drove directly to Eaton Rapids, parked and hurried to Pop's[9] bedside. Everything seemed to be fine. His father sat up in bed and visited with Dave for a couple hours. They had always been on good terms, so they laughed and kidded around and had a lovely visit. Dave did not let on to his father what had happened. Relieved, but somewhat puzzled, Dave left the hospital and drove home to Kentwood. Two days later, Pop died of a sudden complication of the surgery: some sort of internal bleeding. We never knew for sure what happened and Dave's mother declined an autopsy. Dave has always been thankful that something warned him to go see his dad. It must have been a terribly strong premonition to have caused Dave to leave the important meeting so abruptly.

---

[9] Lloyd E Mercer, known to us as Pop (1900-1976)

*   *   *

The very same year, I experienced another unexplained sensation connected with my own father's[10] death. In this case, his end came as no surprise. We knew he was suffering from terminal prostate cancer. It had metastasized to his bones. My siblings and I had been taking turns by his bedside in Foote Hospital in Jackson, Michigan. Dad had been operated on for prostate cancer a year or two before. At that time, the doctor had recommended no follow-up radiation treatments. Dr. Keefer's opinion was that prostate cancer is so slow growing that something else would take him before the cancer did. Doc was wrong this time. Dad wanted to go home, but the boys wouldn't allow it, because they knew mother couldn't care for him. My older siblings thought it best not to tell Dad he was dying. These decisions were out of my hands. That day, after our vigil, Dave and I had left Dad's bedside to go back to Kentwood, a long two hour drive. We were exhausted. The others encouraged us to return to our children. Dad's death didn't seem imminent, as yet.

We arrived home about midnight and watched T.V. in our bed for a few minutes. Dave encouraged me, "Go to sleep, honey. Your dad is all right for the night. You need to get some rest." I drifted off. Shortly after 1:00 A.M. I awakened with a strange sensation of presence about me. I sat up. "What is it?" Dave inquired.

"Dad is dead," I responded.

Dave hesitated. "Should we call his room?"

"No need," I said. "I know he is gone."

"What happened?" Dave knew better than to question my veracity.

"I think he came to tell me good-bye," I answered.

Dad's funeral was held on Sunday, Oct. 31st at Concord

---

[10] Leon Luther Douglas (1889-1976)

Methodist Church, where he had served, in unwavering faith, all of his adult life. The congregation overflowed, unusual for a man in his eighties. The service was indeed a celebration of life. No more kind, gentle, generous, self-sacrificing and humble man has ever lived, except for Christ. All who knew him admired him for those Christ-like traits. I remember the hymn "How Great Thou Art" ringing from the rafters. I remember the sturdy oak coffin we had selected, symbolic of his life and of the hundreds of big, old oak trees on the farm. I remember the many words of kindness, people relating Dad's good deeds and his life. I remember the sunlight streaming through the trees in the cemetery, the rustling of the dry leaves underfoot, not far from where Grandmother Dodes is buried. People commented that the perfect day was fitting of Dad's life.

*   *   *

There is a trite saying, often heard at funerals: "Out of this tragedy, some good will come". In my case, it would turn out to be sad but true. If any good came out of the suffering I experienced over the death of our baby boy, Jeffrey, in 1955, it was that I would always have an understanding and empathy for someone else who suffered the same fate. This equipped me to be of service, should God ever place me in such a situation. As so often happens, life brought me more than one opportunity. One such situation occurred when I had a chance to pay back my dear friend who had stood by me during my hour of trial.

Dave and I were living in our Kentwood, Michigan home on Maple Valley S.E. We were so pleased that our old friends, Bob and Edna Kenworthy had moved closer to us. Portland, Michigan was no more than a 45 minute drive east on the freeway. Bob and Edna lived just west of Portland, about a mile or two from the church and the school where their two girls attended. Lou Ann and Kim were a bit older, but were close enough in age to our girls that we loved to have them over. We exchanged visits with the Kenworthys often. The adults would play cards while the girls entertained themselves. Sometimes we took Kim camping with us in our Steury camper. She and Shelley were close in age – perhaps twelve and thirteen – at the time. Kim was a darling girl with hair even more red than her mother's, sweet and smart as could be.

Bob and Edna were very active in their Lutheran church and had many good friends in the town.

One evening, we were in our kitchen fixing dinner when the phone rang. Again! "There it goes again," I grumbled. "How do those solicitors know when it is suppertime? Grab the phone, will you, Dave? My hands are wet."

"Hello? Mercer's. May we help you?" Dave always answered in a business-like manner. You never knew when it might be one of his customers, a business associate or one of my student's parents. He listened for a full minute. "Oh, my God, how bad is she?" I dropped what I was doing and turned toward Dave. "Uh-huh.... Uh-huh... yes... right... what can we do?...we'll be right over...thank you for calling." Slowly he hung up the phone and turned toward me, a worried frown on his face. "Better get your purse, honey, we've got to leave right away."

"Who is it?" My heart clutched, "What happened?" I demanded to know.

"It's Kim. There's been an accident. So far as we know, she is ok but banged up pretty bad," he said. "Get your sweater. We're going over there."

"What about the girls?" I asked.

"They'd better stay here. They've got school tomorrow and we don't know how late we'll be," he suggested.

"I think you're right," I said. "I'll go get them settled down and see if they have homework to do." I gave the girls their instructions, left a number where we could be reached, finished fixing a quick supper for them and went out the door. Dave was already warming up the car.

After we entered the freeway, Dave told me all that he knew. A friend of Bob's had called. It seems that Kim and a friend were riding their bikes home from school. She had stayed late for band practice on the football field. She was riding straight into the late afternoon sun. A driver was apparently blinded by the sun and sideswiped the bike, throwing Kim several feet. He didn't hit her friend. Kim was taken to the hospital in an ambulance. That's all they knew. I asked a few more questions, but Dave simply didn't know any more. "We'll just have to pray and hope for the best," he said.

"I'll pray," I said. We drove in silence. I prayed as I had learned how, picturing Kim healthy, whole and healed, lifting her up on angel wings before the Lord for his healing touch. My soul was lost in prayer when a strange feeling of not exactly peace came over me – more like a soft presence, a combination of sorrow and peace. I felt a distinct nearness of Kim's spirit. A certainty entered my heart. I knew her spirit had left her body. I breathed quietly for a few minutes, silent tears flowing from my eyes. Then I turned to Dave. "She's gone, honey," I said. "It's no use praying for Kim. She's dead. I'm sure of it." I was absolutely certain. Dave understood well enough not to doubt my veracity.

When we drove up to their house, a few cars were already there and a solemn group was gathered in their driveway. The friend who had called us walked our way. "You're the Mercers, aren't you?" he said, "I'm so sorry."

"Kim's gone, isn't she?" we said.

"Yes," he nodded, "She died instantly. I didn't want to tell you over the phone." He took Dave's hand and introduced himself. Then he gave me a brief hug. "Come. Let me introduce you to the others." The next few minutes passed in a blur as we listened to the same story again and again. There were just a few added details, but the essential facts remained unchanged. The man that hit her was driving alone. Yes, the sun may have been in his eyes, but also, he was drunk.

I visited with my dear friend, Edna. She was recovering from surgery and was laying on the couch in the family room sobbing. I didn't need to tell her that I understood how she felt. We had been through this once almost fifteen years before, only that time it was my baby that was dead. It seemed to help her just to have me sit quietly and listen.

It was so unfortunate that Kim's father was away on a fishing trip in Canada. He and his partner were located at a camp far back in the wilderness of Ontario. Word was sent to the camp manager that there had been an accident and Bob Kenworthy's wife needed him at home right away. The two of them drove straight through the night to the home of the other man who lived in DeWitt, Michigan. Dave planned to meet them in DeWitt and drive Bob back to Portland. Dave recalls that this was a terribly traumatic experience. It fell to Dave to tell a best friend that his daughter was dead. Bob may have been shaken to see Dave here to meet him. He didn't offer his usual friendly greeting. They wasted no time in throwing Bob's luggage into the trunk and getting on their way. There was simply no easy way to impart such devastating news. "I'm so sorry this happened, Bob," Dave began. "The people must have told you there had been an accident, right?"

"Yeah," Bob nodded, "but that's all they knew. We hurried back as quickly as we could."

"You must be tired and hungry," Dave offered.

"I'm OK…"

"I'm afraid it was Kim…" Dave continued.

Bob's head jerked toward Dave, his mouth dropped open. He drew a quick gasp of air.

"She was hit riding her bike home after school."

"Aw, no," Bob's eyes fell shut.

"It was pretty bad…"

Bob's head fell to one side as if he'd been shot.

"She's gone, Bob; … I'm so sorry."

Bob slumped in his seat.

Dave reached a hand over to his friend and gently touched

his arm. They drove on in silence for a long time, until Bob seemed to move a bit and lift his head to look out the window.

Dave said, "Edna and Lou Ann are Ok, Bob, but they are taking it hard, of course. Edna's brother and his wife are staying over."

Bob said nothing, just sort of nodded to acknowledge that he heard and was still again. As they drew closer to Portland, Bob pushed himself up and tried to straighten. He sighed and slowly searched in his pockets. Dave silently handed him a clean white handkerchief. Bob wiped his eyes and sniffed. Dave pulled up in their driveway. "Dorothy and I will do anything we can, Bob, you know that."

"Thanks, Dave." Bob left the car at a dead run for the house, leaving the doors standing wide open.

*   *   *

People sometimes grieve over seemingly trivial things. In this case, it was Kim's tiny silver cross. Kim was an ardent lover of Christ. She had never removed the cross she received on her confirmation day. Somehow, when the EMT people had picked up her broken body, the cross wasn't there.

Edna sighed. "I wish I had her cross to remember her by. She loved that cross."

"Oh, honey," I said. "I wish the police had found it." Just then some visitors came to the door to call on Edna, so I excused myself and went outside looking for Dave. "Sweetheart, would you please drive me down where the accident happened?"

"We don't know where it happened. It could be anywhere along that road into town," he demurred.

"But Edna wants Kim's cross," I said.

"Oh, Ok. What do you mean about Kim's cross?" he asked.

"Sh, not so loud," I said. "Just take me down there, please. We can go look for it down by where she died. It won't hurt anything to look."

Dave reached in his pocket for the car keys. He knew when to cooperate, but he was a bit baffled. We continued to discuss the issue as we drove off. "Ok, I'll drive you into town and back, but I don't know if we can find the spot where it happened without more information."

"No matter, it feels kind of good to get away for a few minutes with you," I said.

"I know what you mean. I miss you, too." He reached for my hand.

"Turn around here," I said. Dave let go of my hand, pulled in and dutifully backed the car around. "See that long stretch up ahead," I said, "Just drive along here real slow... closer... ah, stop right here. I'm getting out."

"I'll go with you." Dave pulled off the road into a little drive.

"Ya' think this is the place?" he asked.

"Yeah, I do. This just feels right to me." I moved off. "Up this way." I was already out of the car and walking directly up the roadside. There were no signs of car tracks or scuff marks, but something else was directing me. Without hesitation, I walked directly to the right spot, bent over and started looking through the gravel.

Dave leaned down beside me, reached down and casually picked up a tiny cross lying beside the road. "Is this what you're looking for?" A slight grin touched his lips, a merry twinkle in his eye.

My jaw dropped, "Oh, my God... you found it!" I offered my hand for the cross. Our steps hastened back to the car, as I held up the cross in triumph. "Thank you, Jesus! Thank you, Lord!" I cradled the cross in my hands like a holy relic as I slid into the car beside Dave. We gaped at each other and started to laugh for the first time in days. "Do you realize what just happened?" I exclaimed.

"Hold on to that thing," Dave ordered. "We don't want to lose it now." He started the car and eased back onto the road.

I couldn't wait to present the cross to Edna. Somehow it felt as if we were returning a part of Kim to her. "Is this Kim's?" I asked, as I held the cross out to her.

"Oh, yes!" her face lit up as fresh tears streamed down. "Thank you, Dort and Dave. Thank you so much." She pulled the cross to her chest, pressed it to her lips and sank back down.

There was nothing more we could do that day, so we said good-bye and headed on back to Kentwood. On the way, we went over what had happened. Dave was curious as to how I knew where the cross was. "Well, we had a few clues. We knew it happened on the way home from town, so it had to be on the north side of the road. She was riding with the traffic."

"Yeah, but that covers a lot of territory," Dave remarked. "We were looking for a needle in a haystack."

"And they said the impact threw her several feet onto the side of the road."

"Ok, so now we've eliminated the middle of the road and the far ditch," Dave pointed out. "I think they said the sun was in the driver's eyes." He adjusted his sun visor.

"If the sun blinded him, he must have been on an incline, because it wasn't that late in the day," I reasoned.

"Ok, Sherlock, so what?" he scoffed, "You know that the sheriff and deputies scoured every inch of that accident site all up and down and sideways for any clues. There couldn't have been a single scrap of dust or blade of grass left unturned."

"Well, yeah," I conceded.

"I didn't see any skid marks, or any blood. Did you?" he asked.

"No, I didn't, but I was afraid I might." I chuckled.

"I'll bet you were. You were brave, Dort, and plenty lucky too."

"It wasn't just luck. The chances of finding that cross were ten million to one. We walked right to it, Dave."

"You're right... it's a miracle we found it."

"Yes... I know." I said.

* * *

As small towns are wont to do, the next few days hummed with relatives, friends and neighbors bringing food and sympathy. Funeral arrangements were made. Kim's pastor would conduct at their church, with burial at the community cemetery. Edna was too ill to attend. I offered to sit with her while others attended the service. She seemed comfortable with that idea.

Dave and I had ordered a large spray of flowers for the church and grave site. But there was one more thing I wanted to buy. "Can we stop at Eastern Floral on the way out of town, please?" I asked as the girls piled in the back seat and I slid in beside Dave.

"Whatever you want is fine," he said as he pulled out of the drive.

I had ordered one single pink baby rosebud with baby's breath tied up with a ribbon. I intended to offer that to Edna as a special gift for her baby. I would place it on the grave for her later. Edna seemed pleased and held on to the flower throughout the hours we waited together while everyone else was at the funeral, the graveside service, followed by the luncheon at the church.

Edna and I visited off and on during those hours. We talked about Kim and reminisced about all our fun times together. I let Edna lead. At times, she would smile over some memory; at other times, tears might come and she would lay back on her pillow and close her eyes. I knew she probably wasn't sleeping but hoped a little rest might come. I prayed with her and read a few Bible verses. That was comforting. Time dragged, but eventually we heard cars drive up. Soon the house was crowded with close friends and relatives. It was a good time to slip away.

Dave drove me up to the cemetery alone. He pointed out the site for me. The grave had been filled in and covered with a huge pile of flowers brought over from the church by the funeral director. This was my time to say good-bye to Kim for her mother and for myself. I stood beside the grave, said my good-byes and a prayer. Then I carefully placed the rose in the middle of the pile of flowers. "Kim, honey, this rose is from your Mom. She loves you so much," I said and paused for a few minutes with my eyes closed. Then I took a deep breath and let it out, squared my shoulders, lifted my head, turned and walked back to the car. We started back toward the Kenworthy's house. "That was a nice thing that you did," Dave said as we pulled away.

Back at the house we joined the others in sharing a few more minutes together and a meal. I offered to help with the cleanup, but there were plenty of others. Bob encouraged us to go home and rest. "We'll be back in a couple days," we said, "after your relatives fly home."

"Ok, see ya," he said. "Thanks for everything you've done."

"Sure, it was nothing. You've done the same for us," I said. "See ya!" we waved as we drove off.

Two days later, we stopped in again for a half hour or so. "We don't want to stay too long," we said, "but we are going to stop out to the cemetery before we go home. Would you like us to bring you some of the flowers?" I asked.

"They will probably be pretty badly wilted," Edna replied,

"but I would like to have that baby rose you bought. I'd like to press it in her album."

"Oh, that's a nice idea," I said. "We'll drop it off before we head home."

"Thanks, Dort and Dave," she said. "You've been great."

We drove out to the cemetery, got out of the car and walked up to the grave. The pile of flowers was still there, wilted but undisturbed. They looked kind of sad, really – the way I felt.

We both stared. "Do you see it?" I asked.

"No," Dave said.

"I'm sure I put it right here, right on top. It couldn't have gone anywhere," I said.

"No. It hasn't rained, or anything, has it?" Dave asked.

"No, and the wind hasn't blown, either," I added.

"Well, if the wind had blown, we'd see it somewhere around here. Besides, the rest of the flowers are still here." Dave observed.

"Would some kid have taken it? Y'know, vandals or something."

"I suppose, but why would they do that?"

"Should I move the flowers and look for it?"

"I don't know. That doesn't seem right."

"Ya' think?"

"Well, maybe you could move them just a little, if you're careful."

"I don't want anyone to see us."

"There's nobody around. Here, let me hold onto your other hand and you just lean over and poke around a bit."

He took my hand and I leaned over and delicately touched the top flower. "I can't do it," I said. "Besides, it's gone. I know it's gone. Too many other strange things have happened. Let's just go".

Dave hesitated, "Good idea. We'll just tell Edna it's gone. What else can we do?" He sighed.

"Yeah, I'll tell her. Let's go, honey."

Dave took my hand and we slowly walked to the car.

*   *   *

Chapter Twenty-Five

"On My Honor I Will Try"

Scouting was an important part of my life, beginning when I was in fifth grade. Mrs. Edith Sanford started a Junior Girl Scout troop in my home town of Concord, Michigan. I couldn't wait to join. We held meetings at her house after school. I regret now that I was somewhat of a cut-up, keeping everyone laughing, thus making it difficult for Mrs. Sanford to keep control of the group. She was the sweetest person of infinite patience. I had a wonderful time.

I learned how to tie a square knot, properly fold a flag and identify poison ivy. I tried my hand at knitting. Every week we recited the Girl Scout motto, "Be Prepared"; the promise, "Do A Good Turn Daily"; and the pledge, "On my honor I will try to do my duty to God and my country, to help other people at all times and to obey the Girl Scout laws."

Definitely the highlight of my Girl Scout career was attending summer camp at "Camp O' The Hills" on Wampler's Lake for one week in 1944 and two weeks in 1945. The first year I was homesick. I looked forward to mail call. Bless her heart, Mom wrote to me every day. The second year, my friend, Judy Kressbach, joined me. Having a friend along has its advantages. It prevents homesickness. However, that doesn't allow one to make as many new friends. I especially loved singing around the campfire. One of our rounds was "Make new friends and keep the old. One is silver the other gold." How true!

Camp was run on a rigorous time schedule, with a set routine throughout each day. Awaken to a bugle call, do personal care, make beds, have inspection, meals, crafts, swimming, k.p. (kitchen patrol) and other duties, flag ceremonies, quiet time, afternoon swim, more duties, build a proper campfire, sing camp songs, canoe, hike, camp overnight and perform Girl Scout rituals and ceremonies. It was great to be a part of a group with wonderful, caring counselors and just the right mix of fun, action, learning, duties, rest, music and food. I learned a lot of things at Girl Scout camp that I took with me throughout life, some of which my grandchildren will recognize, such as how to organize a group of kids to do their housekeeping jobs, how to canoe and swim, how to camp, hike, have fun in the out-of-doors, build a campfire and of most importance: make S'Mores[11].

Swimming was my best sport already, but I learned how to do it properly at camp; that is, how to do the breast stroke, back stroke, side stroke on either side and two kinds of crawl. The butterfly wasn't used at that time. I took an official Red Cross class in Junior Lifesaving and earned my badge and certificate. I was too young for Senior Lifesaving. There were certain tests you had to pass, such as being able to do a shallow dive, swim to your instructor who pretended to be drowning, "subdue" and "save" her using the proper life saving stroke. She weighed a good 60 pounds more than me, too. Another test was the proper technique for reviving a drowning victim. This is similar to artificial respiration.

A third test was to be able to swim for one hour out in Wampler's Lake without stopping. You must use an official stroke, not a doggy paddle. You couldn't stop to rest, or tread water. I passed the one hour swim test on the last day. Mother had already come to pick me up, so she stood on shore and watched her daughter become a tiny dot out in the middle of the lake. Mother wasn't crazy about the water, so this must have given her pause. Of course, there was a safety boat monitoring me all the way. Bless her heart, Mom praised me and said she was amazed that I could keep going all that time.

*   *   *

Judy and I went on an "overnight" camping trip with two counselors and some of the other girls who also had the necessary permission slips, as well as swimming, first aid, outdoor cooking and canoeing badges. We were going to learn how to take care of ourselves in the wilderness. Preparations included planning menus, setting up a duty chart, and learning how to make a bedroll out of three blankets folded in thirds and lapped over each other so they

---

[11] In case you came from another planet: S'mores are a graham cracker sandwich filled with four squares of Hershey's chocolate bar and one marshmallow toasted over a campfire on the end of a green sapling. Never mind if there are a few ashes.

wouldn't come apart when you lay on the bottom folds. (No one had sleeping bags in those days.) Everyone had to roll their clothes and gear inside the bed roll and secure the whole thing with ropes and the proper knots. Gear included a certain list of necessary articles for survival such as a first aid kit, jack-knife, hatchet, poncho, rope, toilet articles, change of clothing and mosquito netting. We were going to sleep under the stars.

On the appointed day, we set out in a flotilla of canoes with bursting energy, trembling hearts and some apprehension. Upon arrival at the wilderness camp, we all went about our appointed tasks. Some were wood gatherers, some kitchen helpers, some digging a latrine, some setting up wash stations and some taking care of "stores": that is, fashioning a bear-proof storage for our food. This consisted of hoisting food in mesh bags over a high limb with a rope. Never mind that bears hadn't been sighted in the area for hundreds of years. One must be prepared.

Once again my creative nature and disregard for the wisdom and experience of my elders got me into trouble. Our intrepid leaders had demonstrated how to cut poles from young saplings for use in propping up our mosquito nettings over our bed rolls. Never one to do things the hard way, I decided that cutting saplings was for morons. I would devise a clever shortcut. I chose a picnic table to serve as the head of my bed. It was just the right height to prop up one end of my netting. I weighted the netting down on both ends with bricks and placed my bedroll within. My friend, Judy, followed suit, fashioning her canopy next to mine.

I congratulated myself and felt rather smug. Judy and I were all nice and tight under our netting, while the morons struggled with leaning saplings, collapsing netting and invading mosquitoes. She and I giggled, whispered and drifted off to sleep as the stars came out. All was well until near midnight, when Judy started to dream and roll around. Twice the netting came loose. I had to get out and fix it, arranging it under the bricks. "Lie still, for heaven's sake, Judy, you're pulling out the netting," I cautioned as I shimmied into my bedroll.

"Mmm," grumbled Judy as she grabbed the covers and rolled over. Suddenly a brick smashed smack-dap across my face. I sprang bolt upright.

"Judy!" I screamed, "Wake up!" She sat up in alarm, wide awake at last. All our beautiful setup fell in ruins. "Oh, Judy," I moaned.

"What's wrong, what happened?"

"I'm hurt. My mouth is bleeding."

"Huh?

"You pulled the bricks down on my head," I cried.

"Are you hurt?" she asked.

Stupid question. Moron! I thought. "My tooth is gone!" I wailed.

Next day the headmistress went into defensive mode. She sent me to a local dentist, phoned my parents and requested an interview. Mother and Dad would never sue. It wasn't done in those days.

I had a toothless grin for some years and still have the artificial front tooth to remind me of just who was the real moron.

* * *

Years later, when my own daughters became of age for Scouting, I started a new Junior Troop, Number 82 in Kentwood, Michigan. Shelley and her friends were in my troop from fourth through sixth grade. Ann started out as a Brownie and "flew up" to my troop. We accomplished a lot of things. We met once a week after school. I took them troop camping twice a year at Camp Anna Behrens in Greenville, Michigan and on numerous field trips, overnights and cookouts. We sold cookies and sponsored events to earn money for all our trips. We wore out our handbooks, earned badges and did many good deeds and service projects. Most of the time, we had a large troop with over twenty girls. We all wore uniforms, something I didn't have as a girl. Several of our girls became official First Class Scouts.

Both Shelley and Ann and many others in our troop attended summer camp at Camp Anna Behrens. When Shelley and her friend Diane graduated from Junior Scouts to the Cadette Level, we started a Cadette Girl Scout Troop. When they were ready for Senior Level, Shelley and Ann decided to leave scouting, so I retired too, but it had been a great run. Diane went on to Senior Scouting with another troop and eventually became a Junior Counselor.

The Scouting organization had strict rules concerning taking your troop camping, such as the correct number of chaperones per student, permission slips and so on. You must have a nurse and/or someone certified in Red Cross First Aid in attendance. Fortunately, two of our mothers were nurses, and one could usually accompany us. Also, I took a course in Red Cross First Aid as a backup at all times. In addition to that, I wanted to take the troop swimming; but according to the rules, you must have a Senior Lifesaver in attendance. My Junior Lifesaving certificate wasn't good enough – besides, it had expired. So there was nothing to do but take the Senior Lifesaving course myself.

I signed up for one at a school in Grand Rapids that had an Olympic-size pool. When I showed up for the first class, I was the only "Mom" in attendance. All the others were tanned and fit young men and women brushing up on their skills in preparation for Lifesaving jobs at Lake Michigan beaches or country club pools. I definitely felt like a Senior citizen in my dowdy suit and pot tummy.

The instructor was a buff young man, pleasant and considerate of my feelings, and all the kids thought I was brave. The class lasted for several weeks. Our last test was the twenty lap swim, similar to the long swim I made in Wampler's Lake as a young girl. The problem was that I was twenty-four years older. The young kids dived in and raced each other with great form and much splashing, just like a bunch of Olympic swimmers. At this point, I knew I was in trouble. I asked the instructor, "Do I have to be using an official stroke at all times?"

"Oh, yes," he replied. "Sorry."

"Can it be any stroke I choose instead of the crawl or butterfly?"

"Well, yes, but what did you have in mind?"

"I was thinking of something easier, like the side stroke or back stroke."

"That would work." By now, the others had completed their swim and paused to listen to this discussion.

"One last question," I asked, "Is there any time limit?"

"No, the rules just say you have to do twenty laps without pausing."

My spirits lifted. "You mean I can take all the time I need?"

"Yes, so long as you keep swimming." He checked his watch. "Better get started."

I dived in and slowly made my way up and down the pool, stroke after stroke, back stroke one way, side stroke the other. *Two… five… ten… fifteen. Breathe deeply. Keep going. Keep going. You can do this. Think of the girls.* By now, my classmates were drifting back from the locker room, fully dressed, holding their duffle bags. *Eighteen… nineteen.* They were actually lining the sides of the pool cheering. *Twenty laps!* Slowly, I hauled my exhausted body out of the pool and stood there panting. The onlookers burst into spontaneous applause. My instructor shook my hand. "Congratulations, Mrs. Mercer. You are now a Certified Senior Life Saver!"

I wore that badge with pride.

*   *   *

Chapter Twenty-Six

"Crafts, Concerts and Canoes"

During my girls' Scouting years, I was also very involved with their school as a room mother and with PTA (Parent Teachers Association). Room mothers assisted the teachers with parties and field trips. The PTA also put on events and money raisers for the school.

Shelley and Ann were both excellent students, making their parents proud. They consistently brought home perfect report cards and stayed out of trouble. We loved them dearly and enjoyed our times together. I was grateful that Dave was able to support us, thus allowing me to be a stay-at-home Mom for their formative years, as my mother was before me, and as they later became with their own children.

Ann was creative and focused on arts and crafts. We allowed both girls to choose the décor for their own rooms. Ann's was done in bright pink. I was amazed at the way she could sit on her shag carpet and paint without spilling a drop. Ann was a neat person and actually enjoyed cleaning out drawers and closets. She couldn't have inherited either of those traits from her mother.

Shelley was energetic, friendly and outgoing. Her room was done up in shades of green with white fluffy curtains. She loved to read. After lights-out she would hide under the covers and continue reading with a flashlight. She had a razor sharp memory. We often thought of her as the family historian.

* * *

"Where are we going to take the camper this year?" was one of our favorite conversation gambits during the parents' private time Dave and I tried to hold nightly. That was when the kids watched television while we just visited, talking over our days or making plans. One evening Dave said, "Let's take the kids to Boundary Waters Canoe Area. I've always thought that would be fun."

"Where is that?" I asked.

"It's this huge pristine wilderness area set aside in northern Minnesota on the border with Canada. There are no roads or commercial developments allowed, just backpacking and canoeing. You can't even have a motor on your canoe. You can rent light weight canoes completely outfitted with everything you need including backpacks, waterproof stowing bags, freeze dried food, down sleeping bags, collapsible fishing poles, etc. Everything is ultra light because sometimes you have to carry it. All you have to bring are your clothes and personal items."

"Wow, that sounds wonderful," I said, "but do you think the girls are old[12] enough?"

That set in motion months of planning for the trip of a lifetime. My job was to contact the Minnesota Chamber of Commerce and request brochures. We selected an outfitter and made reservations. We would take a five day circle wilderness trip, starting from Ely, Minnesota, going across several lakes (involving portages), along rivers, paddling every day to a new site and returning to the take-out site where the outfitters would meet us.

I needed to buy proper clothes for all of us. One of the hardest things to find was hiking boots small enough to fit our petite daughters. I finally had to send away for much of our stuff.

The plan was for Shelley and me to be in one canoe, Dave and Ann in the other. Ann was brave and would paddle hard, but she was so small that we thought she should go with the strongest member of the family. It was important for the two adults to be stern paddlers. We would be weighted down and it would take a lot of strength to turn the canoe.

Before we had a chance to get our sea legs, our very first crossing was the most harrowing. We had a strong quartering tail wind blowing up white caps. It was all we could do to keep our bow into the waves so we didn't turn over. I was scared. Shelley paddled with all her strength, but she was only seven, after all. Dave and Ann had gotten out ahead of us. The wind was blowing

---

[12] Shelley and Ann were ages 7 and 5 at the time of this trip.

us way too fast. Had we tipped over, I doubt Dave could have even heard us scream, much less come back for a rescue attempt.

We made camp early that night. It was a bit like Christmas: unwrapping all the gear, sorting through the stuff and selecting our dinner from among the freeze dried selections. There were no improved camp sites. You just pulled up to shore and looked for a reasonably level spot. You could clear away dead sticks and rocks, but you were not allowed to cut any trees, and the rules said to restore your camp site to its original wild condition. For bathroom purposes a little digging tool was provided. Everything should be buried so many inches deep and covered. Garbage and trash were packed out. All food and odor-causing materials were hung in trees away from camp to discourage animals.

There are tens of thousands of acres in this wilderness, and the number of people allowed each year is limited. We did not see any signs of other people until the fifth day. The wilderness is so clear and so quiet that we began speaking in softer voices to each other. All tension drained away. Daylight lingers late in the day in Minnesota. We were tucked into our sleeping bags, listening to the loons, before it became completely dark.

Portages were a challenge for us, some of them several hundred yards long and not cleared. Sometimes we climbed over fallen logs that were six feet in diameter. The girls carried the smaller packs. The larger packs, weighing up to 75 pounds, were left for Dave and I. Dave carried the canoes that weighed only 40 pounds apiece.

Occasionally, we stopped to fish. We found a great spot populated by small mouth bass. Standing on a huge granite slab looking down into the depths of the crystal clear blue water, one could see the fish schooling around all the way to the bottom, perhaps twenty feet.

On our last day, we were scheduled to paddle the length of a long narrow lake at journey's end. This was the only lake that allowed motor craft from the various outfitters. We were scheduled to paddle it ourselves rather than pay the extra fee to ride in the boat. Packing up that morning, every one of us really hurt, but no one complained. Our kids were such good troopers, we couldn't complain ourselves. After paddling for an hour and a half, into the wind, we looked forward to another six hours before we reached the dock.

Well, perhaps I did groan just a wee bit – memory fades. About then, we heard the faint sound of a motor craft coming. As it grew louder, and drew closer, I may have possibly whined a little. "Gee, it's too bad we didn't schedule a pick up, isn't it, Dave?"

Fast as a cat he answered, "Do you want me to flag him down?"

Whereupon, all three of his girls loudly chorused, "YES!"

Dave whistled and yelled. We girls frantically waved our arms. The boat came to a halt. "Ahoy, there, Mates, do you need a lift?" called the captain.

Strong arms lifted our canoes and stowed them aboard as we scrambled to find seats. Minutes later we were landed, tired but happy, having accomplished a wilderness canoe trip with the youngest girls the outfitter had seen in some time. That night, we were safely back in our camper with warm showers, real food and soft beds. None had ever felt so good.

*   *   *

Both children showed musical promise. My attempt to teach piano to Shelley was a disaster. We would end up in an argument, sometimes with tears. Having learned my lesson, when Ann was old enough for lessons I took her to a piano teacher. Ever after, when asked, I always advised parents not to try to teach their own children. Of course, I have been proven wrong a thousand times over with today's wildly popular home-school movement.

As soon as the school system offered band, Shelley chose to play trumpet and Ann chose the flute. Both girls showed outstanding promise right away. We made sure that they had the best private teachers available, and as soon as they were ready for them, the best instruments we could afford: a silver trumpet and silver flute. We attended all their concerts. Both girls won first chair position in the best band and received the highest marks at the Solo and Ensemble festivals. I was their accompanist for their solos. We often played our instruments and sang for our church and other churches around. We had a singing trio act where we dressed up in long dresses and sang for churches. I always sang the low part and Ann the middle. Shelley had the soprano voice. It was a wonderful time of making music together. By the time they reached high school age, they were teaching private students themselves.

Girls' sports in the public schools had not really come into their own yet. Still, both girls learned to ski. For a small fee, they would ride the school bus to Canonsburg Ski Area north of town. In high school, Ann went out for the golf team. I made sure that they both knew how to swim and canoe. We sent them to summer music camp at Interlochen and Blue Lake. We enjoyed visiting the music camps on the concert days. With so many talented youth to work with, the directors were able to present some amazing concerts.

*   *   *

Michigan is well known for its beautiful lakes, rivers and streams. One of our favorite things to do was to take canoe trips down the Au Sable, the Pere Marquette, or any of the numerous other well-maintained canoeing rivers. Canoe Liveries are located on the designated recreational rivers. For a reasonable fee, you can rent a canoe and everything else needed for a trip down the river. Included in the fee would be the service of transportation to the launch site and pickup at the take-out site. Trips of varying lengths are available, anywhere from 2 to 8 hours or overnight. An ideal length for our young family was 2 to 4 hours. Drifting down the river through picturesque woodlands and meadows, one never knew when one might spot kingfishers, eagles, waterfowl or varieties of small wild animals. The streams are swift-flowing, so one's craft will glide along without assistance, but great skill is necessary for avoidance of rocks and fallen logs. An entertaining feature of such trips is watching neophyte canoeists overturning as they sweep into a sharp bend and smash into some hazard.

Michigan sports streams are noted for their cleanliness and

pristine beauty. It wasn't always so. Before the advent of the ten cent deposit on returnable drink bottles and cans, the bottoms of our lakes and streams were littered with beer and soda cans. That law alone went a long way toward affecting a cleanup. Also, local sportsman clubs sponsor regular cleanups of miles of waterways. Another nice addition was the enactment of the roadside cleanups. Once a year on a designated day, every mile of highway is cleaned of discards. Organizations and individuals can adopt a two mile stretch of highway. The state places a sign showing who sponsors this section. Sometimes people designate their section as a memorial to someone. On the day, workers are provided with blaze orange vests and trash bags with special tags. Commercial garbage vendors pick up the filled bags.

One time when Shelley and her friend, Diane, were working on one of their Girl Scout badges, they had to take an overnight canoe trip as part of the requirement.[13] Of course, I went along as a counselor. They had to plan the trip, menus and gear; shop for food; and assemble everything needed, including tent, sleeping bags, etc. Gear had to be secured in waterproof containers and lashed down in the canoe, in case of an upset. As counselor, I could advise but could not do the work for them. They had to demonstrate skill in bow paddling and stern paddling, setting up camp, cooking out of doors, etc., and I had to sign off on it.

We had taken trips on the Pere Marquette, but never one of this length. I was confident that this river was not too difficult for their skill level. However, I hadn't reckoned on the unusually high runoff in the last few days. The river was higher than I had ever experienced, running much faster than normal. One good thing was that this made for more clearance over rocks. But there were two big disadvantages. One was the dangerously excessive speed with which the canoe traveled, making it harder to steer around hazards in time. If you did collide with a rock or log at that speed, you could easily tip over. The worst disadvantage was that we were riding so much higher up that the many overhanging trees became aerial hazards for us. Trees that we would normally sail right under now threatened to decapitate us. Sometimes we were traveling so fast that we couldn't steer away from it in time and were forced to

[13] Shelley and Diane were working toward their First Class Scout designation.

flatten ourselves down as low as possible in order to scrape under. It went like this: First we would paddle like crazy to try to avoid the tree. Second, someone would yell, "Low Bridge!" Third, everyone would dive to the bottom of the canoe and cover their heads.

Needless to say, life jackets were *de rigueur* for the trip. It was a thrill a minute, but we made great time and managed to stay dry, until the next morning when we had to pack up in the rain and paddle several more hours to the take-out place.

When asked, we liked to tell people that Dave's part in my Girl Scout outings was to keep the home fires burning and have a martini and a bubble bath ready upon my return. I don't know about the martini, but the bubble bath always felt wonderful, and I was so pooped and grubby that Dave had to check on me every few minutes to make sure I hadn't fallen asleep.

*   *   *

Chapter Twenty-Seven

"Vacation Home"

Dave's business was doing well, so we set out to find a place to build a second home on a Michigan lake. We had enjoyed taking our camper to Interlochen State Park, on Green Lake near Traverse City, when Shelley was at the music camp. A woodland path wandered from the park over to the camp. I loved the area, especially the concerts. So the first place we searched for a vacant lot was on Green Lake. We drove around the entire lake looking for signs. The quest was discouraging. Every piece of shoreline seemed to be taken up with beautiful cottages. The girls were getting tired and cross. Dave was anxious to head for home.

"Ok, we'll leave, but can't we just go down this one more street?" I bargained.

"What street?" he sighed.

"The little short one there," I pointed.

Knowing when to give in, Dave turned left. "Oh, all right." Speaking of right, guess what we found at the very end of that street: the perfect pie-shaped lot, water on two sides and a view of Interlochen Music Camp. I pictured ourselves sitting on the front porch listening to the music across the water. We all got out and tramped around. I dug in my purse for a notepad and jotted down the business number of the Realtor whose sign was on the lot.

Next day, I phoned the realtor's office. "I'm calling about the lot you have for sale on Green Lake, across from the music camp."

"Yes, ma'am, I know just which one you mean. It's a brand new listing. Been tied up for years as part of an estate. This one will go fast. You won't see many vacant lots as nice as this one. Most are swampy. Yesiree, someone will move on this one fast. I can let it go for $75,000 – not a bad price, considering. Well, what do you think? Shall I sign you up?"

"Uh, no thanks, that's a little steep for our budget."

"Well, just what budget did you have in mind, ma'am? Maybe I can help you out."

"We were thinking of something in the neighborhood of ten to fifteen thousand," I replied.

"How about something back from the lake," he offered.

"Uh, no thank you. We'll keep looking. Thanks for your time."

"Sorry I couldn't help you."

"Good-bye".

"Keep us in mind, if you change your mind. Good-bye, now"

$75,000 for a prime lakefront lot seems low by today's standards, but in 1970 it was impossibly high. Our four bedroom, two and a half bath house in the city of Kentwood cost only $17,000. So we put our dreams on the back burner.

*   *   *

Dave had a flying buddy by the name of Russ Coté. One day, they took a flight up north of Grand Rapids to a place where Russ had a farm. Knowing a bit about our search for vacation property, Russ flew over a nearby development called Canadian Lakes. When Dave came home that night, he was excited about it. We made an appointment with a salesman to drive us around the Canadian Lakes Club development. After two and a half hours of driving, our butts were getting tired, our bladders full and our salesman discouraged. Nothing seemed to suit our criteria, within our budget limitations. "Well, folks, I don't know," he said. "Maybe this just isn't our day. There's only one more lakefront lot I can show you that some other people bought a couple years ago. Now they want to sell. But I think they may be asking around twenty-seven five".

"Let's just take a quick look at that and then we need to go home," Dave said.

We turned and headed down yet another bumpy gravel road passed some wooded areas. Off to one side were piles of black dirt that had obviously been excavated out of a swamp. "Off to our right is where the lake is going to be," Bob Doerr explained. "Don Bollman is in the process of building another lake. Eventually there will be more lots for sale around here, but I think they are all taken now."

We took a few more turns and came upon a stand of pines. They reminded me so much of the pines on the farm where I grew up. "What's this?" I leaned forward in my seat.

"I'm not sure," he answered.

"Stop," I said. "Please, let me out right here."

He drew up and motioned me out. Meantime, he opened his maps and studied them with a puzzled look on his face. "I'm not sure if there is a lot in here or not," he said. "Why don't you walk around and stretch a bit while I call in and check on it."

"Dave, you've got to see this. Come on, honey," I said as excitement rose in my heart. There was something about this place that called to me. Even though the leaves were off the trees and it was a gloomy cool day, I just knew this had to be it. The ground was high, sloping down to the front and back to the road. Completely wooded with pines and a few maples, the pine scent was fresh and pure. One huge grand old oak tree guarded the rear.

Our salesman was off the phone now. "You people are in luck," he said. "I didn't even know there was a lot in here. This is amazing. There is a special price on it too, because the lake isn't finished yet. You can have this lot for only $12,000 with financing, or $10,000 cash." He went on to explain more details, the size of the lot and where the lake would be. I was sold

.   "Is this what you want?" Dave asked.

"Let's buy it," I answered.

We signed the papers that very day and wrote a check for $10,000.

We hired a contractor, designed and built our vacation home the following summer. We stayed in the club campground while the house was being built. Don Bollman finished up the lake and allowed it to fill with water. We took out our canoe and were the first ones to paddle its length. Our house was the first one built on the lake, and we treasured the privacy.

During those first few years the fishing was terrific. I remember one beautiful June day. It was my birthday, so I asked to go fishing. Dave trolled up and down in front of our house while I caught thirteen nice pike. Dave liked to ice fish in the winter. He would set out his "tip-ups" and watch them from our living room with his binoculars. Whenever one flew up, he got on his snowmobile and went after the fish.

The house was an A-frame with long, solid wooden beams supporting the roof and knotty pine ceilings. The living, kitchen and dining areas had lofted ceilings and a stone fireplace. The color scheme was black, white and red. Our bedroom was on the main floor and the girls slept in twin beds in the loft. Dave finished off the basement with bedroom, bath and recreation room. The entire house was carpeted. It was a perfect place for sleepovers and youth group weekends. We slept the boys downstairs, the girls upstairs and the chaperones in between. Our girls often had their friends up, as did we. We had many grand times with them as well as both sides of our families.

The girls and I lived at our cottage every summer. Dave commuted back and forth to his Grand Rapids office every day. In the evening when he got home, if it was a hot day, he and I would take our drinks down to the lake, lean into our inner tubes and float around in our bayou, cooling off.

Some of the amenities in the development included the

beaches, swimming pools and golf courses. I was a fairly good golfer, having played in the championship section in the Grand Rapids city women's golf league back home. My friend, Bonnie, and I were a team. We won the championship trophy one year. Feeling optimistic, I decided to enter the contest for the club championship at our Canadian Lakes club. The finals happened to be on a weekend when my sister, Anna, and her family were visiting. I asked Anna to come along and caddie for me. She is not a golfer, but she would enjoy the outing. It was a match play tournament.   I had a fairly low handicap, so I was in the championship flight. No worries.

Big mistake! Mercifully, I don't remember the score. I only remember that the pressure got to me. Nothing went right: I hooked, I sliced, I dubbed and I whiffed. It was one of the worst games of my life and ended up in a humiliating defeat. Clearly, I would never be cut out for the pro tour. But I will always empathize with those great tournament golfers who choke on the final nine.

* * *

Chapter Twenty-Eight

"Back to School"

What could be in this huge box?" Dressed in the traditional red Santa hat, Ann stretched her little arms far under the gaily decorated tree. The youngest family member read off the gift tag, "It says, 'Merry Christmas to Dort from Dave'". "Here, Mom, open it!" She struggled with a box as tall as herself. I savored the moment, carefully saving the ribbons and folding the wrapping paper aside for next year.

"Guess what it is," Dave chimed in.

I gave it a shake. "Give me a hint."

"It's bigger than a bread box."

"That's no hint. I can see that for myself." I turned it this way and that.

"Careful," he said, leaning forward. "Need some help?" he laughed.

"Hand me the knife, please." I reached toward Shelley.

Shelley crowded next to me and offered the box cutter. "Hurry up, Mom!"

"Ok, ok, just hold your horses. Your turn is next." I gave the cutter a pull through the first side, then cut along the ends. "Oh. M'Gosh!" I exclaimed as I held up a shiny new guitar. "How did you know this is what I wanted?" I smiled at Dave.

"I pay attention," he grinned. "Ya' like it?"

"I love it! Thank you, honey." I blew him a kiss as I hugged the guitar to my chest. "This is going to be so perfect for my Girl Scout meetings. And it's just the right size to take along on our overnights. Can't you just picture us around the campfire?" I gave it a strum.

"Eeeooh!" The girls covered their ears.

"Well, I guess it needs a tuning. I'll play with it later. Who's next? Oh, yes, find a gift for Shelley."

None of my many Christmas presents pleased me as much as that beginner's guitar. It was the first small step in a path that would lead me into a lifetime of careers. Starting out with a self-teaching book, *Fun With the Guitar*, I figured out how to tune and attempted to make the first few chords: C, G, G7, and D7. None of them were easy, but when I came to the F chord, I was stymied. I soon learned that playing the guitar was not nearly as easy as those long-haired guys on television made it appear. Family members listening to me practice soon left the room. This was going to take time.

After two months of getting nowhere fast, I wandered into the local guitar store and inquired about lessons. Soon I was signed up for weekly lessons with Brian Roberts. We began working with Aaron Shearer's *Classical Guitar Method, Book One*. In my ignorance, I didn't know the difference between classical, folk, jazz, rock or whatever, but I was eager to get started. The first lesson was simply alternating your fingers – i m i m i m (index, middle) – on the top string, while holding the guitar in the proper position. I'd been holding it all wrong. This was going to take years.

Weeks later, I could play a simple melody, and finally got to learn six different ways to play the C chord. Now we were getting somewhere. Would I ever be ready to play and sing with the Scouts?

A year later, Brian left the studio to teach at Grand Rapids Junior College. Larry Middlemas took his place. By now, I had completed Book One and was well into Aaron Shearer's *Classical Guitar Method, Book Two*. Larry was well known locally among guitarists for his recitals at St. Cecilia auditorium. His day job as janitor at one of the schools allowed him plenty of time to practice his guitar back in the furnace room.

After a few months Larry decided to quit the studio to start his own teaching practice. Ted Zaharias, the store's owner surprised me one evening after my lesson to ask if I would like to take over Larry's students. Nearly speechless with shock, I couldn't believe myself capable of teaching guitar. My stumbling efforts were nowhere close to Brian's or Larry's. "I'll consider it, but I would rather teach piano," I said.

"Sorry, we already have a good piano teacher," Ted shook his head.

"Give me a day to talk to my husband," I offered.

"All right," Ted said, "but I need to know right away, before all his students go elsewhere. Can you call me tomorrow?"

More audacious than qualified, I started my teaching career two weeks later. I learned immediately there was no reason to be concerned about my shortcomings. The students were an assortment of beginners with cheap guitars mixed in with an occasional rock guitarist who played entirely by ear, wanting to learn how to read music. That much I could handle, but it became clear that my ¾ size guitar wasn't adequate for teaching.

Every time I entered the studio I passed a row of new guitars hanging by their necks along the wall. In every spare moment, I examined their price tags and lovingly caressed their smooth finishes. Ted let me try them out while teaching, one by one. They ranged from student level guitars to glossy handmade models for several hundred dollars. Price was a concern, so I soon selected a Yamaha student model for just under $100. Thus began the practice of plowing my earnings back into better and better tools of the trade.

Fall turned into winter. A yearning increased in my heart to take up where I left off twenty years earlier at the University of Michigan. *Could I do it? Was I too old to go back to college?* My only option was the local community college. I prayed about it. "Lord, if it be your will, let me enroll as a second semester freshman." I interviewed with the registrar, hoping to begin studying in the music department for the January term. It was necessary to apply to transfer my fifteen credits from U of M. Fortunately for me, the University of Michigan was and is a prestigious institution, known as the *Ivy League of the West*. Credits from U of M. were accepted anywhere. The first door was opened. *Could we complete all the paperwork in time?* Christmas break was starting soon when schools would be shut down until after New Year's. I stayed up late at night completing letters to my old high school and college applying for transcripts, breathing a quick prayer and hoping another door would open for me.

On January 15, 1972, freshman music student Dorothy Mercer, age thirty-nine, braved the freezing cold to enter her first class, Music Theory 102. Looking around at the other students, all of whom were twenty years younger, she nervously took her seat and tried to relax.

Fortunately, I never threw anything away that might possibly be of use someday. I had dug out my old textbooks from the U of M and reviewed Music Theory 101. Having purchased all my GRJC[14] textbooks a week earlier at the campus bookstore, I had studied the chapters leading up to this moment. Now, as prepared as I could be, I needn't have worried. Theory 102 was to be my favorite class.

Classes met Monday, Wednesday and Friday. The only thing scheduled for Thursday was choir and private guitar lessons with Brian Roberts. Brian laid out a heavy lesson schedule. Practice requirements were two hours a day. I would prepare two solos from memory and all the major scales for the mid-term juries, a Bach Suite plus all the minor scales and arpeggios for final juries. Juries consisted of all the music faculty members. The grade I received from them would receive equal weight with the grade from Brian in determining my final grade. For this amount of work, I would receive one hour of credit. *Maybe I had bit off more than I could chew. I hope my other classes require fewer hours.* I had, cautiously, signed up for only ten credits. Three credits each for theory and music literature, piano class for two credits and choir and applied guitar for one credit each.

---

[14] Grand Rapids Junior College

Piano lab met once a week. The piano studio consisted of fifteen electronic pianos wired up with earphones for the students and a master console for the teacher. The teacher could listen in to one or more students at a time or speak to the entire class as needed. At the beginning of the class, we were given today's assignment and then allowed to work individually for the remainder of the time. When a particular step was mastered, we could signal the teacher. She would listen in to our performance and grade it right there and then. I was ready in five minutes, leaving 95 minutes left to fill. This class was meant for piano beginners.

I knew immediately that I was way ahead of this class. So I requested a conference with the teacher, thinking she might be willing to waive the class for me. Sympathetic to my plight, she pointed out that Piano Class 1, 2, 3, and 4 was a graduation requirement for every student seeking an Associate in Music degree, excepting piano majors. My major was classical guitar, not piano. Our compromise solution to the problem was to allow me to take all four classes in one term.[15] I would work ahead on my own time and prepare for all four final exams at once. Bless her, she was willing to give me individual time to take that exam.[16]

Three and one half years later, I received my Associate in Music degree from Grand Rapids J.C. with straight A's. The rules did not allow me to graduate with honors, because I had been a part-time student. I always thought this to be rather unfair, considering that I had a family to care for and held a part-time job in order to pay my expenses. There were no scholarships available for part-timers either, another inequity it seemed to me. In spite of those negatives, I had loved college. School was my element and music my passion.

It was time now to consider going on for a Bachelor's degree. Being limited to colleges within driving distance, I had some experience with the closest one, Grand Valley State in

---

[15] Reminiscent of taking Kindergarten and First grade in one year.

[16] Big advantages of Junior College were the small class sizes, the individual, caring attention given by the faculty and the maturity and skills of the teachers. Contrast this with U.of M. where freshman class sizes were larger and taught by grad students.

Allendale. After Brian Roberts left GRJC, I commuted to Allendale to finish up my applied guitar requirements with Guillermo Fierens, a world class guitarist who was a visiting fellow at Grand Valley. He also taught a class in Medieval Guitar literature. Normally this would be a graduate level class, so we were really lucky to have it. We learned how to send away to foreign libraries in Spain and London to get copies of old manuscripts written in very old ways, before the development of the current ways of writing music on the musical staff. We learned how to translate that into today's musical language and be able to play it. Guillermo was staying with his brother's family in East Grand Rapids. His young niece, Maria Fierens, was one of my students. Because of that connection, Guillermo was willing to take me on. Except for Guillermo, there was nothing more of interest to me at Grand Valley. J.C. offered the same classes, so I had already taken everything Grand Valley had to offer. I wasn't interested in going on for an education degree.

I had also transferred credits from a class at Michigan State University. They had a wonderful music school, but it was too far for me to drive. That left Western Michigan University in Kalamazoo. They had a good variety of interesting advanced music classes, but they didn't offer a guitar major. Very few colleges in the United States did at that time. I consulted with my faculty advisor. She said, "Something has always puzzled me about you, Dorothy. May I ask you a personal question?"

"Of course," I replied.

"Why didn't you major in piano in the first place? Clearly piano should be your primary instrument, not guitar."

I had been the accompanist for the college choir for my final year at J.C. and private accompanist for several of the voice majors for their juries. By this time, I had moved my studio into my home and taught more piano students than guitar. I explained, "When I first enrolled in U of M I was a piano major, but four years ago I switched to guitar because I was only teaching guitar at that time. I thought I needed more guitar skills."

"I see. That makes sense, but if I might make a suggestion," she offered, "maybe you should consider enrolling at Western as a piano major and see if you can finish up a guitar minor or major at Grand Valley".

"Um, that's a great idea," I mused, "but I'm not sure I'm good enough to get in. Do you think I could do it?"

"Yes, I do, but you will need help. You will have to pass a tryout and entrance exam. I'd be willing to help you," she offered.

"It's a deal," I said. "I'll talk to the people at WMU.[17] right away.

Thus, I spent that summer working with her on a difficult piano solo and brushing up on my scales and exercises in preparation for my tryout before members of the faculty at WMU School of Music in Kalamazoo, an hour's drive from our home in Kentwood.

I was a bit disappointed to be accepted as only a second semester sophomore in piano,[18] whereas in reality I was darned lucky they didn't require eight semesters. In all my other classes, I was accepted as a junior. At the same time, I was able to finish a guitar major at Grand Valley.

The day I gave my Senior recital at Western was a great day for me and a culmination of my dreams. I thought back to how far I had come since my prayer at age seven: "Lord, teach me to play the piano." My whole family was there, including parents, siblings and their families. Shelley's fiancé, Tom Watkins was there, as well as much of the music faculty and a smattering of students and residents of Kalamazoo with nothing better to do. I had not taken any other classes this semester so that I could concentrate solely on piano. I had just fifteen weeks to prepare a one hour, memorized concert containing the required variety of difficult classical pieces from each period. Having to memorize worried me the most, as it would most older people. I had prepared for that daunting task the previous summer by memorizing

---

[17] Western Michigan University

[18] I fulfilled the required 8 semesters of applied piano in 5 semesters.

scripture along with copious prayer. The first few verses that I tried seemed almost impossible. I went over and over each word endlessly, getting it right one day only to forget it the next. The second verse was a bit easier as was the third and fourth and so on, until by the end of summer I could recite whole passages. Without that training I never would have made it.

My faculty piano teacher, Steve Hesla, had pity on me in one respect. In consultation with the other staff, he allowed me to use printed music for the Bach French Suite I was playing. He said that Bach was the most difficult to memorize. That left only forty-five minutes of music to memorize –thousands of separate notes and notations. One of the pieces was a long Chopin "Barcarolle". Another was "Argentine Suite" by Ginistera. A unique piece was an extremely difficult piano accompaniment for a Mozart flute solo. My daughter, Ann, played the flute for me. There were others. After the recital there was a reception with gifts and many congratulations. Steve was overjoyed. He gave me a big hug and an A on my report card. My successful recital was as much as reflection on him as on me. I understood that feeling completely, as I held recitals for my own students, their parents and guests once or twice a year.

After the recital, I was able to concentrate on finishing up the requirements for my Bachelor of Music, Summa Cum Laude. Western Michigan University had no compunctions about awarding honors to a part-time student. I had finished in four years, at the age of forty-nine.

*   *   *

Chapter Twenty-Nine

"Empty Nest"

At one time, Dave had all three of his girls in college. He jested, "I'm suffering from *maltuition*," But he was a proud man. Shelley and I were inducted into the Pi Kappa Lamda Honors Society in the same year at two separate universities. Shelley received her Bachelor of Music Education from Michigan State University and also completed some of her masters' level credits. Ann received her Bachelor's in Graphic Design from Western Michigan University and I received my Bachelors in Music from WMU.

Shelley Mercer and Tom Watkins graduated from Kentwood High School in the same class. Tom claims he had his eye on her right from kindergarten, but I believe they actually met in middle school. They didn't court seriously until college and then it was via long-distance. Tom graduated from Calvin College in pre-med the same year Shelley graduated from MSU. They were married right out of college. They spent their honeymoon year in Grand Rapids while both worked and saved their money. Shelley worked as a school teacher. The next year, Tom was accepted into the School of Osteopathic Medicine at MSU. They moved to a mobile home in Perry, a small town east of Lansing. Shelley taught in the schools and finished work on her Master's in Education. After Tom received his doctorate, he interned, then took a residency in family medicine in Columbus, Ohio. Their daughter Amy was born there. Since then, she takes plenty of ribbing for being a "Buckeye".[19] Undaunted, she dons her red OSU shirt, perches herself in front of the T.V. on game days and roots her team home. When it came time for Tom to set up his practice and a new home in Muskegon, they laughingly noted that Amy was a frequent flyer before the age of six months.

Ann Mercer dated the same guy through her senior year of high school and four years of college only to break up with him. So she began her single life employed at Notre Dame University as a graphic designer. After two years of experience, she looked at

---

[19] Ohio State and Michigan State are sports rivals.

several big cities before deciding on Dallas, Texas. She moved to an apartment in Dallas and worked as a graphic designer for an advertising firm for several years. She designed print ads as well as television commercials. She and Bill Cormany met and were married in Dallas at age twenty-nine. Kendal was born there. Later, Bill took a job in Phoenix. They moved to Scottsdale and then built a home in Paradise Valley. Bill and Ann now have three boys and a girl. Tom and Shelley have two girls. Both our daughters have had very interesting lives, families and careers, but that is their story. Let me just say that we love them both dearly, remain very close and consider them and their families our very best of friends.

Dave and I have always taken a keen interest in our grandchildren and could regale you with stories, but I'll try to keep it to just a few facts in order to leave room for them to write their own stories. I spent at least a week with my daughters after each new baby. Dave flew down to Columbus for an additional week when Amy was born. Modeling myself after Dave's Mom, I knitted an afghan for each new baby. Ann would announce her pregnancies by calling me up, "Hi, Mom, it's time to start knitting."

Dave has been a spectacular grandfather.

Here he was called upon to fix a bike as grand- daughter Alden and her dad observe.

Neither of us ever hesitated to change a diaper or clean up a mess. We loved to babysit as much as possible, though living far away. We played together endlessly and took them on trips. We've done our best to create happy memories for them. The time has flown by. They have grown up so quickly. The eldest, Amy, is now in grad school, Emily in college, Kendal and Alden in high school, Byron in middle and Grant in elementary. The four older ones are heading for fascinating careers. The younger two boys have been close enough in age to be bosom playmates. Great fun!

Grandma Dorothy and Amy

Chapter Thirty

"Church Music Careers"

For years, I served as chairwoman of the music committee at St. Paul's United Methodist, the church that Dave and I attended. Our accomplishments were legendary. I was able to raise money to replace all the old clunky uprights in the church with brand new Kawai pianos and a six-foot grand in the sanctuary. We raised money for a new Allen organ and hired a great organist. I often played organ-piano duets with her. Shelley and I sang in the senior choir under the direction of Donald Druart, who also directed Shelley's band at the High School. I often accompanied for Don and his students. Shelley, Ann and I did duets and instrumental ensembles for worship services. I directed the children's choir as a volunteer. It was a golden time.

Once, when Don called in sick, I stepped in and directed his adult choir rehearsal. I fell in love. This was what I must do. I was still a junior at WMU when Don resigned. I applied to our search committee to direct the adult choir myself. They turned me down because they "didn't think it wise to hire a member of the church as an employee." This was the first of many years of unflinching service to the United Methodist Church, only to be rewarded by disappointing slaps in the face. I made up my mind, then and there, to take the first choir director's job that appeared in the newspaper. The lucky church was the Burlingame United Church of Christ in Wyoming, Michigan[20]. Their adult choir was made up of a dozen singers with more enthusiasm than talent. None had any musical training. They told me that when they found me they thought they had "hit the jackpot". I finished out the season with them, for a salary of $20 a week.

The following summer I received a call from Rev. Chuck Shulmer of Grandville United Methodist Church, one of the largest in our area. He offered me a Director of Music position involving a 25-voice senior choir, and two age-level children's choirs. We would perform four Sundays a month. Fifth Sundays were filled by the handbell choir, directed by one of the members who also served as organist and choir accompanist. My salary would be $75 a week, the same as hers. All three of my rehearsals could be held on one day, starting after school and continuing into the evening. The money would supplement my income from teaching private

---

[20] So-called because it was on Burlingame Avenue.

lessons. I could arrange my college classes and my teaching around that schedule. I took the job.

It was a joy working with Rev. Shulmer. He met with me every two months to go over his sermon schedule, so I could coordinate the music with the theme and scripture of the day. He followed the Lectionary.[21] I loved this job and worked hard at it, coordinating with the handbell choir to arrange big productions for special festival days. I joined the Society of United Methodists for Worship, Music and Other Arts, attending their regional workshops and week-long national meetings. At these events, I was able to work under some of the best known directors in the country.

Chuck taught me a lot about worship planning and became a good friend and supporter. He seemed to be extremely pleased with my work. Sadly, he also taught me my first hard lesson in church politics when he failed to overrule a lay committee that set out to get me fired. I hadn't heard the rumor that one of the influential members,[22] upon hearing that the pastor hired me, vowed to get rid of me before she had even met me. Apparently, she took it as a personal insult that she wasn't consulted and adopted a vendetta against a woman choir director. She and her husband both sang in my choir. She never gave me a chance. I had no idea what was going on until one Sunday morning in late May, the phone rang before I left for church. "Hello?"

"Hello, Dorothy, this is Brian W___, chair of the Staff Relations Committee at church."

"Yes, of course, Mr. W___. How can I help you?"

"I'm calling to inform you that the committee has voted to release you from your duties as of today. We won't have you come in today."

I was stunned into silence.

---

[21] A universal guide for preachers, used by many mainline churches, prescribing scripture, psalm, theme and a suggestion for hymns of the day.
[22] translate that: big givers

"Are you still there?" he asked.

"W-w-would you please say that again?"

"We won't be needing your services any further, Dorothy."

"B-b-but why?" I stammered as I sank into the nearest chair.

"Your performance has been evaluated as unsatisfactory."

"But that can't be. My choir members love me. The congregation loves me. The pastor is very happy with my work. Surely, he didn't agree to this."

"No, Dorothy, you're mistaken. Pastor has a voice, but no vote on the committee. The committee believes that, as a woman, you are much better suited to work with the children. Pastor agrees. They are willing to offer you the job of directing the children, while we interview your replacement for the senior choir."

"No, thank you. I won't take the children's choir alone. That is insulting."

"All right, Dorothy, in that case, you may come in one day next week while no one is here and pick up your things. That is all."

"But I've rehearsed the choir. I'm all ready to leave. I want to come in today to direct my choir."

"No, Dorothy, we can't allow that."

"B-b-but, I need to see them, to say goodbye and explain what happened."

"We don't think that would be healthy for the choir. I will speak with the choir. Thank you for your service. Goodbye."

As chief negotiator for the Grandville School District, dealing with the teacher's union, hiring and firing teachers, Mr. W was uniquely qualified for this ruthless volunteer job.

I cannot describe the feeling of broken-heartedness I felt. It was the worst shock since Jeffrey had died. Unaccustomed as I was to the dirty side of church politics, I fully expected my choir and congregation to rise up in defense of me and force a change of policy. Surely the pastor couldn't let this stand. Hope faded as days passed with no word except for one awkwardly worded letter from a minor choir member, inquiring about what had happened. Apparently, the lid was on and the cover-up gears in motion.

I spent one afternoon organizing the music files, bringing the library and records up-to-date and cleaning the choir room from top to bottom. No successor of mine could ever complain that I was messy.

Later, I learned that the Staff Committee had hired an assistant professor at GVSU,[23] who directed one of their choirs, as their new adult choir director and appointed the organist/handbell director as the new children's choir director.

*   *   *

During my grieving period, I received a call from Rev. Ron Fassett of Burton Heights United Methodist Church. It seemed that he needed a choir director. Once again the pastor was allowed to choose an employee who met his requirements, thus bypassing the committee structure. *Apparently, the Staff Relations committee is only called in to handle the dirty jobs like firing.*

Burton UMC turned out to fit my pressing needs at the time, and it became a place of healing. Burton was a dying church in a changing neighborhood. Once upon a time, it had over 500 members. The sanctuary was large and beautiful with huge stained glass windows and a twenty rank pipe organ. Now, the aging adult members had moved to the suburbs, but remained stubbornly clinging to their church home, struggling to keep up with the costly

---

[23] Grand Valley State University

heating bills. I was treated with the utmost kindness and fairness. All I had to do was direct one choir rehearsal and one worship service a week.

Rev. Fassett was a believer in designed worship, and used the Lectionary, the same as Chuck Fulmer. We didn't spend a lot of time in conference. He was prompt in leaving his worship plans in my mailbox once a quarter. I was free to design the music around that, returning my titles to Roberta, the church secretary, in time for typing up the Sunday bulletin. An interesting twist to the story was that Rev. Fulmer's wife was the church organist and was going to be my choir accompanist. Turns out, Margaret Fulmer was the one who had recommended me. Small world. She was efficient, prompt and a very competent keyboardist. Most of all she was quiet, a valuable trait for a pastor's wife. She passed along some of the news to me, but was careful not to gossip. I never learned more from her about why I got the sack at Grandville.

I genuinely believed that God had a purpose in mind for my life, even though it wasn't always apparent. Because of that, I was able to heal and carry on in a new church. One of my favorite children's anthems had been "I Am A Promise" by Bill Gaither.

On my first appointment with Pastor Ron, he showed me around the church and gave me some of the history. I was issued a set of keys. Three different keys were necessary to proceed from the office to the choir room. It was important to keep the various wings of the church locked at all times because of the prevalence of petty theft in the neighborhood. I was cautioned to always lock the doors behind me. On choir nights, I should park close to the back entrance, under the light, make sure my car doors were locked and carry everything with me, leaving no valuables behind. I should lock the entrance door behind me, move along a corridor and up some steps to another locked door into the choir room. After choir rehearsal, at least one of the choir men would wait with me until I was ready to go and escort me to my car. I was to drive directly home so that my husband would always know when to expect me. All this security seemed a bit much, but I was careful to follow procedure. The last thing I wanted was to be responsible for a burglary.

During the year I conducted at Burton Heights, I became interested in working toward a professional designation of "Director of Music" with the UMC.[24] There were some daunting educational and occupational requirements. In addition to a Bachelor's degree in music and further graduate study, a requirement was at least two years full-time service as director of a complete church choir program, from pre-school through adult. Within our denomination, there were very few full time positions of this sort, and most of them were filled by men.

It was during the following summer, after one year at Burton UMC, that I learned that Faith UMC in northwest Grand Rapids was looking for someone to take over from a man who had developed a large music program at the church. They were looking for a director/organist to replace John Potter, whom I had met professionally. Their program included three choirs and a handbell choir. For a church of about 300 members it was quite an ambitious program. The age range of their members made the difference. The church was intergenerational, with many young families to supplement their older, wealthy senior members.

I applied for the job and went for an interview and tryout. I prepared a splashy organ piece by Gordon Young and played that as well as sight-reading a hymn of their selection. I lingered to listen to the next candidate in line, Brenda Wepman, who was a candidate for organist only. I had to admit she was very good, better than me on organ, but not on piano. Organ was not my first instrument. I was self-taught and had only been playing organ a few years.

The upshot was that I was offered the choirs and Brenda was offered the organist job. She would also accompany the senior choir. Brenda was a sweet little thing with dark hair and big brown eyes that melted your heart when she turned them on you. She had influence in Grand Rapids Symphony circles through her husband, who was General Manager. During our seven years working together, she was divorced from her husband and kept custody of her two sons. My only bone to pick with Brenda was her annoying tardiness at choir rehearsals. This directly clashed with my need to

---

[24] United Methodist Church

start punctually on time so I could end on time. Also, I wished I could get her to vary her dynamics instead of playing at one constant volume. Other than that, she was perfectly sweet, without a typical musician's temperament[25], and she seldom made mistakes.

I was experienced now, a college graduate, and conducted myself and my music very well. I infused my conducting with emotion – in respectable amounts, of course. My objective was to touch the emotions of people in the congregation, as I believed that touching people's faith was a matter of touching their emotions. A good day, for me, was when someone told me the music brought tears to their eyes. Rev. Eugene Lewis, the pastor, was another exponent of overall planning, coordinating and following the Lectionary.

Gene was the first boss I had who used the Worship Committee in designing and planning worship. He encouraged regular meetings to plan creative worship situations around the theme, utilizing all the arts and designs. It was a gloriously creative time. We often used two lovely, elementary age girls who studied ballet to enhance the music with expressive dance. One of the girls went on to star in the New York City Ballet. We used storytelling and dramatic readings. We erected crude wooden crosses on the front lawn, draping them with black on Good Friday and exchanging it for white on Easter morning. One Palm Sunday, we assembled the congregation outside with palms and let the choirs lead them in, singing and waving palms, starting with the smallest children's choir. Whatever we could dream up was fine with Gene Lewis. I even volunteered my daughter Ann, now a graphic designer, to design a logo for the church for use on their stationery and Sunday bulletins.

Rev. Lewis remarked that members couldn't wait to get to church on Sunday to see what his worship committee had dreamed up. I became friendly with one of the committee members. We worked together on projects and talked on the phone.

I led money-raising projects for the choirs until we had

---

[25] such as mine, sad to say

raised enough money to buy all new robes and spearheaded the drive to get their ancient but priceless Steinway in the sanctuary completely redone. One year I recorded all our music and took snapshot pictures of their various church wide activities. Dave and I surprised the congregation with one of our first multi-media presentations, blending the pictures with readings of the Psalms and background music of the choirs. We even held a church-wide fast on Ash Wednesday, ending with a service and a breakfast of finger food at night. I taught a six week seminar on the meaning of fasting during church school. A small group of us met weekly to practice the spiritual disciplines. That is a small sampling of my activities. There were more.

Sunday afternoons directly after church, I would grab a sack lunch, then go out to call on all the visitors for that day. I worked tirelessly seventy hours a week. I started a youth choir, a second handbell choir, a cherub choir and chaired the Grand Rapids Children's Choir Organization. Our main effort was to bring in one famous children's anthem composer each year. During the choir season, local children's choirs would learn a selection of the composer's music, using it in their own worship service. In the spring, the composer would come into town and conduct workshops for an entire weekend, culminating with all the 200-plus children coming together on Sunday in one of the big churches for a rehearsal and concert, conducted by the composer. Also, I led my youth choir to be involved in some community-wide activities and sponsored parties for them.

While I was at Faith UMC, I completed the postgraduate requirements and achieved my dream of becoming certified as Director of Music. This was solemnized in a consecration by the Bishop during the ordination service at the Annual Conference held at Albion College. I was especially pleased that my sister-in-law, Joyce Douglas, had brought my aged mother to the program. I'm not sure mother understood what was happening, but she was there and that counted a lot.

Joyce, having been raised Presbyterian, was now a member of the United Methodist Church in Concord, where I was raised. She seemed to be very proud of me and was invariably kind and supportive. An interesting sidelight was that Joyce was the lone family member who kept up the Douglas family tradition in that church where the two stained glass windows gracing the sanctuary wore brass nameplates in memory of my father and mother.[26] So far as I know, her husband never darkened the door except at Dad's funeral in 1976, and later at Mother's in 1992. The ordination service was two and a half hours long, and Joyce opted to take mother home before it was over. Directly afterward, the Bishop appointed me to the Board of Diaconal Ministry for an eight-year term. I also served as chairperson of that board for almost two years.

During this time, I kept up with my private students, at one time teaching as many as forty. My church salary was just too small. I received raises of maybe five percent a year, but 5% of nothing is nothing. The most I ever made was $7,000 a year, with no benefits whatsoever and no expense account. At the same time, a beginning part-time assistant pastor made $18,000 and senior pastors received as much as $50,000 with free housing and utilities, insurance, pension, medical care, expense account, transportation, and every possible benefit. The part-time janitor was paid more than the musicians.[27]

Still, I understood my situation and honestly do not remember complaining about my salary. I naively thought that if I practiced my faith, worked hard, stayed out of trouble, made the pastor look good, and did a good job, the congregation would prosper and everyone would love me.

One year the inevitable happened: Eugene Lewis was transferred to a larger, more prosperous church and an older man was appointed to take his place. It is customary for Methodist ministers to itinerate.[28] Rev. Paul Patterson was a kindly

---

[26] Leon Luther Douglas (1889-1976) and Esther Elizabeth Douglas, nee Dodes (1901-1992)

[27] Michigan churches were noted for paying their musicians poorly. Among my peers in the professional music organizations, my salary was an embarrassment. One of the goals of the Board of Diaconal Ministry was to set high standards and raise the salaries of lay church professionals. They got the first part right, but had a long way to go on the second.

[28] Move from church to church. Historically Methodism was spread across rural America by itinerate preachers traveling on horseback. Today Bishops appoint them to a parish, moving them approx. every 3 to 10 years.

gentleman, balding and built somewhat like Santa Claus. This would be Paul's last parish before retirement. He had reached a point in life where he had nothing more to prove, so he was content to do his job and let sleeping dogs lie. Paul was invariably courteous to me, but had less interest in doing anything particularly creative with worship. Paul preferred that he plan his sermons and I plan the music. He was confident that I could do my job without his micromanagement. That was fine with me – it was less work actually. I knew how to work with any style of management.

During Paul's tenure, I started working on the requirements to be a Diaconal Minister. Paul was Ok with that and gave me the necessary endorsements and signatures. The church provided a small stipend to help with my travel. Meeting the requirements would take several years.

I decided to attend Perkins School of Theology in Dallas for my training. There were six classes in intense three-week terms on campus, taught by the same professors who taught student pastors at the seminary.[29] Our daughter, Ann, was living in Dallas now, so I could bunk in with her. Airfare was cheap: only $79 round trip. The Board of Diaconal Ministry provided small scholarships. The rest of the expense was up to me.

Locally, I would relate to the West Michigan Conference Board of Diaconal Ministry, attending their meetings and retreats. I was assigned a Mentor, the Rev. Bob Brubaker, with whom I would meet regularly. His job was to guide my path of faith through this process. We were provided with textbooks and a thick workbook with lessons in matters of faith and spiritual discipline to work through. We took up the spiritual disciplines one by one: meditation, prayer, fasting, study, simplicity, solitude, submission, service, confession, worship, guidance and celebration. I spent a good hour every morning practicing the disciplines and filled several notebooks with my prayer journal. Throughout my ministry, I kept this up and fasted one day a week.

---

[29] I studied New Testament and Old Testament, Biblical History, Theology, Wesleyan History, the Structure and Organization of the United Methodist Church, Preaching and the Sacraments.

An important part of the mentoring process was exploring my calling to the ministry so that I was sure the calling was of God and I was certain of the path I took. The mentoring process was designed to take three or four years and continue throughout the education and preparation for the ministry, right up until the consecration service. If possible, the Mentor will take part in the laying on of hands. Unfortunately, Rev. Brubaker was stricken with a virulent form of cancer before he and I were able to completely finish. Bob Brubaker died, leaving behind his young widow, Ellen, who was also an ordained elder and a minister in the West Michigan Conference of the UMC. A few years later, she married another minister. I carried on alone for a time until a new mentor was found for me, this time a godly woman, Margaret Foster, a Diaconal Minister.

For each year of candidacy, I was required to attend a spiritual retreat. During the retreat, I was interviewed concerning my progress toward consecration by a committee from the Board of Diaconal Ministry made up of pastors and lay people. A further requirement was to submit a comprehensive written report on what I had done in the previous year. My employing church also had to fill out a report on my work. In some respects, it was a nerve-wracking business, considering everything you had to do to become eligible to do the Lord's work *at little or no pay.*

The symbol of the Diaconal Ministry is the basin and towel, reminiscent of Christ's foot-washing at the Last Supper. The symbol signifies a life of service. We were called to find ways to connect the church and the world, to reach out to the world in service to others and to lead others in the church to do the same. During our interviews, we could expect questions such as, "Tell us about your calling. How do you know that God is calling you to a set-apart and consecrated ministry and not simply to be a lay person? What does consecration mean to you? In what ways are you fulfilling your particular calling? How is this different from what any Christian could do? Define diaconal ministry. Explain what you are doing in your daily life to increase your faith." The hapless candidate had better be prepared to articulate the answers clearly in speech and in writing.

There was a contingent[30] of people at Faith U.M.C. who didn't like Rev. Patterson. They thought his sermons were boring. I had been there longer than Paul and had many friends who brought their complaints to me. I did all I could to deflect those complaints and tried not to get drawn into the conflict. I knew it would be a big mistake to ever let a single negative word pass my lips. In truth, I had no criticisms of his work. His style was merely different, not especially dramatic, but entirely acceptable. I had experienced lots of different ministers and understood that each one is unique.

It would be foolhardy for someone in my position to listen to complaints, because it is human nature to embellish conversations in the retelling, for example, putting words in my mouth that actually came from a different source. For instance, "Dorothy and I were talking about Paul the other day and she agrees... blah, blah, blah." I was walking a tightrope, trying to support Paul, stay out of trouble and refrain from offending my friends.

The woman on the worship committee with whom I had become friends and phone buddies created a particularly touchy problem for me. Accustomed to working with Rev. Lewis, she bridled at Rev. Patterson's quite different style. She took to calling me up and complaining about him. I had to take care to support the pastor and not to join in the complaining without offending her. She was related to a large influential church family with four generations of church members. Her grandmother was a matriarchal curmudgeon who reportedly gave $10,000 a year to the church.

It grieved me to attend professional meetings of church musicians and secretaries and listen to them complain about the pastor for whom they were working. No wonder pastors are wary of employees. In those situations, I remained quiet and hoped not to get painted with the same brush. I believed it was part of my job to make the pastor look good and let him take the credit.

To be fair, there were an equal number of pastor gripe

---

[30] All people in positions of authority have their detractors.

sessions where they complained about the people in their church. I didn't care for those either. It goes back to my upbringing and the way Mother disdained gossip and thought the best of everybody. I'll never live up to her level of sainthood, but some of her attitude rubbed off.

In the end, Paul Patterson was wily and capable enough to escape the clutches of his naysayers and retire to his pleasant home up north with nary a problem. Fortunately for Paul and others like him, the Bishops tend to take local church complaints with a large dose of salt. Things have got to be really bad before a pastor will be removed. Sadly, there are no such constraints when it comes to dismissing lay employees or lay professionals, such as me. The band of busybodies that tried to pull a power play and get rid of Paul had to turn elsewhere for a place to vent their frustration.

By now, I had finished my requirements and was consecrated Diaconal Minister of Music at the June Annual Conference. It was an impressive and dignified ceremony held in conjunction with the Ordination service. All the ordained ministers and candidates processed into Goodrich Chapel, dressed in their flowing robes to the moving processional played on the huge pipe organ amid a thousand voices raised in song. The candidates each had a handmade banner representative of their ministry, carried by a special person. Dave carried my banner. The choir had presented me with my robe, the church had given me a silver cross and Dave had bought me an elaborate stole, embroidered with gold thread. I was wearing the robe and cross, but Dave would place the stole on me after we had all repeated our vows and I was consecrated to ministry by the Bishop.

Later, Faith UMC held a recognition for me, as did St. Paul's UMC in Kentwood, where Dave still had his membership. St. Paul's considered that I had come out of that church. They display my consecration picture in a place of honor on a special wall in the Narthex, alongside the pictures of several others who entered the ministry from that church.

When Paul retired, a younger man, Rev. Douglas Pederson, was appointed to take his place at Faith UMC. Doug's style was entirely different from any of my five previous employers/pastors, but that was ok. I knew how to get along. Douglas met with me and the Staff Parish chairman over lunch a couple of times just to have an informal talk about my job - more or less an evaluation. Was I happy? How could they be of assistance? etc. I took their few suggestions to heart, implemented them immediately and thought nothing more of it. Douglas stopped to chat occasionally while I was at work. He had laughingly made oblique references to his own rotten experience as an assistant pastor. "The new senior pastor wanted to clean house and bring in his own team, ha-ha," he joked. I thought no more of it at the time. I was used to playing assistant to the senior pastor and always got along great with them.

The Staff Parish chairman happened to be the husband of my gossipy friend from the worship committee. Coincidentally, it was about that time that she stopped calling me. I wondered why, but couldn't be sure of the reason. Could be she regretted having said too much in the past about Rev. Patterson. I tried calling her a couple of times. She said she had been busy with a new part time job. She sounded all right, but continued to avoid me.

One day, a few months into Doug's term, I was asked to come into the pastor's conference room when I finished work. Expecting the pastor simply needed to confer about something, I quickly finished up and walked into the room. A group of people was seated around a conference table looking up at me. I was asked to sit, but remained standing, holding on to my armload of music books. I set my briefcase down on the chair and looked into each face. *Oh-oh. I have a bad feeling about this.* Douglas cleared his throat. He had a speech all prepared. "Uh, Dorothy, these folks are members of the Staff Relations committee. We have just completed a meeting in reference to your annual evaluation. They have elected me to be their spokesman, ha-ha." No one smiled. Pausing for breath, he looked around as the members nodded. Doug continued, "We want you to know that you have done an outstanding job here at Faith. We give you the highest marks. You have gone above and beyond the requirements of your job."

"Thank you," I said. *What is going on?*

"Well, uh, Dorothy, now, the committee unanimously agrees that this has nothing to do with your performance here, you understand." He paused and sighed. No one moved. I stared at him, in silent dread. A pin drop could be heard in the room. Doug's hands fidgeted. He half-smiled and looked around the room. Beads of sweat stood out on his brow. "Uh, Dorothy, this has absolutely nothing to do with your work, b-but I must tell you that the committee has decided it is time you moved on to something better, a bigger church, better paying job."

"You mean you're firing me?" I choked.

"Well, I wouldn't want to put it in those drastic terms, Dorothy. We just think you are destined for bigger things."

"But, I've been here seven years. I've been faithful. I've built up the program. How can you do this?" I replied.

"The fact is we think you are overqualified for the job," he admitted. "There are some folks... well, you got on this track of being certified and then you started on the Diaconal Minister program, and some folks think... well, they just don't want a Diaconal Minister working here. Most of the people don't even know what it is anyway."

I must have turned stark white. My limbs began to tremble. I looked at some of my best friends sitting around the table. They looked down to avoid my eye. Sadly, I shook my head, picked up my briefcase, and without another word, turned and walked out to my car.

I was numb. The half-hour drive across the city was done completely by rote. Arriving home I sagged into Dave's arms and cried.

"What's wrong? Darling, what happened?" he said in dismay.

"I can't believe it happened again. They did it again, honey. Oh God, Dave, they fired me." I collapsed in sobs, no longer able to speak.

Dave held me close, "No, darlin', they couldn't have fired

you, not you."

I nodded my head and sobbed louder.

"I don't believe it. You must have heard them wrong."

"They did," I nodded.

"Oh, Dort, I'm so sorry!" he said, "Here, take my handkerchief."

"Thank you," I sniffed.

"Come on out in the kitchen and sit down," he offered. "I'll fix us a cup of tea and you tell me what happened." He pulled out my chair and handed me a box of tissues. "What happened, honey?"

Amid tears, coughs and sniffs and sips, I told the story, using up half a box of tissues.

"I want to drive out there," Dave said, "There's got to be something wrong. There must be some mistake. You've done a wonderful job there, worked your buns off. You've built that church. Good grief, what's wrong with them? I just can't believe it. Your choirs love you. The people love you. Your music has been twice as good as ever. What are they saying you did wrong, anyway?"

"Actually, nothing, they say I've done good work."

"Then what's wrong?"

"Some of them don't want a Diaconal Minister."

"C'mon, they can't be that stupid! For the price they pay you, they don't deserve anything. You're twice as good, ten times as good as they pay for. What's wrong with them?"

"I don't know, Dave," I said. "It doesn't make sense to me either."

"Can you get help from the Conference?"

"Well," I said, "the rules say that they can't fire me in the middle of the season. They have to keep me on until the end of the choir year."

"You aren't going to stay, are you?" he asked.
"Yes, I'll finish my contract. I won't descend to their level."

It took three more months to finish out my year. It was tough, especially with the children. I held my head high and continued the excellent level of music to which they were accustomed. It hurt when they offered my job to Brenda. When she came to me for advice, I gave her my best wishes, advised her to do a children's musical next year, and make sure that the church paid her no less than what our combined salaries had cost them. She did both.

My last Sunday at Faith, I conducted a wonderful combined number using all my choirs. When I was through, I cracked my baton and left it on the music stand. My vow was to never direct another choir, not ever. No other choir could come up to this one. The sound we achieved in that sanctuary was pure heaven. The building was built for music, the reverb so pronounced and prolonged that it was hard to understand spoken words in there. My adult choir had been made up of young to middle-aged adults with good voices, dedicated to singing. One of the men worked a supervisory position on the swing shift way across the city, a thirty-minute-plus drive each way. On choir nights, he took a break from work to drive to choir practice and return. Is there any wonder I carefully planned my rehearsals so as to start and end on time?

When I walked out of there for the last time, I never looked back and never went back. I couldn't bear to drive on that side of town. The expressway to Muskegon went through northwest Grand Rapids. We took that highway whenever we went to visit Shelley and her family. Whenever we drove that expressway – five miles away from Faith UMC – my heart would be so overcome with sadness and pain that I had to hide my tears from Dave.

Dave had been so supportive during my Sundays away from home. It had been especially difficult for us on holidays such as Christmas Eve, when our scattered family would be arriving at home, and I was still at church conducting a 7PM early service plus a midnight service. We lived too far away for me to drive home and return. Easter was another difficult time because of the sunrise service followed by two services with a breakfast in between. Of course, any preacher worth his salt knows that if you can get the children's choirs to sing, their parents will fill up the pews. Sometimes on those special days, Dave would drive out and sit with me while I rested between services. Then he would go home and attend his own church. In many respects, Dave bore the brunt of our pain and suffered for me, far worse than I did. He blamed it on Rev. Doug Pederson and felt an almost vicious hatred for him. Dave thought Doug should have stood up for me. He believed that Doug had acted with jealousy, wanting to get rid of me and selling the committee a bill of goods to convince them that they were doing me a favor. I don't know whether that was the case at all. We can't know what the inner workings were. I tended to accept it as the Lord's will.

I can say this much for certain: so far as job security is concerned, the jobs I held were about on a par with professional football coaches. There are a lot of wonderful Christians, that's for sure, but churches tend to attract more than their share of wackos as well. An attractive, popular woman, up front, doing a good job is a perfect target for a power play and/or professional jealousy. As a lay professional, I did not have the protection of the Bishop's office the way that Ordained Deacons and Elders did. The mother church[31] sets standards that protect their clergy, but makes no particular inquiry into the hiring practices of the local churches. By definition, Diaconal Ministers and other Lay Professionals[32] had to find their own jobs. They could also be fired easily. Churches are not subject to the laws of the United States that

---

[31] United Methodist Church hierarchy organization, including clergy, Bishops, Annual Conferences, General Conferences, National Committees and other professionals.
[32] For more on this general subject see Appendix I, "The United Methodist Church Struggles With Orders".

protect other people from discriminatory and unfair employment practices. Employees can be fired without cause, mistreated, abused, underpaid, discriminated against, made to work in unheated rooms, etc. There is no such thing as unemployment insurance. Only a few of the larger churches provide their lay employees with a pension.

*   *   *

Chapter Thirty-One

"Alaska Bound"

"She suddenly realized that she felt a tranquility about that period of her life...she regarded that time and its events as merely an unfortunate episode...and no longer felt pain."[33]

In the spring of my final year at Faith, I pondered what to do next. Important to my consideration was my desire to spend time with Dave. We both needed adequate time to heal and put this behind us. I'll take credit for hitting upon one of my better ideas. There were a few things Dave had dreamed of doing in his life. One had already been taken care of: his dream of flying. Another was his dream of going to Alaska. Sometimes, during our conversations around the fireplace, we would fancy ourselves doing something adventurous. Whenever he brought up going to Alaska, I resisted, saying how much I hated to be cold. Besides, I couldn't take that much time off work.

As my thoughts turned toward the solace of our marriage to salve my wounds over being fired from my job at Faith UMC, I thought about how I could make it up to Dave for all his support for me. "Honey," I asked one day, "What would you think about taking the summer off with me and driving to Alaska?"

No need to repeat that offer. With lightning speed he agreed and we began making plans.

I continued, "I've been thinking of one or two options. Either we could fly up there in your Cessna, or we could take the Steury camper."

"You've got this all figured out," he grinned.

"Not entirely." I tried to appear innocent. "You are certainly allowed *some* say in this."

---

[33] From Aaron Fletcher's Outback Station, pg. 463, © 1991 Dorchester Publishing Company Inc.

"Thanks a whole bunch,' he laughed. "I'll have to give it some thought, but off the top of my head, I can't fly the Cessna to Alaska. I've read too many horror stories about flying in the bush. Also, we'd be flying over a foreign country. That takes special permits. Besides, it wouldn't be fair to Russ[34] to keep the airplane away for two months. No, I just don't feel confident enough to fly us to Alaska and back."

"Well, what do you think about taking the camper?" I asked.

"Um, well... No, I don't think I want to drag a trailer five thousand miles either."

This was working out well. It was time I suggested the thing I wanted to do all along. "Well, I'd rather not fly commercially," I said, "Driving the Al-Can highway has always been one of our dream trips. Maybe we should look around for a new camper of some sort. What do you think?"

"I won't buy anything used." He halfway agreed.

Thus began one of our great adventures. At the same time as I was winding down my career at Faith UMC, we were already looking ahead and planning our next trip. We had so much fun visiting camping shows as well as all the car dealers near and far. We had almost decided on a van conversion for $45,000.[35] On the way home from making a deal on a real beauty, decked out with all the goodies, I remarked to Dave, "Honey, do you think it would be a good idea to look at some motor homes before we put money down on that van? We're talking about big money here. For the same amount, we might be able to get a real motor home."

"I've got time today. Let's drive out on South Division Street and take a gander." He smiled at me. "We'll grab some

---

[34] Russ Cotè and Dave were partners in owning a Cessna 182. See chapter, "Come, Josephine in My Flying Machine."

[35] Specialty shops can take a regular van off the assembly line, chop off the top, and raise it up, then, outfit the inside with a tiny kitchen, potty, seating/dining arrangement, bed and storage areas. It was crowded, but, it had all the basics.

lunch on the way back."

One look at the array of spacious and comfortable motor homes was all it took to quickly dispel any thoughts of buying a van. We spent the rest of the afternoon learning all there was to know about C models versus A models, Chevrolet engines vs. Ford Econo-line truck engines, 22-foot models vs. 29-foot models, priced from $15,000 and up. The sky was the limit.

Soon, our heads were spinning and our arms loaded down with brochures and floor plans. We were like kids in a candy store. Over a *very* late lunch, we agreed there was no point in looking at vans anymore. Clearly, we could buy a much nicer motor home for less money. We congratulated ourselves for avoiding a big mistake.

In time, we decided on a 29-foot C Model over the 22-foot. It was a bit roomier than we needed, but the longer chassis had a smoother ride. Also, this one had the bigger engine. We would need that in the mountains. Also, we could picture taking our grandchildren in this someday.

As soon as the spanking new vehicle was delivered, we set about outfitting it for our trip. We were so excited, we had to initiate it by sleeping in it together, our tradition for any new home. The first day we brought it home, we had to phone the girls and tell them our plans. They couldn't have been happier for us. "Have a wonderful time, Mom and Dad! You deserve it. By the way, when can we borrow the new camper?" they joked, trying to sound as if they didn't really mean it. "Well, not just yet," we retorted. "Let us put the first scratch on it, OK? You know the Steury is yours any time you want it."

Dave slyly pointed out that he had to get back to work sometime soon to support my extravagances and save up for our big trip. So, as was our usual practice, I set about doing the planning. Soon the maps and travel brochures started filling up our mailbox. We consulted any friends that had been to Alaska. Everyone said, "You must get a copy of 'Milepost'". This was something I planned to borrow, but our kids went together and gave us a fresh new copy as a going-away present. They were tickled to discover that we had provided them with a host of fresh ideas for birthday, Father's day, Mother's day and Christmas gifts.

We subscribed to Alaska magazine and soon became fluent with a host of strange new names, such as Skagway, Talkeetna, Clinglet, Denali, and Ketchikan. We learned the difference between Southeast Alaska and Alaska proper. I read an article about traveling the Marine Inland Highway and immediately became intrigued with the idea of taking the ferry up to the capital city, Juneau, with connections to Haines, Skagway and Glacier National Park. This seemed like a far better plan than driving the Al Can highway in our brand new vehicle. Horror stories about the damage to vehicles had turned me off from attempting that. The cost of taking our motor home on the ferry was prohibitive. Besides, there was no place to drive in Southeast Alaska, so why bother? The ferry stopped in Prince Rupert, British Columbia. We could have taken another ferry up the coast from Seattle, but why not drive through the National Parks, then over to Prince Rupert, park the motor home and proceed on up the coast from there?

I read everything I could find about the ferry service. It sounded like a backpacker's dream. Most of the ships were equipped with special deck lounges designed to let down into beds. There were showers and lockers available, and a cafeteria. For longer trips, small bunk rooms could be reserved. All the authors cautioned to make your reservations early. Deck lounges were on a first come, first served basis. Wise travelers should try to be the first to stake out their lounge bed, as the prime locations were under the overhang. Southeast Alaska was *not* noted for its clear, sunny days. We learned a new term: "temperate zone rain forest". Warm currents coming up from the South Pacific brought with them yearly rainfall amounts in the three digits.

The day he picked up the motor home, Dave couldn't resist driving it over to Faith UMC to show me. I gave my children's "beginning keyboard"[36] class a recess and we all piled into the camper to check it out. They peered into all the closets and

---

[36] I had purchased a half dozen or so child-size keyboards for a beginner piano class at Faith. We were learning rudimentary scales and chords harmonies, so they could play and sing. There was a waiting list for the class.

cupboards, hammered me with questions, bounced on the furniture and climbed into the overhead cab. One of the sweet little girls inquired, "Why did you get fired?" She was a fourth generation church member. "Honey, you need to ask your Mom and Dad, Grandmother or Great Grandmother about that." I deflected her question as I had every other such question I had received from church members.

As the kids "ooed" and "ahed" over our new toy, I guess they thought I was pretty lucky. Maybe it was more than simple luck. The Lord knew I would never leave that church voluntarily. Perhaps he had more lessons in mind. It was time to move on. It wasn't the first time I had compared myself with Jonah, or the last, actually. [37]

Splurging on the motor home was just the beginning of our shopping spree. There were all kinds of special equipment for it. I nearly went crazy in the retail store attached to the motor home sales showroom. *Oh my gosh, you can't believe all the neat stuff they had.* Dave learned to limit our trips, lest I bankrupt us buying all the cool stuff. Some things, however, were essential, such as chemicals for the onboard black-water storage tanks. (You don't want to know.)

Dave vetoed such elaborate toys as folding canoes, outdoor artificial grass carpets, decorative lanterns and leveling jacks, but he agreed we needed two aluminum folding chairs. *Whoopee!* I felt like a new bride, lining my cupboards and filling them with special dishes that wouldn't break or rattle, while Dave concentrated on the all important male department of engine spare parts, tire pumps and outdoor barbeque grills.

We needed to acquire everything for the backpacker from tent to sleeping bag. Good friends from my choir loaned us their handmade feather-down sleeping bags. I spent hours poring over the Campmor catalog, selecting just the right pup tent, portable lights, hiking boots, sox, rain gear, clothes, water bottles, freeze-dried food, cooking gear, bug repellant, clothes line, wash basin,

---

[37] From the O.T. story of "Jonah and the whale". Having refused the Lord's call, Jonah was swallowed by a big fish and thrown up on the shores of Nineveh.

towels, first aid, binoculars and the all-important backpacks. Dave specialized in the camera equipment, cell phones, film, the collapsible tripod, hiking poles and fishing gear. Everything had to be ultra light, every ounce weighed and counted. In the end, we were able to take everything needed, including our food, for a 15-day stay in Southeast Alaska in two packs. Mine weighed 45 pounds, Dave's 55.

Preparations went beyond shopping for gear. Our bodies had to toughen up. We began practicing hiking with packs, slowly allowing our bodies to accustom themselves to more and more weight and more and more distance. We got so acclimated that it almost felt strangely light when we removed the packs.

Business arrangements and coverage for Dave's agency were made. Neighbors would watch over our house. A service would take care of the lawn. Everything inside was shut down.

Final goodbyes over, we took off across the northern tier of states toward Glacier National Park. From there, we turned north through the entire long chain of the Canadian Rocky Mountains and their fabulous National Parks: Waterton Lakes, Kootenay, Banff, Yoho and Jasper. I could write an entire book about those parks. But for now we'll move on. Otherwise, we'll never make it to Alaska.

Not many people drive from Jasper National Park west to Prince George, and even fewer go on to Prince Rupert. In the words of our hill country cousins, "It's a fur piece." Not only that, it is beautiful and rugged. The further west you go, the rougher the roads. I'm glad we did it, but have no wish to go that way again. There was no competition for camping spaces. Most were cheap and on the honor system. You put money in an envelope and pushed it through a slot. The grounds would be freshly raked and a fire set in the fire bowl.

When you came upon a gas station, it was a good idea to fill up. Thankfully, we had allowed plenty of time to reach the ferry station at the appointed hour. We couldn't believe our luck when we saw our first eagle, just sitting there on top of a freight building, gazing around at a town, seemingly unconcerned with people and traffic noise. We were to see hundreds more eagles and wildlife of all sorts.

It felt good to arrive at our destination of Prince Rupert and settle into a motel for the night. We had plenty to do in the next two days, preparing our gear before we had to meet the ferry. We spread everything out on a big plastic tarp, took inventory and carefully loaded our backpacks, taking care to balance the load, put soft goods next to our backs and the things we would need most often on top. Outside pockets were loaded with small items easily reached. Next we had to do laundry, clean the motor home/camper and stow things away. We made arrangements with our landlady to park the motor home in her upper lot until we returned. The fridge would run on battery while we were gone. Our freezer was still packed full with food we had brought from home. That would keep, but we had to throw away milk and any fresh food that might spoil.

Grateful for a clear day, we laced up our hiking boots, hoisted our packs and hiked down to the waterfront. Tickets and passports were in order. The first officer welcomed us aboard and we headed up the gangway to stake claim to two lounges. Some folks smarter than us had already claimed the best spots. Oh well. Undaunted, we grabbed two and dragged them as close as we could get to the overhang. That would have to do. We would be spending two nights aboard, but had our tarps. We hoped some people would get off in Ketchikan.

With much coughing and grinding of gears the ferry took off. We leaned over the rail and gawked and waved at the townspeople as we passed by. It wasn't long before we entered the state of Alaska, as Prince Rupert is right on the border.

The big advantage of riding the ferry over taking a cruise ship, aside from the price of a ticket, is that it is smaller with a shallow draft. The ferry weaves in between the myriad islands that make up Southeast Alaska and never takes to the open ocean. Thus, you are always within view of the shore, with its spectacular mountains, green forests, glacial inlets and sheltered waters brimming with wildlife. The captain was quick to point out sea mammals whenever they passed by. A park ranger, well-versed in local lore, was available to answer questions. She also entertained the passengers with travelogues and talks on the area, pointing out landmarks and preparing us for the sights to come.

Our first stop was Ketchikan, Alaska. We would be in port forty-five minutes to an hour. Passengers could disembark to look around town, but were warned to be back in time. The ship couldn't wait. It would blast a five minute warning whistle before leaving. Dave and I were eager to set foot in our first Alaskan town. The quaint main street was bordered by small businesses. We didn't stop to shop, but set off at hiking speed down the hill, pausing to snap pictures right and left. The harbor was loaded with eagles and other shorebirds, fishing vessels of all shapes and sizes, and airplanes on pontoons. There were no roads inland from these Southeast towns, as the mountains to the east are impenetrable. The only transportation is by water or air.

We were having a wonderful time and it seemed as if no time had passed when we heard the ear-splitting blast of the ferry's horn. Too late, we checked our watches. We had lost track of time. There was no mistaking the message. We had five minutes to make it back to the dock. In panic we realized we were a good half mile away. Uphill. "C'mon, kid, let's run!" Dave grabbed my hand and we took off.

"What'll we do if we don't make it?" I gasped.

"We charter a plane and catch up with the ferry at the next stop," Dave said.

"But our extra money is on the ship!" I protested, feet flying.

"Run like hell!" was his advice.

Chests heaving and sides aching we charged up the last block, just in time to see the heavy gangplank rising with a heart-sinking grinding of gears. The sight gave us an extra burst of speed. We starting screaming, "Stop! Wait for us!" while frantically waving our arms. Just as the gangplank was about to slam into place it halted and slowly began to reverse directions.

We came to the end of the dock, gasping for breath as it lowered for us alone. "All aboard," called the purser, a huge grin splitting his face. "You folks almost got left behind," he chided, stating the obvious.

"Thanks, man! Thanks a million!" Dave pumped the poor guy's hand, reached in his back pocket and pulled out a large bill.

"Naw, keep your money," said that wonderful man. "It's just part of the service."

"What time do you get off duty?" Dave asked slapping him heartily on the back. "I'll buy you a beer." He had made a friend for life.

As we slowly progressed, I leaned against the ship rails gazing at the fog-shrouded shoreline. My thoughts would turn back to my experience at Faith UMC. The further we went, the less important that became, but the hurt remained. On through the straits and around the islands, I couldn't wait to see the spectacular mountains that graced the covers of all the travel brochures and witness the huge whales breaching beside our ship, a là Sea World. Would you believe, we never saw a single mountain or whale while on board? Oh, the mountains were out there all right – we just couldn't see them. The fog prevented that. Two and a half days of fog made it a long trip, but we still enjoyed what was visible along the banks, waterways and towns. The ferry boat stopped in Petersburg and Wrangall, ending at the capital city of Juneau. We hitched up our packs and headed for the Juneau campground, set up our little tent, laid out our sleeping bags and sighed. "Well, here we are! What next?"

Juneau's bay is an eye-popping Mediterranean blue. Dave spent one day on a charter fishing trip. We attended a United Methodist Church and were invited to stay for dinner; we also visited Mendenhall Glacier and various parks. Dave and I took a boat trip up to Haines, where we camped, attended a Salmon Bake with entertainment by Natives, looked for eagles and chartered a plane to fly over the mountain range to Gustavus International Airport. The flight was an awesome trip through snowcapped mountain peaks. Note I said *through*, not around or over. Our pilot weaved his way around the peaks, skimming the sides of mountains because the peaks were shrouded in fog and were too high to fly over, anyway. We had to find a path through, never knowing for sure whether a given hole would stay open long enough to sneak through. Forget about turning around and going back – that pathway had closed already.

We always laugh when we think of Gustavas International Airport. The terminal was little more than a one room shack. The level ground was treeless and barren with little cover but a few scraggly bushes. When we entered the terminal building, I politely inquired directions to the ladies room. "Out the door and turn left or right," pointed out the clerk.

I was in a bit of a hurry. In no time I was back. "Excuse me: did you say left *or* right?" I inquired.

"Makes no difference. Just pick out any bush you want," he said.

"C'mon, Dave," I said. "You go first."

A long, dusty, bumpy bus ride reminded me of the school buses we rode as kids. It could have been the very same bus. We were delivered to a very fancy resort lodge at the entrance to Glacier Bay National Park. We stayed overnight in the campground and prepared to board a tour boat the next day up the bay to the headwaters generated by tidewater glaciers of tremendous power. Our tour boat served lunch and paused for an hour so we could watch the gigantic icebergs breaking off the mile-wide glaciers. In Glacier Bay, we at last got our fill of whales, seals, and exotic birds such as Puffins.

We had a permit to outpost camp on Glacier Bay's shores. Every five, ten or twenty miles, the tour boat would stop to let off campers, along with their gear. Some had kayaks. We disembarked on a narrow stretch of windblown, rocky beach: completely isolated from society, hemmed in by sheer mountains, a grandiose, vast, beautiful, wild space, all ours alone to enjoy. We set up our tent, using rocks to hold it down as best we could. We built a tiny windbreak of rocks for our ultra light stove and hurried to boil water for our supper. We carefully opened a foil packet of freeze-dried food, gingerly poured boiling water into it, stirred and waited for the dried food to reconstitute. More boiled water made tea. A cookie and a reconstituted apple compote completed our meal.

A park ranger had given us the required training for wilderness campers. The theme was how to avoid attacks from grizzly bears. Every effort is made to close any areas where there have been bear sightings; however, there is no guarantee that the bears pay attention to that. We were required to check our gun with him for the protection of the *bears*. It behooves the camper to hide all evidence of cooking odors and body odors as much as possible. Cooking and washing takes place far away from the tent on the tidal plain, so that when the tide comes in those odors are washed away. Likewise, soap or any scented lotion, tooth paste or cosmetics are stored in tightly sealed plastic containers and stored far away from the tent. Body waste is buried or stored in plastic and carried out. Food is separated into several containers and hidden under a rock pile as far away as possible. There were no trees in which to hide it.

The sun set rapidly and with it the ice moved in, dropping the temperature precipitously. There was no help but to don all our clothes and dive into our sleeping bags. I was cold all night. No amount of layers of wool and insulation could keep the body heat in.

We spent the next day preparing meals, cleaning up and watching sea life, birds and one cruise ship go by.

I found a place to sit and meditate on all that had happened to me. It was a profound time for me, as I felt that I had fled as far as I could go to get away. This was the end of the line, when I planned to face up to the hurt and shed the necessary tears. It wasn't a matter of forgiveness. I had forgiven them. Rather, it was more a matter of reliving and finally letting go. From time to time, Dave glanced my way, but he knew I had to do this by myself. After that, I was ready to move on.

We survived one more night. Dave remembers smelling and hearing a grizzly bear pass by in the night. He wisely kept that little tidbit from me for years. The same tour boat was scheduled to pick us up the next day. Believe me, it was a sight for sore eyes. Returning to the lodge, we splurged on a room for the night and a restaurant meal. I can tell you, never has food and water tasted so good, a bath felt so wonderful or a real bed been so heavenly. Just two nights under the stars did that for me. Imagine what our soldiers on a mission have to go through.

The next time we were fated to return to Alaska, it was in a great deal more luxury, but no more memorable.

From Glacier Bay we took a catamaran back to Juneau. We returned to the same campground, but this time, I requested that we rent-a-wreck. There is actually a rental car business by that name. The cars are as the name implies, but it felt like a limo to me. In addition to the city streets, Juneau has about 30 miles of highway running out of town in an easterly direction. We spent one day going as far as we could each way, stopping every mile or so to gaze at the scenery – sparkling blue waters, clear blue sky, deep green trees and crystal white mountains. Driving east to the end of the highway, we came to the Shrine of St. Theresa built on a point of land jutting out into the sea. There was a little native stone chapel. The fourteen stations of the cross were built of native stone and copper and placed along a path hewn in the woods. Dave and I made a story in pictures there that we showed around later to various churches in Michigan as a Lenten program. Along the shore, waves crashed onto huge boulders. Dave stood out on those boulders and cast out his line. He was thrilled to catch a beautiful Dolly Varden trout. We took it back to camp with us. Having no pan large enough to cook it, we gave it to one of our fellow campers.

The following day, we drove west as far as the highway would go, passed a rusted-out shipwreck and gorgeous mountain scenery along a rushing glacial stream. The salmon berries were ripe and hanging from large bushes. We picked and ate them by the handful. We'd been warned to watch for bears, as these berries are dessert for them too. We made as much noise as possible and hoped we wouldn't meet a bear picking around the other side.

On our return trip along the Marine Highway, we rented a bunk room for one night. It wasn't anything great, but a big step up from sleeping on the open air deck. I requested better accommodations, as I had grown weary of roughing it. We had experienced some rain every day. It didn't rain all day, and it didn't rain heavy – just a steady mist that wouldn't have been a problem if you weren't out in it all day. It was a great adventure, but I was ready for a bit of an upgrade. Having a clean, warm bed enhanced the pleasure of the trip immeasurably.

Arriving back in Prince Rupert, we were anxious to check out our motor home. It had survived nicely, but the fridge had quit. Neophytes that we were, we didn't realize that the battery could only keep the fridge alive for about four days. Oops! Live and learn. Everything in the freezer section had thawed and run down into the refrigerator section and onto the floor. After the clean up, we left the next day to return to the States via the eastern side of the Canadian Rocky mountains. From Prince George, we drove south on Route 97 through Williams Lake, cutting over to Whistler. Every mile is marked on the map as "scenic". Beautiful British Columbia lives up to its name in every sense. The lakes and streams are dotted with pristine campgrounds which are never crowded. The road over to Whistler was a 13% grade in places, with boulders as big as a bread basket.

We loved Whistler, a millionaire's paradise. We took the tram up almost to the top of the mountain, had lunch at a restaurant and walked up another 1,000 feet where the air was very thin. The U.S. Olympic ski team was practicing still farther up.

I would have to rate the drive down the coast to Vancouver as the most beautiful drive I have ever made, and also one of the crabbiest. The mountains on one side and the blue water on the other blew me away. However, I was mad at Dave over some trifle and maintained a wounded silence while glaring out the window, sniffling from time to time. Wisely, he remained quiet and kept driving. Perhaps we'd reached our limit of togetherness. Fortunately it blew over as swiftly as it started and we enjoyed a few days in the city of Vancouver, with its spectacular parks and beautiful convention center.

We drove our motor home onto a ferry to cross the bay and spend a glorious week on Vancouver Island. Highlights of this period were three days fishing during the salmon run at the mouth of the Campbell River, killer whale watching in Johnson Strait and the gardens at Victoria. All were world-class and every bit as good as advertised. I would do it over again in a New York minute.

Back in the States, we had a family reunion with the Seattle branch of the family. Aunt Grace was still living then, as were first cousins Carol and Shirley, all gone now. We provided the salmon and they knew how to cook it. Yum! They took us all around Seattle and showed us the sights as only natives can do.

I had dreamed of seeing Mt. Rainer. We camped on the mountain for a week and climbed not to the very top, but all over. So beautiful, so clean and pure. I can close my eyes and smell the air. I actually drove the motor home up the seven mile twisting, turning road, sheer drop offs on one side, cliffs on the other. Dave drove it down a week later. Actually, I think it is less frightening to drive than to be a passenger.

A side trip to Crater Lake National Park was another "must do". A week spent in the spacious camp ground afforded plenty of time to drive the thirty mile circle trip around the lake, take the charter boat tour, climb to the top of the mountain and take a rest day in between. We must have snapped hundreds of pictures. If Crater Lake isn't one of the Seven Wonders of the World, it should be. I'm told it is the deepest lake on the continent. We spent an entire day on the circular drive. Frequent pullouts allowed us to alight from the motor home, climb up the natural earthen berm that surrounds the lake and view the awesome beauty of the huge, bottomless blue lake that fills the caldera formed by the extinct volcano. It is unfortunate that I've forgotten the name of the 4,500 foot mountain above the lake. It is one of the few that I've managed to climb all the way to the top. We took dozens of pictures and shared a picnic lunch.

The park service allows only one vessel on the lake. It is a commercial tour boat. One wonders how the service was able to get the boat in there in the first place. A long pathway leads down to the launch site with several hundred steps. No problem for us.

We were in great shape. The tour boat slowly circled the lake, allowing plenty of time for picture taking. A park ranger gave interesting highlights of the history of the area.

We continued south to the mighty Columbia River and drove along it to the mouth, where we camped and watch the surging surf at the miles-wide, treacherous entry into the ocean. Many an unwary seaman has met his fate there. We went back to where we could cross the river. We then motored along the Pacific Coast of Oregon with its mammoth black boulders, tall as buildings, with foamy blue surf pounding around them. We had made a mistake by not getting advance reservations for a campsite along the coast: It was a very popular place. Again, a scenic highway travels almost the entire length of the coast of Oregon.

Our final west coast state was California – the giant redwoods, Monterey Peninsula, the Pacific Coast Highway, sea lions, whales doing bubble fishing, the never-ending drive across Los Angeles, turning east toward Palm Springs, riding the tram, visiting a date farm, tasting each variety and driving in the desert. We saw Utah and the Great Salt Lake, Colorado and the high Rockies, heading home through Kansas, St. Louis and the arch, Illinois and Indiana.

Altogether, we were gone for two and one half months, drove 12,000 miles and took 1,700 slide pictures. What a trip! What an adventure! Home sweet home.

I dragged him to all the waterfalls. Dave, all smiles. What a Guy!

*   *   *

Chapter Thirty-Two

"Healing Ministry Career"

"Among primitive people, as well as among many who considered themselves anything but that, rituals produced results simply because they were considered effective. The actual agent of change was the mind, with its capacity to perceive what it believed."[38]

A s part of my preparation for the Diaconal Ministry and during national meetings of the FUMFMWA,[39] I had been exposed to aspects of meditation and spiritual healing. I attended a week of training taught by a psychiatrist from Ft. Worth, Texas and learned that I had a gift for it. After I had left Faith UMC, I needed to find another job in order remain active as a Diaconal Minister. It so happened that the United Methodist organization now offered a new certification in the Healing Ministries, called "An Adventure in Healing and Wholeness". I signed up for the training.

As one might expect for any Methodist offering, there was a complete and thorough "method" in place. We were issued thick notebooks with lesson plans, outlines, references, etc. If we graduated from the course, we could choose to be certified to teach the course in local churches. When a local church requested someone to put on a retreat called "An Adventure in Healing and Wholeness", one of us would be assigned to conduct the retreat. As part of our training, we were taken through the whole course by the author, Rev. "Jim," a really nice man dedicated to this ministry. The culmination of the event was a healing service. As part of the service, we were assigned to prayer teams of two or three people. After Jim issued his "altar call," members of the congregation could line up before the healing teams and await their turn to be prayed over. We had been carefully taught how to do this prayer, with laying-on of hands, and had practiced on each other. The praying was done quietly, nothing like the flamboyant style that we have come to expect from watching so-called "healers" on television. People didn't fall over in a dead faint and they didn't

---

[38] Aaron Fletcher, "Outback Station", p. 463
[39] Fellowship of United Methodists for Music, Worship and Other Arts

throw away their crutches and "walk." The praying was designed to appeal to the more middle class, conservative members of mainline churches, not to embarrass anyone. I decided to sign up for the ministry.

Over the course of the next seven years, I taught the "Adventure in Healing and Wholeness" in several churches, including my own. The national committee tried to assign instructors who lived close by; however, I particularly recall one seminar in St. Louis, Missouri and another on Cape Cod. During every event, I would live with a host family. This was by design, but it did put an extra strain on the presenter. I would have gotten more rest in a hotel. Instead, I often ended up dealing with the problems of my hosts.

We were taught to pray protection around ourselves in preparation for listening to the problems of others, much the same as anyone in the healing profession must do. Otherwise, if you are too empathetic you drain yourself of the energy needed to help others. I put on "Adventures in Healing" in churches around Michigan. A fun one that sticks in my mind was in an inner city church in the all-black ghetto of downtown Detroit. My hostess was a white woman who lived in a wealthy suburb but remained active in the downtown church.

It was amazing how people would open up with their most intimate prayer requests. Even more amazing was how, in just a few minutes, I could zero in on the correct words to help them. I heard all kinds of confessions running the gamut of the human condition. A couple of personality traits that I had were helpful. One was that I was able to divorce myself from their problems, while remaining understanding; another was that my memory fades quickly, so I can't gossip about the problems I have heard. I forget them quickly.

One that stuck in my mind, however, was when a young woman confessed to me that she was homosexual. She was "in the closet" as the saying goes. She asked to speak with me privately, whereupon she poured out her suffering and anxiety over her situation that, so far, she had kept entirely to herself. She pleaded with me to tell her what the church thought, what Christ thought, what the Bible taught, what she should do, why she felt this way if it was a sin, what would happen, could she be healed, etc. She was trying to live a pure life, but was thoroughly confused, poor thing.

In time, I realized that I was not receiving enough assignments from the "Adventure" people to keep me busy. Most of my assignments were those that I developed myself. Eventually, I developed retreats and seminars of my own in a variety of subjects that better suited my clientele. Often, I designed a retreat just for the occasion, or adapted one I had already used. I handed out business cards and began to develop a reputation and a following. It wasn't always individuals who needed healing. Sometimes it was an entire congregation.

Once, I was called in by a pastor who had been ousted, thus causing a split and infighting in the congregation. Friday evening, I met with the central committee of elders and lay leaders. For them, I designed a ceremony based on a foot washing. I've seen this done by others where the leader washed a hand meant to represent the foot or had people wash each other's hands. This doesn't work for me as it is not as meaningful. It is too big a stretch to ask people who wash their hands several times a day to imagine they are washing a foot. I insisted on getting on my knees and washing a foot, drying it with a towel tied around my waist, just like the scripture says. In those days a servant actually washed the dusty feet of the guests. Thus, it had meaning when Jesus did it.

First, I asked the members to be seated in a circle of chairs and instructed them to remove one shoe and sock. If the lady had on pantyhose, that was no problem. The hose dried almost instantly. I passed out the pertinent scriptures on slips of paper so that the story in scripture was read in their own voices around the circle as I acted out the moves and progressed around the circle myself. I instructed them not to hurry or worry too much, but if possible to just try to match the words to what I was doing as the spirit moved them. It was amazing how people got into the drama of the thing. I had it timed just right so I ended up when the scripture finished. It was best not to cover the act with music, but to let the silences speak for themselves. It was so moving that tears were common.

When I started the demonstration, there was good natured kidding by the men and reluctance by the women. However, I left enough mystery that they were curious to see what I would do. Of course there were some pretty ugly feet. After everything was assembled, in readiness, the readings began. At just the right time in the scripture I would pour water from my pitcher into a large bowl. As I took each foot I would use enough water so that they knew they were wet, but not too much. The foot rub was the part that mattered. Each foot was lovingly massaged and dried, no matter how crippled and beat up it was. In the end some of the men took off their other shoe and sock for me to massage.

When we were done I had instructed the pastor to pray a dismissal blessing. After that I left in silence.

Saturday morning and afternoon, I conducted a seminar. Sunday morning I preached, using scripture and hymns on the subject. The ceremony I designed for the congregation to end that service was based on the scripture of Jesus marking in the sand and challenging those without sin to cast the first stone. I had some sand that I had brought from Alaska, from the shrine. I spread that in a shallow bowl that had some significance. It was the bowl that was used for baptisms.

Members were invited to come forward and make their mark in the sand as representative of whatever they needed to let go, then to smooth the sand and erase that mark. I stood back and closed my eyes. I heard the shuffling of feet and sniffing of noses, but I didn't peek. Later, I learned that every single member of the congregation came forward. From that point on, the congregation forgave themselves, each other and their pastor and became dynamic.

*   *   *

Dorothy Mercer: Diaconal Minister of Music, Healing & Wholeness

A fun seminar weekend retreat that I designed was on the interpretation of dreams. It's amazing how you can dig out old hurts that are holding a person back or making him sick by working with dreams. I always used my skills with the keyboard and my hobbies with the camera and computer to assist my classes. That was especially useful in dream work, because you had to relax people enough to open up their minds. By necessity, this retreat had to start in the evening. People had to be taught first how to prepare themselves to dream, how to interrogate the dream and how to keep a record. The next day, we did more teaching and worked with our dreams. Everyone dreamed, even those who claimed to never dream, and everyone learned a great deal about themselves. Somewhere in my store room I've kept all of those retreat outlines and writings. If God gives me enough time I plan to publish those.

During the seven years after I left the ministry of music at Faith UMC, I renewed my attendance at St. Paul's United Methodist Church in Kentwood, just a half mile from our house. This had been Dave's church during all the years I worked elsewhere on Sundays. It was so good to be with him now.

I started up a church orchestra. We weren't all that great to tell the truth. There was a diversity of talent: some good artists, some...well... less good. But we had fun and we met regularly. Also, after the church sponsored "An Adventure in Healing and Wholeness," I headed up a healing service once a month on a Sunday evening. There was a faithful core of people who always came, and others who came as needed. As is often the case, Dave was my sidekick. I always thought he had more healing hands than mine, *at least for me. The fact that he doesn't realize it may be the best part.* Together, we experienced lots of healings.

These efforts, along with teaching upwards of forty private students in piano and classical guitar, together with my work for Conference Boards, and my retreats and seminars... all this together made up my work as a Diaconal Minister. It was a full-time job and was evaluated every year by the Conference and General Board in Nashville. There was never any trouble with my evaluations and this ministry was considered excellent within the definition of service in the Church and in the world.

* * *

Chapter Thirty-Three

"Mentoring and the Boards of Ministry"

Through my work with the Board of Diaconal Ministry of the West Michigan Conference of the United Methodist Church, I took a special interest in mentoring candidates into the ministries of service. During my time as chair of the Board, I took charge of recruiting and training new mentors and assigning them to our candidates. Ideally, the same mentor stayed with the candidate all through the process, which takes several years. Usually, a mentor would work with just one candidate at a time.

When my term was up as chair of the Board, I continued with the mentoring work in the same fashion. Even after I had left the Board, I still continued as a mentor to two different candidates. Interestingly, one of them realized halfway through the process that she was meant to be a preacher instead of a Diaconal Minister. It was a happy decision for her and the right thing to do. I was gratified to have helped her through that process of self-understanding.

There were many other things our Board did besides mentoring Diaconal Ministers. We were also responsible for candidates for certification in the professional areas I have mentioned before. Part of our job was education. Resources were available through the division offices, such as brochures, books, and videos describing the various types of ministries and the routes to becoming a professional in the different areas.

We worked hard to find ways to educate the churches, their congregations and employees to the value of this type of training and education. We kept track of the requirements for each professional status, where classes were being held, helping candidates understand where they were and what they needed. We kept records of each prospect and candidate, and we kept in touch by telephone and personal visit. We interviewed each person in the process at least once a year, more often as needed. And in the good old Methodist tradition, we filled out copious reports and filed voluminous records. Our Board designed and held retreats twice a year for all the candidates, certified persons, consecrated Diaconal Ministers and members of the Board. These were held at Methodist camps and various retreat centers. Once a year, we attended the West Michigan Annual Conference lasting for nearly a week, where all the business of the Conference took place.

In addition to the Board business, each of us was required to keep up with our own spiritual life and earn twelve continuing education credits every three years. Each year, we gave written reports on all this, plus a report on our work and evaluations by our superiors. These were kept in a file in the Conference headquarters, with copies in the General Board files in Nashville.

After my ten years of working as a certified Director of Music and a Diaconal Minister, the mother church had a change of heart about the Diaconal Ministry. They decided to phase out the designation. After a certain date, no more candidates would be accepted. A new office was being created, that of the Permanent Deacon.[40] Those in the process could continue if they chose, or they could switch to the Permanent Deacon track.

Those of us who were Diaconal Ministers would have the option of becoming Ordained Permanent Deacons or remaining as Diaconal Ministers. All of the Diaconal Ministers in the West Michigan Conference decided to be ordained. We were required to attend a one-week orientation where we would be taught everything for which it stands, attend workshops, take part in small group discussions, read, meditate on our calling and spend time deciding which way we were called to go and what we were called to be under this new set of orders. We also had to meet the new educational standards, but if I remember correctly, none of us had to take any more classes.[41] The education and requirements for

---

[40] The old idea of temporary Deacon as being a step into Elders orders would continue for the time being. Eventually, that would phase out and there would be Elder candidates and Ordained Elders who are ordained to the Ministry of Word and Sacrament. The Permanent Deacon would be considered equal with the Elder. This Deacon would be ordained to the ministry of Service, connecting the Church and the world, and would take the place of the Consecrated Diaconal Minister. Both offices would be appointed by the Bishop. As before, Elders would itinerate and Deacons would not.

[41] The new Permanent Deacon would be as highly educated as the Elder, but the classes would be different. Neither one would be a step above the other. Deacons would have a profession and would be trained and educated in that profession before taking the

Deacon would not differ a great deal from that of Diaconal Minister. The ministries of service were all pretty well defined. What differed was that the church had now decided they should be ordained. A chapter on the story of my personal ordination comes later.

After we were ordained as Deacons, three of us were switched over to the Board of Ordained Ministry. The Board of Diaconal Ministry would be phased out. The new B.O.M. would take care of both Deacons and Elders and candidates for either track. In fact, a person was not expected to make a final selection between the two tracks until well into the process. The mentoring process was designed to help the candidate explore their calling for some time before making a choice.

This system was *so* much better. Now, people who were called to be teachers could be ordained without having to be Elders. Ordained Deacons could also be administrators of churches, colleges, hospitals or seminaries. Deacons could be psychiatrists, nurses, physicians, missionaries, musicians, church school directors, secretaries, principals, or community workers. The list was almost endless. The point was they must be called to be of service to others in a particular area, be educated and prepared, and have experience and gifts in that area.

The idea was that in this way, the Church was being made visible in a needy world, rather than hiding behind cloistered walls. I liked these new ideas very much and felt that the mother church had finally gotten it right. Now we would be ministering in the church and in the world after the example of Christ.

The new B.O.M. had much work to do. We were all assigned to a particular area of work on the larger board and on sub-committees. The most demanding time consuming job was the annual interview retreat held at Wesley Woods Camp. At this retreat, we would interview candidates and make judgments. For

---

seminary classes leading up to ordination, very similar to a Diaconal Minister. For instance, a nurse took nurses' training, a musician took music, and an administrator took business administration, and so on.

those already in the process, the interview would simply be a matter of checking up on their progress, addressing any issues or concerns that had been raised either by themselves, their supervisor or the required psychological evaluation. We might decide to keep them on probation a year, continue their candidacy or recommend they be discontinued.

The most demanding cases were those that were in their last interview before ordination. Before our arrival at the retreat, we were assigned to either listen to the taped sermons or read the essays. Either route took many hours. We had to prepare a report on each one and evaluate it on several counts. Once at the retreat, we became part of a team of three to interview a list of candidates.

Every day for a week, we rose early, breakfasted, carefully dressed in professional clothing and drove into town to a church where we worked all day doing interviews and discussing each candidate among ourselves. At the end of the week the full board met and hashed over each candidate, sometimes at great length, until we came to a decision: thumbs up or thumbs down. It was somewhat similar to being on a jury, that is, exhausting work. Once we got back to our retreat center, we had dinner, more discussions and devotions, and then fell into bed, usually too keyed up to sleep properly.

Another job I did for this board came about because of the problem of stress among clergy. Clergy are no different from anyone else. They have the very same family problems – sin and sexuality, dropouts and drugs, debts and divorce – as the rest of us do. Two big differences are that expectations are probably higher and they have no pastor to turn to – they are the pastors!

What could be done to assist them when personal problems occurred? More was needed to help clergy to stay emotionally fit and to assist those in need of help with personal problems. My response was to ferret out retreat centers within Michigan and nearby states. I interviewed the directors, investigated and wrote a brief description of the services they offered, costs and an evaluation for a printed brochure which we made available to all clergy in the conference. It was thought that this would encourage clergy. They would now have a handy resource of places where they could go for personal retreats and/or to find help when needed. It would be a step in maintaining good spiritual health, as well as being available in times of crisis. Recently, I was pleased to notice that the retreat brochure I designed is kept updated and is still in use.

After three years, I resigned from the Board of Ordained Ministry, feeling that I had paid my dues. I was weary of it and needed a rest myself.

*   *   *

Chapter Thirty-Four

"Come, Josephine, in My Flying Machine"

D ave had a dream of one day learning how to fly. Early in our married life while residing in Kentwood, MI., for his birthday present, I gave him a surprise. He had to trust me enough to get into the car and let me drive. We proceeded north of Grand Rapids on the expressway and pulled off at the Sparta exit.

"Okay, Dave, we are getting close, so you have to close your eyes. Are your eyes closed?"

"Yes, my eyes are closed. This had better be good."

"Oh, it will be good," I assured him. "Keep them closed – no peeking!"

"Should I make a guess?" he asked.

"Sure, if you want to," I answered.

"We are going out to a restaurant," he offered.

"C'mon, you can do better than that," I coaxed as we pulled into the drive of a small town airport with a tar runway.

"Well, let's see, we are going shopping," he tried again.

"Just like a man, no imagination," I taunted, as I parked in front of the General Aviation office and gave a friendly beep on my horn. A good looking man in his mid-thirties appeared, wearing aviator sunglasses and carrying a small briefcase. I shifted the car into "Park" and opened my door. "Okay, Dave, open your eyes".

Stunned at first, Dave said, "What's this? What are we doing here?"

"*We* aren't doing anything. *You* are going for a ride. C'mon, Dave, let me introduce you to your flight instructor."

"O my God! You're kidding me."

"No way. Today is going to be your first flying lesson. Surprise! Happy birthday, Darling!" I crowed. "Here, you are going to need these." I handed him his sunglasses.

After completing his 40 hours of dual instruction and taking his solo flights, Dave joined a flying club at Kent County Airport. For an initiation fee and so much a month, he was entitled to flying hours in one of the club's Cessna 172s. Through the club, Dave met other fellows with the same hobby. After a couple years, the club went bankrupt. All the members lost their initial investment.

Dave was invited to join with three other men as partners in owning a Cessna 182 single-engine private airplane, housed at Kent County Airport, not far from our house. This seemed safer financially than joining another flying club. The arrangement worked well for several years, until one of the guys died and one pulled out. This left Dave and Russ Cotè to buy out the others and become sole owners in the airplane. Eventually, Russ and Dave decided to step up to a newer Cessna 182. They remained partners until Russ died. We were very fond of Russ and loved our airplanes, calling them by name. Dave owned "4895 Delta" for 8 or 9 years. We took many family trips together with our girls and by ourselves, until Dave retired from the General Agency and from flying.

Often today, we will drive past a small town airstrip and Dave will remember when he flew into that airport. I think he remembers every trip and every bump in the air. For myself, I can remember some of the high points and that is all. We flew to Florida more than once to attend a convention of the John Hancock Life Insurance Company that Dave represented for more than fifty years.

At first, Dave was a leading salesman, later promoted to supervisor, and finally to General Agent, which is the top field position available. That meant that he had an exclusive right to the West Michigan territory and the Upper Peninsula of Michigan. He owned his own building, hired an office staff and had a couple dozen or so salespeople working for him throughout the territory. Dave used his airplane to visit his people, flying into small airports all over his territory.

He represented several other companies in addition to the Hancock. I mention all these achievements to illustrate why Dave qualified for multiple opportunities every year to attend conventions at company expense at the very finest resorts in lovely locations. For many years, I accompanied Dave once or twice a year to a nice convention. When the girls were older, they came with us once or twice as well. Sometimes we drove or flew commercial, but there were other occasions when we took our Cessna.

I recall flying over the Smoky Mountains. How different they look from the air! It is readily apparent how they came to have the name smoky. From the air, low-lying clouds are visible lying between and among the peaks, creating an illusion of smoke.

Another beautiful sight is flying into the Florida Keys. The many shades of aqua blue are even more stunning from the air than they are from the bridges. One can see so much farther, out into the Gulf and the Ocean, where the fluorescent white caps provide a contrast to the blue water and green palm trees.

Once or twice, we flew across Lake Michigan and landed at Chicago Midway Airport. All Dave's nerves were at attention as he was vectored in and around the commercial flights. I was able to help out by reading the charts and watching out for other planes, but was useless so far as the radio was concerned. It sounded like so much squawking to me.

Favorite trips were up north to Michigan playgrounds such as Boyne Mountain, Shanty Creek Lodge, Sault Saint Marie, Traverse City, Mackinac[42] Island, Pentwater, Gaylord and others.

There are many advantages to owning your own plane for business, in addition to the tax write-off. You could quickly get

---

[42] Pronounced Mackinaw

into small towns where there are no commercial flights available, and on your own schedule. Obviously, the disadvantage of owning your own plane was that, once you landed at the airfield, some other means of land transportation became necessary in order to get to your destination.

Some of the fancier resorts had their own airstrip. Others had a shuttle service. Since Dave used his plane primarily to fly for business, whenever he was visiting an associate or a client, he made prior arrangements to meet at the airport or for someone to pick him up. Other than that, private pilots are resourceful and share a certain camaraderie. There was usually someone to give you a lift into town.

The small town of Baldwin, Michigan, had a favorite ice cream parlor where the owner dipped up huge cones so high they threatened to topple over. The place was about a one mile walk from the airstrip – not enough distance, we figured, to walk off the calories. It was fun on a Saturday or Sunday afternoon to fly up to Baldwin for ice cream.

Longer trips were into West Virginia to a convention at the Greenbrier[43], into Wisconsin to the Playboy Club, to Lake of the Ozarks, Missouri to the Four Seasons Club, to Fort Lauderdale and the famous old Palm Beach resort, the Breakers, to Phoenix and the Arizona Biltmore (designed by Frank Lloyd Wright), and across part of the Atlantic to a casino resort on Bimini Island.

Once on the way home from Florida, we were grounded in a small town in Georgia for three nights waiting for the weather to clear and the ceiling to lift high enough to allow us to legally take off. While there, we visited Mercer University. That was rather neat, but we came to rue the cliché, "If you have time to spare, go by air." After that experience, Dave vowed, "Never again," and enrolled in a course of instrument training including long hours of required dual instruction. After receiving his instrument rating, we were never grounded unnecessarily again.

---

[43] The famous 5 star Greenbrier Resort and Golf Club is still there, more beautiful than ever. We went there several times. Back then, Sammy Snead was still the golf pro.

One of Dave's instructors, Art, was full of wise sayings. "Whenever you take up a passenger for the first time, be careful to give them a smooth ride. That way they may ride with you again. Also, be very careful you don't kill them, for in that case they definitely will never ride with you again." Too bad, Dave forgot that advice when he coaxed his elderly father to go up for his first airplane ride. It happened to be a bumpy day. Pop never went up again.

Dave made certain that I could fly the plane and land it if anything ever happened to him during a flight, but thankfully I never had to do that. We never had any close calls, but it was reassuring to know that a Cessna can glide a long way if the engine ever conks out. If necessary, it can land in a grassy field or on the freeway in a relatively short space. One would need to take care not to run into any wires, overpasses, autos, lakes, birds or cows, of course.

Flying over large bodies of water made Dave more cautious than usual and a bit nervous until he could sight land. In those cases, he would fly as high as the air flight controller allowed in order to give himself a longer glide path in case of emergency.

I wish I had some exciting narrow escape to add some spice to this story. Not so. About the most exciting thing I can remember is landing and taking off from Mackinac Island. You fly in over the water, gauging your touchdown as close to the end of the runway as you dare, as the strip is not overly long. Having avoided the trees you are okay until take-off.

That's when it gets fun. You taxi out all the way to the far end, in order to allow yourself the longest take off possible. You have no choice of direction, so the ever-present wind had best be on your nose, not a tail wind or cross wind. It is not as bad as taking off from an aircraft carrier, but gives the same sensation, because at the end of the runway a cliff drops straight down into the Straits of Machinac some 300 feet below.

There is an abrupt change of temperature over the water as compared to the land. Depending on the time of day, it can cause a sudden updraft, or worse yet, a downdraft. The well-trained pilot is prepared to compensate for either of those contingencies, but the passenger is not. The only thing the passenger can do to prepare is to wear "Depends".

Dave had eyes like an eagle and could spot other planes and point them out to me long before I was able to focus on that tiny distant speck in the sky. He was also an excellent pilot and prudent too. Among pilots, there is a saying, "There are old pilots and there are bold pilots, but there are no old, bold pilots." I can truthfully say that Dave is now an old pilot. He would probably respond, "What chu' talkin' about *old*!"

At one time, he was offered a Vice President's position with the home office in Boston, but we preferred to remain in Kentwood and raise our girls. After some twenty years as a General Agent, Dave retired from that and returned to being an award-winning commissioned salesman and multi-million dollar producer, Life Member of the Million Dollar Round Table and C.L.U.[44]

*   *   *

---

[44] Chartered Life Underwriter is the highest professional certification in his field, requiring the passing of ten levels of study and a final exam, somewhat equivalent to a Certified Public Account.

Chapter Thirty-Five

"Phase Three Camping"

Our third camper purchase was a 33 foot, wide-body C model motor home with the largest engine possible, an "Ultra-Sport" by Damon, all done up in a pretty lavender décor, with oak cabinets, sofa and two overstuffed chairs, queen size bed with pillow-top mattress, separate closets for each of us, bath and shower, lots of storage inside and out, air conditioning and fancy decorator marks on the sides. We installed extra heavy duty batteries so we would not run out of power ever again. By now, we had sold our Kentwood home and were living in our remodeled and expanded vacation home at Canadian Lakes, Michigan. While on our various travels, we had noticed other motor home campers going down the road towing a car. Reasoning that must save a lot of trouble by not having to use the camper whenever you wanted to run to the store, I bought a red Mazda 4 X 4 pickup truck that we could tow behind the Ultra Sport. The pickup came in handy for all sorts of purposes. Besides, I felt rather "sporty" in the thing.

We towed that little red truck a lot of miles. We loved the mountains out west and in Canada. When asked, Dave explained that we drove the Ultra Sport as high up as we could go, then took the truck to the end of the road, then put on our backpacks and walked even higher. There were times when that was literally quite true. The truck could go up some really rough two-track roads with its four-wheel drive, high clearance and heavy duty tires. A few times, we slept in the back of the truck as well.

We have hiked, camped and slept in most of the Rocky Mountain states and Canadian provinces, the Cascades in Washington, the Big Horns in Wyoming, the Black Hills in South Dakota, the Bitterroots in Idaho, the Appalachians in Virginia and Tennessee, and the Grand Tetons in Wyoming more than once. Twice we climbed and camped on the Grand Teton itself.

Also, we took our camper and little red truck east to New York, Vermont, New Hampshire, up the Maine coast, through New Brunswick to Nova Scotia and Newfoundland, returning along the St. Lawrence River Drive through Quebec, Montreal and the province of Ontario. Romantic that I am, Niagara Falls is one of my favorite places. I can't tell you how many times we've been there.

In 1999, I reluctantly gave up my darling little red truck and bought a new Ford Ranger pickup. We wasted no time in installing the proper tow bar so it could be pulled behind the camper. Also, we bought a cap for the back to keep it waterproof. Some Yakima cross bar attachments were added on top of the cap to which we could strap and carry our canoe. Now that we were all set, we could haul everything but the kitchen sink.

Pickups had become so essential to our way of life that in 2002 I traded the 1999 model in for another Ford Ranger exactly like the first one, same color and everything. Surely, this pickup would last forever. Meanwhile, for the record, Dave had given up his obsession with Cadillacs and started driving Hondas.

Not all our camping trips have been to the mountains. We also enjoy the beaches and forests, lakes, streams and K.O.A. campgrounds. Twice we camped on the sandy beaches of the Gulf of Mexico. One time was on a barrier island near Pensacola, FL, another time in Texas, near the Mexican border, at Padre Island

National Seashore. We were close enough to the channel entrance that we could sit in our folding chairs and watch the ships.

Our most ambitious camping trip so far has been our two month long trip to mainland Alaska in 2004. I got up my nerve to

try the Al Can Highway, now known as the Alaska Highway. This was a fabulous trip. Many people have done it before us, but we still felt like pioneers. I have written all about this in a separate publication so I won't repeat it here.

We have camped all over Michigan, from the far western end of the Upper Peninsula, to Tahquamenon Falls, to the upper shores of Lake Michigan and Lake Huron, Sault Saint Marie and Drummond Island, the circle tour around icy Lake Superior, numerous state parks in the Lower Peninsula such as Wilderness, Sleeping Bear Dunes, Ludington, Pere Marquette, Hartwick Pines, Allegan, South Haven, and Grand Haven, among others. Just last summer we camped two times in Muskegon State Park on beautiful Lake Michigan. Michigan is the best state in the union for its parks and its golf courses, in my humble opinion. Come to think of it, I guess we have camped on all of the Great Lakes and numerous inland lakes. You must be getting bored with this recitation, so I will pause, but believe me, this is not the entire list.

Owning a camper of any type is no easy task. If you have owned a used car or a used home, you have some idea of what sorts of mechanical things can go wrong. Look at it this way: a motor home is a car and a house in one. Double the fun equals double the trouble. Try changing an inner tire on a dual wheel, parked in the scenic view, after climbing to the very top of a ten mile mountain drive. Imagine the problems when you happen to be hooked up to the sewer in a commercial campground when their sewer backs up. Or consider the flood upon opening the door of your motor home after you accidentally left the inside water running for an hour – we have.

Have you ever returned to your overheated car in the desert to find the back window cracked out from the heat? How many times has the water pump quit 3,000 miles from home? Did you ever drive down a mountain road where the curves were so tight that you had to zigzag back and forth to get around the turn? We have. Were you ever chased down and pulled over by a cop for being *falsely* accused of robbing a gas station? Consider what it's like to have the customs inspectors go through your entire house.

You think it costs an arm and a leg to fill up your gas tank these days? Try filling up a motor home and pickup truck all at one time. Ka-ching, ka-ching. $50.. $100...$150...$200... Then there's the time that... well, you get the idea.

Lots of scenic campgrounds are on lakes, rivers and streams. The premier spots are on the water. It is wise, however, to think ahead. Pay attention to where you park lest the water rise in the night. Once, when the girls were little, we took the Steury camper out West. On the way, we found a beautiful camping site right on the banks of the mighty Mississippi. During the night, it rained so hard we almost got washed into the river. First, we rescued the girls into the car. Having no time to waste, I had to get out in my white nightgown and push while Dave gunned the motor and spun the tires, spraying me with mud. Speaking of mud, we also got stuck in the sticky stuff in northern Alberta, on the way to Alaska. That time the *pickup truck* had to pull the motor home out.

My Mountain Climbing Man

I wouldn't trade those memories for anything.

* * *

Chapter Thirty-Six

"Mercer Publications, Inc."

W hen I first started publishing music, it was well before the age of computer software publishing. I learned to typeset the music, one note at a time. The only store that sold the "rub-off" letters and notes was an art store in downtown Grand Rapids. One could purchase sheets of letters in various typesets, such as Times New Roman, pica or elite.

Each new sheet cost about three bucks and once you used a letter it was gone. All the notes and music symbols had to be rubbed off one at a time. Woe unto the composer who made a mistake or changed her mind. Errors had to be corrected by carefully scraping off the note with a razor blade and covering any residue with white-out. It was a great advancement when IBM came out with a typewriter that would center a word directly under a note.

I also invested in expensive art pens, ultra black ink, various templates and tools. I could do a darned good page of music by hand, if I do say so myself, and much faster than rubbing off each letter, of course.

Artisans who worked for the big music publishers had their own carefully guarded sets of type. Rules of the trade were kept secret and passed down from father to son, or to an apprentice.

When I started, I had to do a lot of digging to learn the practice of typesetting music. Eventually, I came across two out-of-print and obscure texts that told me all I needed to know. I studied these books from cover to cover and kept them right by my side as references.

Typesetting music is an art, a creative design as well as an expression of music. The things that I learned during that time period remained useful for my entire musical career. No music software can substitute for basic knowledge of the rules of typesetting, design and music theory.

After the cumbersome method of rubbing off one note at a time, I purchased a great invention: a music typewriter. It was costly, heavy and cumbersome, but it was a marvel in its time. You could actually type the music staves and all the symbols as well as the notes. This was *so* much faster and more accurate than the former method.

Dave and I began using computers early, before everyone did it. The first PCs [45] for home and business use were made by IBM[46]. Competition soon began, but the knock-offs would be advertised as IBM compatible. Then Apple got into the business with machines that used a different operating system and were advertised as being better for graphics; but Dave and I always stayed with the IBM compatibles because we used them for business as well.

In those days, you had to know how to use DOS commands, because computers were not user-friendly at all. The first ones had 20 megabytes of memory, then 256. Now, we figure in gigabytes. It reminds me somewhat of the federal deficit. It used to be in millions, then in billions. Now, it is in trillions. What's next, gazillions?

You didn't waltz into a Best Buy store and walk out with your computer loaded with all kinds of software. Oh no, you loaded the software yourself. And it wasn't easy. The software was issued with thick books of instructions. When you bought new software, you spent hours and days studying the books and practicing with the software. One advantage was that you could load your software onto as many computers as you wanted. Not anymore. Now, if you want to reload your software, you had better remember the original code number that you forgot to write down in the first place.

A common occurrence was when the computer crashed or locked up. It was essential to purchase your software with free "tech support". Computer magazines and radio shows made money reviewing just which companies had the best tech support. We

---

[45] Personal Computers

[46] International Business Machines

followed those reviews avidly.

Dave had more patience with tech support than I did. It was common to be put on "hold" for a couple hours until you finally got to a service person. After you explained your problem to that person, they would say that they had to switch you to another department. More than likely, after being switched a few times, you got cut off and had to start all over. Another ploy was that they promised to call you back by, say, five o'clock. You waited all day and they never called back. Another ploy was that they would leave the line to check with a supervisor. After a long wait while they probably went on a break, suddenly you were cut off. We grew to despise that lady who came on the line next and informed you, in her nasal twang, "If you wish to make a call, please hang up and try again."

We happened to live on a street named Maple Valley. Ours was a sloping lot that led down into a swampy area. Many were the times when we threatened to throw our computers "down in the valley".

Personal computers were very expensive, and the manufacturers were smart. Computers became outdated rapidly, with more power, faster thing-a-ma-jigs, or whatever. Dave and I kept the companies in business single-handedly, I swear.

Dave was wise enough to always buy desktops. I preferred laptops. They were nice and portable, but they were more expensive, had less power and tended to wear out really fast. The worst thing was to get your laptop loaded down with all your precious documents and then have the darned thing quit working. Arrrrgh. We were told to "back up", but who had time for all that? Besides, just when you got everything backed up on floppy disks, they went out of style. Next it was CDs[47] and the new computers wouldn't read your old floppies. Then CDs went out and it was DVDs, but there were several different kinds and not all the computers read every kind. Besides, you got your DVDs all mixed up and forgot to label them and couldn't find the one you wanted.

---

[47] Compact Disks

Now we have memory sticks that are so small there is no room for a label, and you have to have an adapter because they don't fit all computer slots. Besides that, they get lost; and who can figure out the new-fangled filing system.

I decided to publish all my precious pictures online on a web site so they couldn't get lost. I paid plenty for that, too. After three years, I got a notice that the host server was going out of business because their equipment was hopelessly outdated. They weren't much help either. I had a deuce of a time figuring out how to save my pictures and had to buy more software to download them onto my computer. Of course, the new company who bought the server out would be happy to help me, transfer it over and design a pretty new web site for a hefty fee. Oh well, we must keep that money circulating.

As a music publisher, it was best to keep mum about it when meeting someone new. The world is full of amateur composers who have made up a song and wonder if you would like to arrange and publish it for them. (Lord, save me!) I've been sucked in on that one, more than once. I started telling people I charge $75 a page. Even that doesn't cover your time. Moving on...

At first, I simply did business as "Dorothy Mercer Publications". Soon, I incorporated under the name of Mercer Publications and Ministries, Inc. I learned how to incorporate by myself, and also how to apply for a copyright. This was before the age of "Google". I actually had to go to the library and do research. Once upon a time, I taught a workshop on how to publish your own music. I just ran across the outline and handouts for that workshop recently and tossed it out because I needed the file case for some other purpose. *That was a trip down memory lane.*

Many of the pieces I published were sacred works, but some were for piano and guitar. My primary goal was to publish my own compositions, but I also published a few other composers: Mark Webb, Dolores Hruby, Lucille Panse, Thelma Bass, Paul Donelson, Robert Antecki and some others, all Michigan folks.

Often, I received submissions from strangers, but I turned

them down. Once, Robert Antecki and I were interviewed on local television about the music publishing business. In addition to music, I also published brochures and catalogs. Sometimes I hired a graphic designer, sometimes Ann Cormany designed things for me and sometimes I did it myself.

I developed a file case full of several hundred clients long before the advent of software for keeping track of your customers. Sometimes Dave and I went out to meetings to put up displays of our offerings, or sometimes I went alone. Occasionally, we would stop at music stores and leave off samples on our various trips.

There is no question that the hardest part of any business is marketing. Anybody can write a song. It takes years of hard work and marketing skill to make money at it. I can't say that I made a lot of money. We still have a checking account for Mercer Publications, and I occasionally get an order, but once I stopped marketing, orders dried up. Marketing is dull work for me. I prefer the creative end of things.

Back in the days of cassette tapes, I was fairly successful at marketing a series of meditations. I advertised these in Prevention Magazine, before meditation became popular. I was ahead of my time, I guess. Now, it seems as if meditation is mainstream. I composed the meditations, read them into one track, and then recorded the music onto one or more tracks. Then I mixed them together.

You had to get it right the first time or do it over again, because there was no such thing as loading it into the computer and erasing the wrong notes. If you tried to patch over a mistake, it made an unfortunate click in the line. It wasn't as if I had a sound-proof studio. I did my best to unplug the refrigerator and turn off the furnace, but sometimes the phone would ring just at the wrong moment or someone would flush the toilet. Then you had to start over.

I composed a series of exercises and some nice pieces for classical guitar and piano. I also wrote several sacred choir numbers. Sometimes I used these with my choirs, but I was careful not to overdo it, lest the choir members complain. I heeded the proverb, "A prophet is without honor in his own home town." At national sacred music conferences, we got a chuckle over that sad fact. Even the most prestigious composers admitted that their choir members balk at singing too many of their compositions.

One of the things that Dave and I did while camping in Wyoming was to make a series of healing meditations with our video camera. We had the digital camera work all done. All that remained was to compose the musical background. I felt as if my life wouldn't be complete until I finished those and published them. For a time in my life, it was a burning ambition. However, I never seemed to have the time or the money to buy the expensive equipment needed.

I decided to wait until computer software advanced enough that it could be done on computer. Also, I hoped my grandchildren would grow up and be able to help me figure out how to load the camera work onto the computer so I could edit it and add the music. At least three of my grandchildren could do it now. They are smart and show a great deal of promise. In fact, they are miles ahead of me. I'd like to finish it, but somehow it just doesn't seem so important now.

It seemed that whatever choir I was directing or whatever show I was putting on took up all my creative energy. I always thought that once I retired, I would finish up those tapes. Well, now that I'm retired, what excuse is left? I have done a lot of things, but that is just one thing that is left unfinished. Maybe, someday…

* * *

Chapter Thirty-Seven

"Health Matters"

Normally, I prefer to think and speak little about any health problems, except to Dave and to my doctor(s). However, in fairness to my descendants, it is only right to let them in on some of the genes they may have had the misfortune to inherit.

This chapter is for adults only. The rest of you readers may skip this. I intend to have done with health issues in this chapter. Compared to the general population, I have had better than average luck with good health. But this is a "not quite tell-all book". Everybody has problems and I've lived a long time.

You older women are lucky if you take after me, because I have always looked younger than my years. Not so lucky for you young women. Perhaps it was because of my light colored hair, my young-sounding high voice or my good skin that I inherited from my Scottish ancestors. In our younger days, whenever David Neal and I went into a cocktail lounge (which was seldom) I had to show my ID to prove I was old enough to be allowed in. Neal was never asked, even though we were the same age.

Back when my girls were teenagers, Shelley, Ann and I went out to sing trios together. We dressed alike as part of the act, each of us wearing long dresses and long, blonde hair. Folks who didn't know us mistook us for a sister act, not a mother and two daughters. I was flattered, of course. I'm not so sure that my daughters should have been pleased, but they went along with it good-naturedly. Now that I am in my seventy-seventh year, I don't mind being mistaken for a younger person. Usually, I take this as mere flattery, but when your own woman physician, as part of her analysis of your health, tells you that you look twenty years younger than your age, you tend to give it credence.

This aspect of my being was a nuisance for me during my time working for churches. A few of the married women close to my age tended to resent me being around, looking better than they did. I was very conservative in my behavior, my dress, makeup and jewelry and was super careful to be circumspect around the men, but it didn't seem to stop the jealousy. Maybe it made it worse, who can say? Women tend to outnumber the men in churches, so male employees get along much better than women, unless the women are ugly and masculine. I'm not claiming to be a beauty. I simply aged gracefully and didn't get fat, wrinkled and gray-haired at an early age like some do.

As a bride, I weighed 107 pounds, was 5 feet 4 ½ inches tall and had a 23 inch waist. People told me I was too thin. I worked hard to gain five pounds. Now, I work twice as hard to lose five.

Certain conditions were hereditary, I believe. For example, I bleed and bruise easily. I'm not a hemophiliac in the worst sense, but there will never be a need for me to be on an aspirin regimen. I have since learned that there are milder forms of hemophilia. Recently, when my darling granddaughter researched our family tree, she discovered a tie-back to lines of kings and queens in England and France. When she included Russian kings in that mix, I realized where the bleeding came from. The older I became, the longer my menstrual periods were until it seemed no sooner had one tapered off when the next one began. Also, I bled so heavily at times that I needed to wear two heavy duty tampons, plus two of the hospital overnight pads, put together.

Over the years, my doctors tried to control this with estrogen and progesterone. They did a lot of experimenting with the dosage and duration, but were never completely successful in stopping it. Finally, at the age of 65, I had a complete hysterectomy. After that, I was a happy camper and so was my husband.

My flat feet led to bunions and lots of sore, tired feet, until I learned about orthotic foot lifts. I'm never without them now.

Another genetic condition was the difficulty in digesting certain foods. The main offenders were milk products and wheat products. I'm not as intolerant as some people are. I can cheat a bit. But if I overdo things, it gives me diarrhea. I suffered from diarrhea every morning for years. I planned on getting up an extra hour early to get ready for work. Various doctors tried different things to cure me. I've had colonoscopies[48] and diagnostic tests that show up negative. The top specialist in Grand Rapids had me doing anal exercises and taking Imodium every day, regularly. That helped. I was allowed to take up to eight capsules a day, if needed. Usually one or two did the trick.

Finally in my late sixties, a P.A.[49] told me about the "Blood Type Diet". I read the book and started on the Type "O" diet. Joilé! No more diarrhea, no more bloating, no more gut cramps and noxious gas emissions. There was a perfectly normal explanation. People with certain blood types can't digest certain foods well. I still keep the Imodium in my medicine cabinet, for occasional use, but never had to buy another bottle. Also, I go through a box of Depends every couple years, needing them only when I get careless about my diet. It's a curse, but there are worse things: constipation, for instance.

Two other conditions I inherited from mother. She was hard of hearing and was partially blinded by glaucoma in later years. I have successfully worn hearing aids for twenty years, and have been on Timoptic eye drops to control my eye pressure for ten years. Tests show that I have lost a bit of vision in the lower area, but so far, I don't notice it. Mother also had high blood pressure and died of a stroke at age 91. I have been treated for high blood pressure and high cholesterol for years, but so far, so good.

One curse of older women that I have escaped is osteoporosis. So far, my bones have tested extra strong and I've never broken one. But the old-age osteo-arthritis hasn't left me alone. I've worn out both my thumb joints typing and playing guitar. I had the right one repaired surgically and it has been successful. I had a D & C[50] a couple times, trying to fix the bleeding problem. Other surgeries I've had, in addition to the hysterectomy, are a successful hernia repair, a bunionectomy, removal of ingrown toenails twice (I still have them), and a hemorrhoidectomy.

---

[48] Not my favorite thing to do. The preparation is worse than the test.

[49] Physician's Assistant

[50] Dilation and Curettage

When you add it all up, it sounds like a lot of health problems. But I don't think of it that way. Rather, it has been a lot of years. I feel very healthy and plan to live to be 102 so I can beat Aunt Grace, who lived to 101. I enjoy being active, hiking and skiing, going to the fitness center, playing the piano and making love with my husband.

We have always had a healthy sex life. Today it is better that ever; although maybe not as often as when we were both nineteen. But quality counts more than quantity, right? He has become a magnificent lover, father, husband, provider, protector and jack-of-all-trades. I've always felt that if all husbands were good lovers and made it their mission to keep their wives satisfied and happy, the way Dave does, there would be far fewer divorces in this country. When I'm satisfied, he's happy. We have both been faithful too, so we don't worry about STDs. Simple as that.

That about sums it up.

* * *

Chapter Thirty-Eight

"Building, Buying and Selling Houses"

Canadian Lakes was our vacation paradise for eighteen years. We were part of the weekend group, the "trunk slammers". In 1991, it became obvious that we needed to do something to get rid of the burden of two homes. Dave summed it up this way: "I'm too old to have six bathrooms."

The quandary was, which house do we get rid of? We couldn't bear to let the vacation house go. We loved it too much. But living there permanently would call for drastic changes in our lifestyles. Dave could move his business without too much trouble. He had retired from the General Agency and was working as an independent producer. Much of his business was done by fax, phone and computer. Driving distances would lengthen for calling on clients and shopping, but that could be managed. We would be leaving our church home, but we could continue the healing services by making the one-hour drive into town once a month. The big change for me would be giving up my students.

I dreamed about it and sometimes lay awake nights worrying the problem to death without coming to any conclusion. Finally, I decided to make a prayer pilgrimage to Canadian Lakes alone. I prepared the week before by laying the problem before God, journaling about it, fasting, praying and asking for guidance. On the appointed day, I drove up to Canadian Lakes alone, praying, singing hymns and reciting the Psalms as I drove along the freeway.

It was amazing how my turmoil seemed to quiet the closer I came to the cottage. As I pulled into the drive, parked and got out of the car, I sensed a peace beginning to settle over me. Deep breaths drew in the refreshing fragrance of the pine trees – so quiet, except for the friendly chickadees that greeted my arrival. As I slowly walked around the yard and all through the house, a profound peace settled around me. This was it. This felt so good. I just knew it was right to move here.

Even though we had designed the original house, we hired

an architect to design an addition. The original house was an A frame. Adding on was no job for amateurs. It hadn't been originally designed for permanence, so there was no garage and a general lack of storage space. We would both need offices and I would need a studio.

Our architect came up with great plans for a new entry and garage on one side and a two story addition on the other. This addition would contain a large storage room or studio downstairs, plus an office for me and a nice dressing room with plenty of storage upstairs. There would be a staircase between my office and the studio/storage area.

The original bathroom was remodeled into one full bath with a bubble tub and a second half bath. The front door was moved over, enlarging the kitchen and allowing us to add cupboards and a dishwasher. The side porch was torn away and a three season screened porch, a breezeway, a new entrance and attached garage were added with a storage attic above. The front deck was replaced with two much larger decks, both upstairs and downstairs.

The new house would have 3,800 square feet and a completely new roof. The downstairs recreation room would be refinished for Dave's office.

We took bids. In 18 years, prices had gone up enough that the addition would cost almost four times as much as the original house. This was the third time we had built, not counting the numerous times we had done major remodeling projects. Far more experienced and savvy, we knew that all contractors must be monitored. Dave spent a lot of time at the building site, sometimes camping out up there, even though, theoretically, we couldn't occupy the house again without an occupancy permit.

We have never quite understood why it should take longer to remodel that it does to build a house from scratch, but it did – an entire year, in fact. Toward the end, there was plenty of frustration. One of the hardest tasks is to get the builder to come back and fix all those little things that weren't done right in the first place. Fortunately, we had withheld the final payment until we were satisfied. Even so, there was a bill for twenty thousand dollars for so called "extras" that we had ordered, over and above the original bid, such as built-in shelves, a better grade of floor covering than the bid allowed and perimeter insulation.

Perhaps this was a mistake – remember, get those extra bids in writing – but it isn't easy to catch the contractor when he leaves the house before dawn and doesn't return your calls – well, you get the picture. There is always the option of suing. Would you sue over twenty thousand dollars? Remember, you can't move into the house until all the builders' liens are satisfied.

It so happened that this was the year after my mother passed away. Part of my settlement from her savings and the estate sale was twenty thousand in cash. We finally decided to pay the bill. I reasoned that a big part of the addition was for my offices, so mother's money would go for that. It hurt to write that check, but it meant that we could move forward at last.

We began moving the "little stuff" in my red truck, figuring it cost $12 in gas for one round trip. We planned to hire movers for the final move of the big things. A lifetime of stuff had to be sorted out. What would go into the garage sale, what would go to Canadian Lakes, what would go to charity and what would be thrown out? I never had to pay to advertise. We lived close to a busy street, Breton Avenue, so when my garage sale was open, I would simply put a sign down on that street. The customers would pour in.

Likewise, I tried to sell the house myself. On weekends, I would put a sign down on Breton Ave.: "Open House →". We had lots of "tire kickers", but no offers. Professional realtors[51] made it

---

[51] In 2009, the so-called "housing bubble" burst. The blame was placed on Fannie Mae, Freddie Mac, unscrupulous bankers, politicians, homebuyers, mortgage interest rates, etc. That is part of it, but no one has mentioned the fact that realtors tack their 7 % commission on to home prices. They are motivated to sell high. Every time a house is resold the price has to go up. The state and local sales tax may be another 5 %, and then there are the title insurance and inspections, the bank fees, lawyer fees, mortgage fees, fixing up costs, and moving costs. Selling and buying a house is costly. No wonder people try to recoup!

almost impossible for a "Sale by Owner". People are naturally somewhat leery of buying from owners. We learned that most had been working with a realtor already. If so, their realtor would simply drive by our house and advise them against it. Sometimes the realtor would knock on the door and say that Mr. and Mrs. Smith had requested that she inspect our house. Either we agreed to give her the listing or she would blackball our house.

We were constantly plagued by realtors telephoning us, claiming that they had several "clients" who were looking for a house just like ours. It was just part of the sales talk. Basically, they were trained to get listings. Because of the multiple listing service, they didn't need to actually sell houses. If they got the listing, their agency was guaranteed half of the sales commission regardless of who sold the house. So some salespeople made a nice living without ever selling a house. All they did was sell listings by calling up all the owners who ran ads in the Sunday classifieds. Frustrating!

Forgive me for maligning all realtors. They provide a service and no doubt can make a very effective argument in favor of it. But I think that a person ought to be able to do their own selling if they want to. I enjoy it and have learned enough to type out a legal Warranty Deed, do my own closing, recording, etc.

For two years after we moved, we couldn't sell the house in Kentwood. The extra expense was burdensome. The Kentwood house was empty now, but we still had utility costs, taxes and a mortgage. We had to keep up the lawn and garden and do as much as we could to increase the curb appeal of the house. Sometimes we stayed overnight painting and fixing up. We slept on the floor in sleeping bags. I made new curtains. We did a lot of work on the house. Eventually we listed the house with a friend in the business and lowered the price a lot. After several months, he sold the house for much less than it was worth, but we were out from under.

Dave and I kept up the healing services at St. Paul's United Methodist Church once a month on Sunday night for two years after we moved. When they had a change of pastors, their new pastor had no interest in a healing service. She was most gracious and willing to let us continue, but frankly admitted it wasn't her thing. Without her enthusiastic support and without our being there on Sunday mornings to promote it, interest died down, so we decided it was time to retire from that.

In the meantime, I had made arrangements to teach out of a studio room at Farrell's Guitar Store in Grand Rapids. I drove in every week to meet my students there. Occasionally, they would assign me a new student from a "call in". After a couple of years, they decided they needed the space to remodel their store, so I moved down the block to Keyboard World, a piano store.

I was allowed to charge whatever I wanted and paid them $1.00 per student. It was a good arrangement, but eventually I became too busy up at home and decided to retire from teaching in Grand Rapids. Some of my students had been with me twenty years. Meanwhile, I had developed a nice studio in Canadian Lakes and was becoming busier there.

In time, we invested the money we had gained on the sale of the Kentwood house into – you guessed it – another cottage.[52] We learned that if you move into your vacation home, it is no longer a *vacation* home. Now that we both worked out of there, it morphed into a combined office and primary residence. We needed another vacation home.

*   *   *

---

[52] See chapter: "Gregory Lake House".

Chapter Thirty-Nine

"Life at Canadian Lakes"

L iving at Canadian Lakes full-time was a whole new experience. As "trunk slammers", we had, quite naturally, acted as if we were on vacation: swimming, fishing, golfing resting, reading, dining out, entertaining, playing cards, watching T.V. and making love, not necessarily in that order. We attended the Independence Day fireworks, but that was about the extent of our participation in town activities.

Now that we were full-time residents, we discovered a whole community out there we hadn't known about, a retirement community in full swing. Whatever your interest, whatever your hobby, there was a group you could join, be it book clubs, Bible study, bowling, tennis, fishing, golf leagues, travel clubs, drama groups, writers, motor-cyclers, dancers, Bridge players, Euchre players, gardeners, political groups, or anything else. And if they didn't have a group, you could start one. There were service organizations, with cancer walks and Habitat for Humanity being the big ones. Every church denomination within a few miles was supported with money and volunteers from Canadian Lakes. We soon realized we had made more friends in a few weeks of living here than in all our years living in the city.

Canadian Lakes has golf courses, swimming pools and four community buildings. One is called the Castle, because it looks like a castle. It is large enough for an audience of 400 and has a stage for large events such as plays, concerts, dances and programs.

I ventured a tiny ad offering piano lessons in the Canadian Lakes area. My first student was "Chuck" Mueller, a sweetheart of a guy, retired from the Navy and a little older than Dave and I. He had always yearned to learn to play the piano. As you might expect, he was a bit timid about learning at his advanced age, but I convinced him that age was no barrier and no problem for me.

Chuck was a member of the Northland United Methodist Church. He told me they were in dire need of a pianist. I definitely wasn't interested. I had had enough of working for churches. "Never again!" I vowed. He wasted no time in "ratting" on me to the choir director. She hastened to call me up before some other organization heard that a new pianist had moved into town.

Thus, I listened to her sad tale of woe. Her pianist, who wasn't very reliable, had left her high and dry right in the middle of preparing the Christmas Cantata. Couldn't I please reconsider? It had only been a few months since my hand surgery. I didn't know if my hands could take a full rehearsal. Foolishly, I agreed to try it for just one rehearsal. Next thing I knew, I had agreed to stay through Christmas. After Christmas, the director left for Florida and the church asked me to stay and direct the choir until she returned. I had never directed from the keyboard, but I had received instruction in it from experts, so I agreed. I became the church organist as well.

Turns out I was very good at leading the congregation from the organ and in conducting the choir from the keyboard. I really enjoyed it. Not the least of it was that it saved me from having to work with a variety of accompanists. Unless the accompanist was top notch, I preferred to do it myself anyway. I was patient and kind to all my accompanists, but being an excellent accompanist myself made me more than aware of everything they did, right or wrong. Was I critical? Only to Dave, I hope. Working with a *good* accompanist was a joy because I loved to conduct, more than (almost) anything, but I can only name one – maybe two – that have lived up to my standards. The rest needed practice and training in one way or another.

I was impressed by the size of the Canadian Lakes volunteer male choir called the Merri-Men Singers. Such a choir is a rarity, even in much larger communities. Listening to them sing, I thought to myself *I knew how to improve their sound*. As fate would have it, their director was leaving. A search committee heard about me and asked for an interview. This position tempted me. I decided to take over the Merri-Men. So here I was again, directing two choirs. In terms of the Diaconal Ministry, it was a perfect connection between the "Church and the World". Several of my men sang in both of my choirs.

The Castle auditorium

The Merri-Men put on two concerts a year at the Castle. We sang at nursing homes, churches and an occasional funeral. During my 15 years with them, the most we had was 45 singers. The men were *so* good to me, I became spoiled. Having worked for churches, I was accustomed to having to set up the room, take down chairs, order music, take care of the library, sort out the robes, pick up the trash – you name it, I did it.

But with the Merri-Men, I never had to open a door or carry a music stand. I had a manager, a librarian, a stage crew, and someone who did research and placed orders for me, made concert arrangements, raised money and took care of wardrobe. It was heavenly. They were perfect gentlemen and I never had to worry about being competition for women. Most of these men were well educated and retired from responsible jobs.

There were two drawbacks to men singers. One was that singing interfered with their golf games. The second was the frailty of older men, in general. They got sick, they had knee surgery, they had heart attacks and bad backs, they moved to nursing homes and, worst of all, they died. Now and then, a younger guy moved in and joined up. By younger, I mean 55 and up. But, the really young guys with the best voices were too busy working and raising a family to have spare time to sing.

Also, fewer men than women had musical training. Many of the schools had cut music and art from the curriculum due to budget restraints. Let's face it, in high school, real men played sports, not sissy stuff like music. So, over the years, natural attrition reduced the size of our choir to 25, then 18, 15, and finally 10 (and three of them were women tenors). So, in 2008, I put on my last Christmas show at the castle. It happened to be the day after a blizzard and a lot of people couldn't get out of their driveways. We still had a good sized audience. It was a wonderful show — the best ever — if I do say so myself. Actually, we had a rave review in the community e-newsletter.

In thinking about the theme of the Diaconal Ministry, I asked myself, "What more could I do to connect the Church with the world?" It seemed to me that the one thing lacking in Canadian Lakes was a chance to worship together as a community. Sure, we played together and we did hobbies together, but that is not enough. All the churches were located outside the community, so we were fractured into a dozen or more different worshiping groups. There was no community Thanksgiving service, for example. Even the funerals were outside.

I considered various options and finally approached the association to see if they would like me to put on a Memorial Day service at the Castle. After my presentation, they were thrilled with the idea, so I became the chairperson. I utilized my years of training and experience in putting on worship services to design a unique program that was ecumenical in nature and combined the themes of patriotism, sacrifice, heroism, giving, and remembrance. I used my Merri-Men choir, the ladies choir, a joint choir, people from the drama group, instrumentalists, readers, decorators, members of the military, veterans, girl scouts, flag bearers and lots of displays, banners, flags, and red, white and blue decorations. I wrote, produced and directed the thing. It was hard work, but very creative and fun. Each year, I had a different theme, different music and program, but the format was successful, so I didn't change that a lot.

It had to get better every time and it was the biggest event at the castle each year, with standing room only crowds. I was told the Castle seats 250. After the paid crew had set up 250 chairs, I would go in, shove the rows closer together, dust off every chair I could find tucked away in storage areas and set up another 100 to 150 seats. In time I got the buildings and grounds crew trained to do it my way.

The last two years, we combined video with the music and drama. I spent months assembling and preparing the shows. Dave would run the computer device that controlled the pictures. He practiced so as to get the timing down perfectly.

We learned a lot about our country's history. For example, one year we took our vacation traveling to Civil War battlefields and taking pictures for the program. The theme that year was (surprise) the Civil War. Through my research, I chose three dramatic true stories of heroism and/or sacrifice that were the right length and fit in with my theme. I would always rewrite the stories myself, as I didn't trust anyone else to do it. Sometimes I wrote them in drama form or a reader's theater type of format. I recruited various people from the community to do the parts.

Occasionally, Shelley, Tom and the girls came up for the weekend and I persuaded the girls to participate in the show, either playing "Taps" on the horns or as a trumpet accompaniment in a stirring choir number. The year we featured the Civil War, Emily read an excerpt from her great-great grandfather's memoirs of his Civil War service on the Union side.

In addition to employing all the arts, we used all the traditional elements of worship in our services.[53] *Response* was included in several ways such as singing, rising, cheering, flag waving, wildly applauding and giving. One particularly successful element of *giving* was collecting an offering for the World War II Memorial on the mall in Washington D.C. In addition to gifts of money, people were assisted in registering themselves or a friend or loved one in the WWII Registry. We had people standing by

---

[53] Such as gathering, processional, call to worship, invocation, scripture, prayer, the spoken word, response and sending forth etc. We didn't call them by those names, of course.

with computers and entry forms. Dave and I made donations in honor of his brother, Alfred, who served in the Navy and my mother who worked in a factory making parts. Altogether we registered upwards of one hundred people.

As a pleasant byproduct of this activity, I became chairperson of the Canadian Lakes WWII Memorial committee. I received phone calls, letters and packets of information and beautiful posters to display. Dave and I received an engraved invitation to the groundbreaking ceremony for the Memorial. This trip was a highlight for us. We stayed at a near downtown Washington D.C. hotel. We took the subway to the mall and spent two days visiting all the sights and taking pictures for the following year's hometown Memorial Day service.

We attended receptions and events leading up to the ground breaking. Elizabeth "Libby" Dole appeared at one of them. I shook her hand and got her autograph. On the third day we were given V.I.P. passes and privileged seats only sixteen rows from the front mixed in with WWII veterans in their various old uniforms.

The ceremony was done with pomp and patriotic flourishes as only Washington can do. The flag ceremony with spit-and-polished military honor guard was enough to send my poor heart a-flutter. There was a military band, appropriate speeches and a multitude of celebrities including President Bill Clinton and some top ranking brass. Bob Dole and Tom Hanks were co-chairmen of the money raising effort. We sat close to the big screens that showed a stirring multi-media presentation produced and directed by Steven Spielberg, a famous Hollywood filmmaker.

Even waiting in line at the porta-john was an experience, *par-excellence*. As is usually the case, the women's line was four times as long as the men's and moved at a snail's pace. Spying a men's john with no line, I picked up my feet and moved over in front of it. *What the heck, it all goes to the same place,* I thought. The little sign on the door read "occupied", so I waited a moment for the person to emerge. Imagine my chagrin when out stepped Colin Powell! I resisted any impulse to shake his hand. He carried on with dignity, as if I wasn't there.

There might have been as many as a hundred people altogether working on the Canadian Lakes Memorial Day program in various capacities, but I was the overall director and producer. I didn't summon people out to a lot of boring committee meetings. I preferred to work one on one, appointing someone to be in charge of a certain part, training them and letting them go at it. If they did well, I asked them again the next year. Individual segments would rehearse by themselves. Then we pulled it all together in one dress rehearsal and put it on the next day.

It was the ideal way for me to work, with my particular talents and personality. I *can* work in a committee system, if I have to. Lord knows I've had enough practice, but it is cumbersome. The Memorial Day Service was my baby and I did it for ten years. It was very successful and, for once, I thought no one else wanted my job, until the last year, 2008.

I had asked my favorite accompanist to do the show again, for me, and she agreed. I had hired her for several years and we worked together beautifully. She took my direction well and seemed to enjoy accompanying for me. Early in the planning, I felt I should pay the ladies choir the courtesy of inviting them to sing, if they cared to. They had done so in the past. So I sent the choir director an e-mail. She didn't answer right away. Dave and I were off to Hawaii on vacation. With one thing and another, I didn't follow up. I was passing my personal deadline for having certain things in place.

Thinking the ladies weren't planning to sing, I went ahead with other plans. After everything was set, I learned that the ladies choir director would like to help out. Somehow my e-mail had gotten lost in her inbox or something. I was glad to move things around a bit so the ladies choir could be included.

They had their own accompanist which was fine with me. However, she got her nose out of joint when she learned that she would be sharing the spotlight with *my* accompanist, whom I had already engaged for the rest of the show. She got herself into a jealous snit, called me up and told me off in no uncertain terms. She said she was "highly insulted" that I had not asked her to play the entire show. She felt that it was her place to do the whole show and that I had a lot of nerve to bring in an outsider. She stated, "If I can't do the whole show, you certainly can't expect me to be there for one or two little songs. It would be too insulting".

I was cordial and as polite as possible, but firm in my resolve. I already had my accompanist and wasn't going to change at this late date. I kept these thoughts to myself. *When I am in charge I don't have to put up with nonsense. I've had a lifetime quota of that, thank you very much.* When it ceases to be fun, I quit. So after ten years, I retired on a high note with the very best show ever. [54]

Now, in 2009, they have a new committee and an excellent new chairperson, who asked for "volunteers". Guess who has volunteered to be the accompanist? You got it. Hopefully, everyone is happy now. Sometimes the kindest thing is to graciously step aside.

I didn't mean to boycott the show this year, but it so happened Dave and I have another commitment. We needed to be at the Marriott Desert Ridge Resort in Scottsdale that week attending our first grandson's graduation. Wild horses couldn't keep me away.

*   *   *

---

[54] See chapter: "Small Recognitions and Large Blessings"

Chapter Forty

"Northland United Methodist Church and Ordination"

M eanwhile, I was working at Northland UMC, resolved that this was definitely going to be my last church job. I took the job with a great deal of trepidation. The job was a bit unusual in that I shared the directing job with another church member. Lydia[55] and her husband spent the winters in Florida. So while she was gone, the choir was my baby. When she returned I became her accompanist.

The organist job was mine as well. Rev. Jack Bartholomew was the pastor. His wife gave the children's sermons. They were both real sweethearts and wonderful Christians. They were very kind to me and I loved them.

For a while, I thought that I had finally found the perfect church job. We worked together in harmony, supporting each other and having fun. The not-so-secret ingredient was an abundance of Christian charity and absence of jealousy among the staff. One wouldn't have thought it possible for two strong choir directors to share a choir, but I was able to make the transition from being in charge to sitting in the accompanist's chair rather seamlessly, if I do say so myself. That does not mean that it was easy.

It fell to me to prepare Lydia's anthems for six weeks before her return. She would e-mail a list for me. I would begin preparing and rehearsing the choir, as they needed to work on a piece for several weeks in advance. When Lydia returned, she would step into the role with ease. Naturally, she directed in her own style and with her own ideas. I had to sit quietly while she changed things around, sometimes biting my tongue.

It was a matter of pride to me that I behave in a professional manner, so I worked hard at adapting to her ideas. It may have been difficult for the choir members as well. If it was,

---

[55] Not her real name.

they never said so. Lydia did not have her college degree in music the way I did, but she was and is a very bright lady and had picked up the trade quite well, moving from piano lessons as a youth to volunteer church choir leader with ease.

In smaller churches, that was the way it worked. The pastor picked someone out of the congregation to lead a choir and that was it. Lydia was a volunteer. She had a music budget but no salary. I was paid but I graciously took the small stipend they offered, reasoning that if I accepted that with contentment and remained a humble servant, they wouldn't fire me.

* * *

This system worked well until Jack retired. Changes in pastor have never boded well for me, and this new pastor was no exception. I made as small a target as possible, but I soon realized he was uncomfortable with me as organist. Like many pastors, he loved to talk. I, on the other hand, was a quiet person. He told me all about his wife, the *organist*. Experience taught me this wouldn't work. I could endure until he maneuvered me out of my job, or I could quit. The choice was flight or fight. I chose flight. Within a week, Mrs. Pastor X, the organist, was working for her husband again.

I stayed with the choir and was willing to sub for her when necessary. It turned out that Mrs. X suffered from long bouts of clinical depression. She would be hospitalized for weeks and months at a time, during which I would graciously step into her place without a ripple of disturbance for the church. There was only one little hitch: she continued to receive her salary, but mine didn't increase from the merely symbolic $15 per rehearsal and $15 per Sunday that I received already.

The idea of paying someone to serve the church didn't sit well with some folks. They thought we should support ourselves in some other way and love the situation like a good Christian should. I consoled myself with the thought that I had chosen to work in a rural church where people volunteered and the Lord would bless me in other ways, which He did, pressed down and running over.

I had some fun at Northland, writing and, with Dave's help, producing sacred musicals. This was a new custom for them and they were delighted. Church members and people from the Canadian Lakes community attended these plays and contributed generously to the free will offering. These offerings were astounding in comparison to the typical Sunday offering at Northland. I remember one time the offering was $7,000.

For some unknown reason, there seemed to be no connection between these kinds of offerings, the church music budget and my salary. Our offerings went into the general fund. I still had to beg for funds to buy music and raise my own funds to buy new choir robes. In fact, there was a school of thought that money was a finite resource and that any money-raising activities that I had would eat into the regular giving of the members. I knew that idea was pure poppycock, but it illustrates the parochial thinking I had to endure. Dave and I were generous givers to every church I served, exceeding by far what they returned to me in salary. In short, I was a huge financial asset to Northland and every church I served.

Dave had plenty of complaints about Pastor X, but I kept my own counsel. I knew that all United Methodist pastors got moved, eventually, although the better ones, being in greater demand, were moved more often. Unfortunately, there were also some small rural churches that became dumping grounds for the less successful pastors. It was extremely rare for the system to ease these guys out. If a pastor got into trouble, the bishop found it easier to move him to another unsuspecting congregation than to move him into the "private sector". Thus the system worked against itself.

One poor pastor could ruin a succession of congregations, one after another, until he retired. So far as Pastor X was concerned, I was a good employee. I worked tirelessly, made him look good, raised lots of money to pay his salary, took direction well, and didn't complain behind his back. He and I were business-like in our dealings with each other, but stayed out of each other's way as well. We rubbed along fairly well, I thought, until something happened that changed the dynamics of staff relationships.

*   *   *

During my stay at Northland, the mother church made the momentous change from Diaconal Ministry to Ordained Deacon. I had already established that my work combining the Church and World was a full-time diaconal ministry. I took pride in this, and we all know what happens to pride.[56] I questioned those who were teaching us whether that status would change if I became an Ordained Deacon. During the national training session held for us in Chicago, I made an appointment with the National Director to discuss this question. After I had described what I was doing in detail, he thought that what I did fit perfectly with the Deacon's calling. Full-time status was extremely important to me. I needed the assurance that it would not change.

When the formal interviews took place back in Michigan, I continued to seek reassurance on that issue. We Diaconal Ministers discussed it at length among ourselves. All of us were concerned. Only the two who were full-time in charge of Christian Education in big churches felt confident.

One of the women had the same problem I did. She worked part-time as a church musician and part-time writing for a newspaper. A third job was one day a week as a church secretary in another church. Everyone we talked to saw this as no problem. However, the final decision was always up to the bishop and he was incommunicado. His assistant recommended we all go ahead with ordination, but that choice was ours. We could each remain as Diaconal Ministers for life or become Deacons. Thus assured, we all decided to become ordained. However, once it was done, we couldn't go back.

Ordination was a big deal for us. We worked separately and together to prepare. Someone would be selected for the honor of carrying our banners. I selected Dave, of course. He would stand beside me, but was not allowed to join in the laying on of hands. Only ordained persons were allowed to make that symbolic gesture, having been passed down in unbroken succession from

---

[56] "Pride goeth before destruction." Proverbs 16:18, KJV

Saint Peter himself.

The Merri-Men made a gift to me of my stoles, in the different colors representing each liturgical season. The church made a cash gift to me that I decided to use to buy a special paten and cup for their communion table.

Our small group of eight would be the first class of Permanent Deacons ordained in the West Michigan Conference. We were feted at a special dinner hosted by the bishop. We were allowed to attend the closed-door annual meeting of the clergy where we were formally presented to the group and accepted into fellowship by a loud vote of confidence. There were no "Nays". Dave came down to Albion to stay with me. We posed for lots of pictures. Some of my friends from Canadian Lakes made the long drive to Albion to surprise me by attending my ordination and the reception following. They didn't go home until the wee hours of the morning.

This was one of the most stirring spiritual experiences of my life. We new Deacons sat in the front pew and our sponsors sat directly behind us. Flash cameras were forbidden and any camera was frowned upon, but Dave managed to sneak a few pictures of the event with his sensitive lens from his position behind me. I was completely enthralled and lost in a spiritual fog throughout. If I could have glowed, I would have. The laying on of hands lifted me into space.

I was ready to go serve the Lord and wash the feet of his people. It seemed significant to me that I was ordained on my 65th birthday, June 12, 1997. My prayer and private promise to God was that I would serve for five years until I was seventy. It turned out to be six years.

After the service, when the appointment sheets came out, my friend Janet and I were listed under the column of "Part-Time Appointments". Janet was furious and I was crushed. It seems that bishops operate within their direct connection to God and, much like Popes, pay no special heed to the policies and opinions of mere mortals. After a cursory review of the various jobs in which we fresh new Deacons were employed, the Bishop opined that

Janet and I were engaged in only part-time ministries of suitable nature for an ordained person. His opinion was true for elders, who are appointed to "Ministries of Word, Sacrament and Order", whereas this new order of Deacon was created to be of "Service to the Church and the World". Clearly, the message had not filtered up to his exalted ears.

For some unknown reason, after three years, when the annual appointment sheet was printed, Janet was inexplicably listed as full-time. She never knew how it happened, unless some mole friend of hers made a "filing error".

In my case, the bishop was unbending. No amount of pressure brought to bear from Nashville changed his opinion. My case became rather notorious with the higher-ups in the diaconal division. In fact, whenever I ran into one of my friends from the home office they would ask me, "Did you ever get that problem with your appointment resolved, Dorothy?" after which they would shake their heads in wonderment. I "fought the system" for justice for six years and continued at Northland until my forced retirement in 2003.

Do you suppose my experience has anything to do with my dogged support of charities fighting for justice for various of our servants – such as police officers and service men and women – in prison for doing their job?

*   *   *

A huge change in Lydia's circumstances gave a hidden enemy of mine the opportunity to get rid of his or her misperceived competition. It just wouldn't do to have me around always giving the members someone to which this person might not compare favorably.

Lydia had been married to her second husband, a dear Christian man, for many years. They owned a place with acreage in the township and a winter place in Florida. He had the misfortune of developing a rare form of cancer in his sixties. After a long struggle, he eventually succumbed. This brought about an awful change in Lydia's lifestyle. Taking care of two homes was too much for her. It took another year, but she sold both of their homes and bought a small condo in Canadian Lakes.

Thus, she became a year-round resident. It was no longer necessary for her to leave the choir every year to winter in Florida. There was no question of who was going to direct the choir now.

This worked perfectly for Pastor X. He was never comfortable having a popular Deacon working alongside him, even though he wasted no time when it came to asking me to sub for him and assist in various ways as needed. I preached and tended the flock, free of charge, when he had his six weeks of paid vacation. Otherwise, I knew well to step aside when he was present. Even when one of the parishioners died, he drove home from wherever he was to take charge of the service. I could make the arrangements behind the scenes, but he took the spotlight as befitted a man of his distinction and position.

When Lydia came back, I was relegated to choir accompanist, subbing for Pastor X, and subbing for Mrs. X. It was not lost on me that I hadn't received so much as a tiny raise in several years. The church was in a financial squeeze, and it was all they could do to give the pastor his required raises. Once, I had the temerity to inquire of the lay leader why they gave the church secretary her raise and not me. His astonished answer was, "After all, she keeps the church together."

Meantime, I had been fighting with the bishop's office to get my poor excuse of an appointment increased to full-time. Well, not exactly fighting. I had written to her. I appealed through my district superintendent, who was the widow of my first mentor, Bob Brubaker. Ellen was not helpful. She completed her six-year term as D.S. and Rev. Joe Huston replaced her.

I was sure Joe would help me, because we had known each other back when he was pastor at St. Paul's and Dave was chair of the staff relations committee. The retirement rules say that clergy have to retire at 70, but I put it off for another year. What difference did it make? I wasn't going to receive any pension from the church and I wasn't getting paid much by Northland, so I saw no point in retiring.

I was hoping that the bishop would appoint me full-time before I had to be listed as retired, so that my name would appear in at least one copy of the Conference Journal. It may seem like a silly request, but being listed in the official record meant that my name would live beyond my lifetime. I longed to be recognized for my work, even if it was only a small thing. Being listed as "part-time" was insulting and humiliating.

Joe was very sympathetic to my case and instructed me just how to prepare an appeal. It would be a written presentation that he could take to the bishop, showing all the things that I do and relating that to the mission of the Deacon. I spent a year doing that. There was a beautiful scrapbook and an essay, plus the completed reports you have to fill out every year, letters of recommendation from my pastor, the staff relations chairperson, and one of my students.

It was degrading to have to ask for the letters because I had to explain why they were needed. Joe kindly stopped at my house one day to look everything over. He was very impressed and hopeful that I would be appointed. I had given it my best shot.

Weeks went by while I waited to hear from the bishop. I consoled myself, knowing that she had a lot of material to review, and needed time for thought. *Ha.* Then one day an official letter came from the bishop's office. I looked at it but couldn't open it for a long time. Finally I opened the letter, burst into tears and cried out, "Dave, oh Dave!"

"What is it?! What's wrong?!" He looked at me in alarm.

"Oh no, it's a letter from the bishop."

Dave came to me and took the letter. It was typed on a single piece of official-looking paper. Someone else had typed the letter of two brief paragraphs. It sounded like a simple "bed bug" letter that her secretary had programmed into her computer. "This letter will inform you that your work does not qualify… etc. Please accept my best wishes in your endeavors."

"Is this all there was?" Dave asked. He couldn't believe it. "No more explanation? Just this? Why that no good *(bleep)* ungrateful *(bleep)*! I'd like to *(bleep)*!"

I knew how he felt, but that way wasn't going to help. My despair was complete, but I knew that forgiveness was the only way to peace. I had to put it behind me, accept it as God's will and move on as soon as I could.

There was no choice but to file my retirement papers. The Conference has a practice of showing video of each retiree's life work and allowing them to speak to the Conference. There is a retirement dinner and lots of baloney passed around. I had attended the Annual Conference for fifteen years and had learned to avoid the retirement afternoons, if possible. Some of those old geezers went on well past their allotted five minutes, causing us to be late for dinner.

Feeling that I had nothing to celebrate, I boycotted my own retirement festivities. The gentleman in charge was quite frustrated because I wouldn't send him any information. He must have made up a good story because I received a video of it in the mail. I never looked at it.

Pastor X got wind of my official retirement and called me one day to say that the church wanted to honor me. Being suspicious, I wondered what he was up to. I told him I preferred not, but he insisted that they hold a coffee for me after worship the following Sunday. This is really no big deal because they have coffee most Sundays anyway. In the end, I had little choice in the matter. At the coffee, he quieted everyone down and gave me a plaque to hang on the wall. I smiled and thanked him graciously, thinking that was the end of it. *This wasn't so bad, after all.* It was later when he dropped the other shoe.

Now that I was "retired", Northland Church took me off of salaried staff status and put me on retired status, cutting my already meager pay to an insulting level, like leaving a penny tip for a poor waiter. Retired pastors are allowed to hang around, but that was all. I wasn't notified of this, but discovered it for myself by reading the annual report tacked up on the bulletin board. This was the final insult. I wrote a letter to the chairman of the church board and told him that I was being retired against my will and that I would leave the church.

Some months later, he called and asked for an appointment to see me. He drove out to our house and talked with Dave and me, expressing his profound regret over how I had been treated, and went on about his complaints against the pastor. Dave joined in but I demurred. At last, I spoke up saying, "I truly appreciate your coming out to visit and accept your apology, but," I pointed out, "I would prefer that this not degenerate into a gripe session over the pastor." He said, "You're right," and changed the subject.

One other gentleman from my former choirs has remained a fast friend, although we seldom see him anymore. I still exchange Christmas cards with one woman from Faith UMC too, but no one from Grandville has stayed in touch. Isn't that amazing?

The lesson to be learned from all this is that, "You too can be replaced," and quickly, too. No one is that valuable. Your work seems so terribly important at the time, but its effect vanishes as quickly as a pebble in the ocean.

*   *   *

Chapter Forty-One

"Separation of the Church from Our World"

An important disadvantage of working for a church is that once you leave, you no longer have a church home. Same goes for spouses. The discharged church employee loses a job, church and any church friends that you had. It's a triple whammy. From most of your friends, there is an awkward silence. You miss the people that you nurtured, loved and cared about, especially the children who don't understand. Some of your friends will be wounded as well, but they have to choose whose side they are on. Most choose to stay in their church. I do what I can to encourage that, because I know it is best for them.

However, one of my closest friends left the church too, because she was even more incensed by my treatment than I was. That was sad, but there wasn't much left there for her. The choir numbers dwindled and no one kept up the burgeoning children's choir that I had started. They were so cute. Oh well, moving on…

Dave and I looked for a new church home for a while. The one that appealed to us most was a large, new church in Big Rapids where we could sit in the back pew and listen. The preacher was really good, but I didn't care for their modern music program (rock band) and it was a long drive. I lost interest. Neither Dave nor I ever wanted to be active in a church again as long as we lived. I thought for a while that I might like to try the Catholic Church where we could be like sheep with a minimum commitment, but Dave vetoed that idea.

Once or twice a year we attend Shelley and Tom's church, and I don't mind that. They have a great preacher and a full-time minister of music with a wonderful music department. Shelley and Tom are extremely active in their church. *God bless 'em.* I've never heard a critical word of their church experience pass their lips. After a few months, Dave and I gave up going to church. We really didn't fit in anywhere.

Now, Dave watches television church faithfully every Sunday morning, while I do something else. Recently, it was

Easter Sunday. I asked, "Dave, do you want us to go to church next Sunday?

He seemed surprised at my question. "Why would we want to do that?"

"Well, you know, it's Easter Sunday," I replied.

"Oh no, I'd rather stay here. They'll probably have something special on Crystal Cathedral."

I am more happy and contented than I have ever been. I feel called at this time of life to devote myself to learning how to love Dave well and to spend my time doing that. This is Dave's and my time together. We've been waiting a long time for this. I know it won't last forever, but I'm content that this is what God wants me to do now.

After a lifetime of church service, when Mother was in her twilight years, she didn't care to go to church. She had lost interest. She couldn't hear. The younger generation in the church with their new ways made her uncomfortable. I was somewhat dismayed because, at the time, I was so involved in the church and thought it was essential to one's faith. Now, I understand why mother felt as she did. It was Ok. She had paid her dues. If there is a heaven as billions of people believe it to be, I'm sure Mom has a place of honor there.

*   *   *

Chapter Forty-Two

"Dad, Mom and the Family Farm"

The story of the family farm is long and complicated. Perhaps I will have to put it into a separate book. It starts long ago and spans many of the events in this book. The farm that Mother inherited when her mother was killed in 1934 became the place where she and Dad finished raising their family and lived out their lives. Eventually, it was to go to us four siblings.

The original 90 acres was homesteaded by Mother's ancestors. What's left has been nibbled almost to death. The first nibble was when Grandmother Dodes sold about 30 acres to Jackson for the Swains Lake County Park. She probably needed the money and may have thought the piece worthless for farming. There was about 1,000 feet of lake frontage in that piece, some low land and a high hill next to Pulaski Road.

Dad and Mother borrowed money to buy an adjoining 60 acres. This piece was mostly low and marshy, containing more water front. Dad fenced it in, scattered rye grass and used it to pasture his dairy cows. He fenced in a lane along the property line all the way back to the cow pasture. This covered most of the perimeter of the property, a couple miles of fence. Every post was cut and hewn from his own trees, then hauled with his horse and wagon. Every post hole was dug by hand, an incredible undertaking.

In addition to surface water, there were two springs on the cow pasture that flooded a goodly portion. Using a team of horses, Dad constructed two ditches that drained the spring water and other runoff. The ditch carried water into a lake and a stream. Those drainages are still there today and flow year-round.

Dad added a barn, storage sheds, a large chicken coop and tool sheds. It was necessary to try to produce some cash to pay the mortgage and buy some basic essentials. The eggs and milk helped with that. Still, life was a struggle during the depths of the Great Depression. It wasn't a matter of making ends meet. It was a matter of keeping the wolf from the door one more *day*. Dad hated those annual trips down to see "Dwight" who had inherited the bank from "Frank". (In those days, the local bank was *locally* owned and passed down, father to son.) It was never a matter of paying off the note. Rather it was a matter of begging the banker to extend it one more year. Imagine being in debt for $5,000 and having to beg the local banker, sitting there in his suit and tie, to allow you to grub out a living for one more year while you prayed to keep your wife and kids from starving!

When my brothers married and started their own business as partners, they each chose a lot for themselves, and cut lumber from the farm. Dad helped them to build their houses. Meanwhile, Dad had leased some of the lake frontage for $25 a year to people who wanted to build a cottage. Having given the boys each a lot, Dad and Mother arranged for my sister and I to each have a lot in the woods. Somehow, Dad arranged for the county to have enough land for a one mile-long road skirting the lakefront. At this point, there were four small fields of cropland, ranging in size from four to seven acres, plus the cow pasture.

Dad and Mother raised their family, tithed and worked tirelessly for the church, survived the Great Depression, two World Wars, the 1918 flu epidemic, the Korean War and Vietnam.

Dad died of prostate cancer in 1976. Mother died of a stroke in 1992. My sister did a great deal of the personal care side of things during Mom's old age: doctor and dentist visits, shopping, beauty shop trips and generally being helpful. My brothers helped, as well. My niece balanced Mother's check book.

Dave and I lived much farther away at that time, but we did what we could. One of us accompanied Mom on many of her Florida trips. Someone needed to be with her when she flew to her winter home. I made a point of writing to her and calling every week. Also, I occasionally drove down to take her to her doctor appointments, in order to relieve the burden on the others.

I visited Mom at her house and did all sorts of things when there: canning, cleaning, administering medication, or whatever. While she was still able, I had her up to stay with us for a week or two at a time, several times a year. While she was with us, I tried to take care of shopping trips and appointments for her.

Eventually, Mother had to have a live-in companion. Next, she had to be put in a care facility. At that point, the trips to Florida ceased. I visited her at the nursing home at least once a month. However, she got so that she didn't remember who had been to see her. She knew us, but got lost in the details.

Sometimes I would contact my sister to tell her that I had been down to visit Mom. I might mention, "Mom said she hadn't seen anyone from the family lately." We would laugh because Mom had just told her the same thing the day before. We made it a point to tell each other, mainly so as to evenly space out our visits. We were rather sure Mom wouldn't remember who had been to visit her. She was not diagnosed as having Alzheimer's, but rather the more common, Dementia. Also, her hearing was almost gone and her eyesight weak.

After the holidays in December 1991, Mom had a stroke and became unconscious. While she was in the hospital, we siblings took turns sitting with her. During my turns, I did her bath, applied lotion on her skin, washed her hair and trimmed her nails. I gave her tiny sips of coke or water and she would swallow. I prayed with her, read the Bible, sang hymns and played my guitar, gave her holy communion and the ritual for the end of life and anointed her with blessed oil. She was not on life support, excepting an I.V. and oxygen.

On January 7, 1992, I requested an appointment with the head nurse and the social worker for help with the matter. We three met in mother's room and discussed her fate as she lay there in a coma. The entire discussion escapes me, but they were saying that mother could not be left in the hospital. After so many days, Medicare insists that patients must be moved to a long-term care facility. I told them that I wanted to take Mother to Grand Rapids, where Dave and I lived, and put her in a facility there, so that I could take care of her. There would be problems moving her so far away. It would be a long, expensive ambulance ride.

We were at the point of discussing the logistics of that

when I noticed that Mother's chest was no longer moving. I stopped in mid-sentence. "Oh... I think she's gone. Look, she isn't breathing."

The head nurse stared at Mom for a couple minutes. "You may be right. Let me just listen to her heart."

Mother was dead.

*   *   *

Chapter Forty-Three

"Swains Lake Farms, Inc."

M y preference is to sell the farm," I stated as pleasantly as possible. The four of us were having our first business meeting to begin the process of settling Mother's estate. I was determined to be pleasant and cooperative. The vote was three against one. It would be the first of many. This was going to be a long and difficult process, I thought, but I didn't know the half of it.

There were many problems with management of the leased lots. People had been allowed to build, helter-skelter. The place was junky looking. Some unsavory people had moved in. Others were in default. Moreover, the leases had been written for long terms at incredibly low prices. The worst was for 50 years at $25 a year. I had the software and expertise to make comprehensive printouts and analysis of the leases, their terms and where we stood.

We decided to form an S Corporation and deed our shares to Swains Lake Farms, Inc. Then we each drew 10,000 shares of stock and another 10,000 were held in reserve by the company. We ratified the bylaws unanimously.

We met again to elect officers. I became President, Anna was named Treasurer and the brothers were Vice-President and Secretary. Anna and I remained in our positions for the rest of the time — sixteen years, to date. At times, issues came up with the leases and the lessees. Most were cooperative, nice people, but a few were a lot of trouble. Some things needed to be settled through lawyers.

The State of Michigan allows only so many sub-divisions without having the property platted. This law prevented us from selling the lakefront lots. I set out to try and convince the township board to order an assessor's plat. This is a Michigan law that allows an exception to the usual zoning laws in the case where the assessor determines that homes have been built before the current zoning laws took effect in such a way that proper boundary lines were impossible to ascertain with certainty.

In preparation for my presentation, I researched the laws and made charts, copies and binders for each member of the board. Dressed in my power suit, I had a 180 mile trip each way. The meetings are at 7:30 PM, so I had to stay over. This was the first of hundreds of such trips.

The township agreed to go forward with the assessor's plat, however, it was clear that they expected me to shoulder the burden of the work. Thus I became the supervisor and go-between for the many people involved. This included the township supervisor, the members of my board, various lawyers, county officials, State of Michigan officials, attorneys, judges, surveyors, realtors, title companies, members of my board, owners of cottages, buyers and lessees.

After the surveyors had done their best to reconcile the deeds' and leases' descriptions with the actual ground, there were still some people who were unhappy.

One evening, we were in the kitchen preparing dinner, when a uniformed officer came to the door. "Are you David and Dorothy Mercer?" he asked.

"Yes," we answered and froze with alarm. He extended a paper in our direction. Dave stepped in front of me and reached for it. "What's this about?"

"You are being subpoenaed to appear in circuit court. Thank you, sir." He turned and left.

My stomach clenched and my face lost its color. "Oh my God! Who is it?"

"Let me get my glasses," Dave said. "Here, you read it."

My hand shaking, I took the paper and read, "You are hereby ordered to appear in Jackson County Circuit Court, Monday, December 27th at 9:00 A.M. in the case of Mrs. Jacqueline Douglas and Mr. and Mrs. Donald Ward, as plaintiffs vs. Swains Lake Farms, Inc., Mid-Michigan Engineering and Surveying, Inc., Pulaski Township, Mrs. and Mrs. David N. Mercer and one other couple, defendants."

"What are they suing us for?" Dave wondered.

"They want to stop the assessor's plat. They claim it is encroaching on their land."

The lawyers had a field day. Each defendant had to have their own lawyer— five in all— plus the lawyer for the plaintiffs. I had to work with three different lawyers.[57] The lawsuit was set for eight months hence. During that time, our lawyers prepared me to testify. I studied and researched stacks and stacks of papers, made notes and asked questions. Work on the surveying came to a screeching halt.

The problem was an ancient one. Mrs. Douglas and Mr. and Mrs. Ward thought that they had more land than the surveyors had allowed. Three other lots just happened to be in their way. If the plaintiffs were to have the number of feet that they thought they should have they would need to take some feet off of the three other lots to make that up.

When asked, the surveyors said, "Sorry, people, but there's only so much land. If it ain't there, it ain't there. Maybe it was there sixty years ago, but it ain't there now." Indeed, they said, land can shift and change due to natural forces. Roadways can change due to vehicular traffic and the wear and tear they cause.

A nervous day for me was the taking of depositions. At this meeting, all of the possible witnesses were called before all of the lawyers. A court stenographer was hired. Imagine the cost! Whew! I was told to raise my right hand, "I swear to tell the truth, the whole truth and nothing but the truth, so help me God." The plaintiff's lawyer asked me a long series of questions, some of which didn't seem pertinent. He went over my complete educational background from kindergarten on up. Of course, he asked me about my position with Swains Lake Farms, Inc., about

---

[57] Our business lawyer; our trial lawyer and Dave's & my personal lawyer.

the Plat and about the case. I answered truthfully, as I saw it.

The Wards simply testified that they had bought and paid for a certain size lot and that was what they were entitled to. They didn't care about the Douglas family history or whatever. They wanted what was theirs. They paid their taxes and had the papers to prove it. They had bought from a real estate agent. They had relied on her word. A title company had issued a policy and that proved it, so far as they were concerned.

Part of the court reporter's income came from sales of copies of the depositions. I was learning a lot about "hidden costs". So much a page added up to $150 to $200 apiece. I poured over each one, my blood pressure going up. What a waste! I think the stupid things are up in the attic now, gathering dust.

*   *   *

Several months passed before the trial date. During this time, we got more bad news: Another case had gone bad at the lake. This time one of the owners had defaulted on his mortgage. A second bank in Lansing, Michigan, actually held the paper. Their lawyer wrote us a stiff letter stating they had been stuck with a $55,000 note on the property. Because Pulaski Township would not issue a tax number on the parcel, the bank could not sell the property and recoup their loss. They suggested that Swains Lake Farms, Inc. purchase the whole thing back. Otherwise, they would be forced to take the case to circuit court for adjudication.

*   *   *

Chapter Forty-Four

"Gregory Lake House"

How'd the meeting go?" Dave inquired.

"Oh, you know, the usual." I sighed and sank into a soft chair.

"That bad, huh?" He touched my cheek and pulled up a stool for my feet. "Let me get you a glass of wine and you relax. I want to hear all about it."

"Just half a glass," I said, "and mix it with water or something."

"You think I don't know that by now?" he retorted.

"I'm sorry. Of course you do," I said.

"Not to worry. Here you go." He pulled up a small table and set the wine glass down with a small bowl of nuts.

"Thanks, honey," I said.

"Now, tell me what happened." He took a seat on the sofa opposite me and took a sip of his Diet Coke.

"Well, the big thing was that letter from the bank in Lansing about the Gregory Lake house. [58]

"Oh yeah, I remember that," he chortled.

"The bank is willing to sell it to us for $55,000. I thought we should have jumped at it."

"What did they say?"

---

[58] Gregory Lake was a small lake, an outlet out of Swains Lake, situated at the end of Swains Lake Drive.

They were sorry but shook their heads."

"Well," Dave said. "We'll just buy it ourselves."

I gulped. "We'll buy it? You're willing to buy it alone?"

"Sure, why not?"

"There's a lot of work that has to be done on that house. You're not thinking of doing that, are you?"

"Maybe we can just turn it around. Sell it 'as is'. "

"We can't sell it until the township says so," I said.

"Oh, well, maybe we'll just have to keep it until the plat is finished or sell on a contract," he said.

"That might work," I mused. "We'd still own the land and we'd sell the house on a contract."

"We still have that money in the bank from selling our house in Kentwood," Dave remarked.

"Well, ok, I kind of hate to use that," I said, "but I guess we could do that. We probably couldn't get a mortgage in the condition it is in."

"You're right about that."

"It's decided then. Thanks a lot, honey. You are a jewel," I said.

"Aw, shucks," he grinned and gave me a quick peck on the cheek. "Sit right there and I'll bring you your dinner."

*   *   *

Dave spent three years rehabbing our Gregory Lake cottage. He hired a helper and got a few volunteer hours from me and my side of the family. When finished, he had $100,000 invested and figured he would sell it for $175,000. Only one problem: I had fallen in love with the house. Even years later after Pulaski allowed a tax number, I couldn't bear to sell it. Once again, we had a second home, this time with only two bathrooms. I guess we are just "vacation home" people.

*   *   *

Chapter Forty-Five

"The Trial"

The day of the trial arrived. Dave and I had stayed at the Holiday Inn the night before. I knew that I would be called as a witness. Mr. McDonald, attorney for SLF, Inc. had requested an early morning meeting over breakfast coffee. He drew breath and paused before dropping his bombshell: "I have some bad news."

Oh, no. "Like what?" I asked.

"Well, this was a really smart move on their part," he began. "They waited until Friday night to do it, so that I wouldn't learn about it in time to counter their move."

"What did they do?" I couldn't begin to imagine to what he was referring.

"Mid-Michigan pulled out," he said.

"How could they do that?" I was astonished.

"They settled. We don't know the terms, but they settled and pulled out."

"I still don't understand."

"We were planning on Kaye, the engineer on our project, being called as an expert witness to defend Mid-Michigan's version of the plat. I expected Mid-Michigan's lawyer to carry the ball and do the questioning. He's not even here. By waiting until the last minute, they effectively destroyed our case. I was left holding the bag. I don't have another expert witness. I haven't researched the law. I don't have a line of questioning. I'd be going in there skewered and cold as yesterday's fish."

I wiped my sweaty palms on my best pair of black slacks. "So, what do we do?" I asked.

"Dorothy, I'm sorry. I recommend that we settle. It's all we can do at this point."

"But that would mean that they win." I stiffened. "No, we aren't going to settle. Their claims are ridiculous. You have to win this case!"

"If I go in there today, I'm not recommending it and not guaranteeing you a thing. You could still lose and you'd be out the expense of a trial." His prediction was a portent of things to come.

I dismissed his advice, "So be it." I set my jaw. "I'm not giving in without a fight."

"Is that your final word?" He needed to know.

"Yes," I nodded.

"Well… I will just have to play it by ear. The only witness we have is Kaye, and she may actually be a hostile witness now." His brow wrinkled.

"You can do it," I prevaricated.

"I'm glad you think so," he said, "but I'm not so confident."

My stomach was in such knots that I couldn't eat. Dave drove us downtown to the courthouse as I gazed morosely out the window, deep in thought. Dave pulled up to the entrance to let me off. I grabbed my heavy briefcase and opened the door. "Give me a kiss for luck," he said. I offered my cheek. "You'll be great!" he assured as he pulled out into traffic and blew me one more kiss.

A uniformed officer stood inside the entrance next to an airport-style screening gate. I opened my briefcase and set it on the belt along with my watch and shoes. As I stepped through the gate, an alarm screamed. The kindly officer instructed me to come on through. "I'll just run this wand over you to see what is causing the alarm to sound," he said. "We've got this thing set too sensitive. It keeps going off on me." He swished the wand up and down my body. "You pass, lady," he said. "Have a nice day!" *Nice day. Yeah, right. Let's hope so,* I thought as I sank into a straight chair by the ladies' room door while I waited for Dave to park the car and join me. *I hope I don't run into anybody from the other side.*

As I waited, my gut churned and began a familiar cramping sensation. I dug an Immodium out of my purse and swallowed it dry. *Oh, jeez, not now.* I tightened my buttocks and wriggled in my chair. I hadn't had my morning bowel movement. *I'm going to have to go. Can I make it into the ladies' room in time?* I made a dash for the door. *Thank God, no one else is in here.* I hurried into the first stall unzipping, pulling down my pants and covering the toilet seat in one swift move. *Whew, just made it.* I sat there chin in hand praying the Imodium would take effect soon. *I'd better swallow another Imodium.*

The bathroom door opened and footsteps entered another stall. I didn't dare breathe, hoping it wasn't someone who could recognize my shoes. I heard a flush and steps receding. She didn't take time to wash her hands. *Probably had to hold her breathe the whole time.*

I washed my hands thoroughly and checked my face in the mirror. *You're white as a sheet. Put some more makeup on.*

Taking a deep breath, I opened the exit door and turned left to smile, wanly, at Dave.

"Where have you been?" he demanded. "I was getting worried."

"Yeah, I know. I'm sorry," I said, "Had to make a quick trip." I gestured at the ladies room sign. "The men's is around the corner," I offered.

"No need. I already availed myself of that opportunity. We'd better go up." He took my briefcase and grabbed my arm.

* * *

We sat in the hall outside the courtroom. I had already

sneaked into a judge's empty chambers, locating a private bathroom, just in case.

The plaintiff's lawyer walked up. Mr. T. was all business, dressed in his hand-tailored suit, Italian shoes, and carrying an expensive alligator briefcase. He paused above me purposely standing too close. In a practiced stare he skewered me with eyes that bugged out like a bad facelift. "How do you do, Mrs. Mercer," he smirked.

"I'm excellent," I announced as I stood up and faced him nose to nose and eye to eye. "And you?"

"I'm expecting a very good day, Mercer. Make no mistake, we have an airtight case."

"I wouldn't be too sure about that," I retorted, narrowing my eyes and looking directly at him, refusing to blink. *I have never seen eyes that intimidate like that. They were inhuman.* It was a standoff as we both glared at each other, inches apart, neither one looking away. Abruptly he turned on his heel and stalked off with as much feigned dignity as he could muster. *Chalk up one for our side.*

*   *   *

"All rise," intoned the bailiff. Ceremoniously, he threw open the rear door and a black-gowned man entered the room, solemnly took the high throne behind the imposing judge's desk, adjusted his robes, donned his glasses, frowned, looked around at the audience and announced, "Ladies and gentlemen, you may take your seats." There was a rustling of bodies and purses and a few coughs as throats were cleared. A hush fell over the room.

"We are here in the case of Ward and Douglas vs. Pulaski Township, Swains Lake Farms, Inc., David and Dorothy Mercer, and others," he announced, in a monotone voice. "Is that correct?"

"Yes, your honor," a chorus of male voices answered.

"Are you prepared to present your case?" He peered at the plaintiff's table.

"Yes, your honor."

"Ladies and gentlemen, the court is very busy. I expect this case to last no more than two days. Let's move it along as swiftly as possible."

"Yes, your honor."

"You may call your first witness." The judge looked toward the plaintiff's lawyer expectantly.

Mr. T rose "I call John Smith".[59]

*   *   *

The last witness of the day was on the stand. Kaye, our engineer, had answered a grueling series of questions by the plaintiffs' lawyer, Mr. T. She was our last hope. So far she had not helped our side.

Our corporate lawyer, Mr. McDonald, was attempting to frame his last, and most important, question in a way that would get passed the judge. It was important to find some reason to refute the plaintiff's expert witness.

"Objection!" bellowed Mr. T. "Mr. McDonald has not laid a foundation."

"I withdraw the question," said Mr. McDonald. "Did your surveying crew find the monuments that Mr. Smith found?"

"I'm sure they would have found them, if they were there," Kaye responded.

"*At last! A point for our side,*" I thought.

"No more questions."

"Your witness," said the judge to Mr. T.

---

[59] Not his real name.

"No more questions."

"No more witnesses," said Mr. McDonald

"Court will adjourn until twelve noon tomorrow," said the judge. "I will render a verdict at that time." Bang! Sounded the gavel as the judge rose, gathered his papers and left in a swirl of black robes.

I sagged against Dave. Mr. McDonald turned to us. "You will have until noon tomorrow to try and settle. I would like to see you settle this case. The judge is not going to find in your favor. I'm sorry." I shook my head sadly. "I'm advising you in your best interest to give some serious thought to what you want to get and what you are willing to give."

I turned toward Dave. He read my mind. "We'll talk about it tonight," he said.

Mr. McD nodded. "Ok, let's meet back here at eleven o'clock tomorrow"

My shoulders slumped, "Don't you think we have a chance?" I glanced at our personal attorney who hadn't said a word throughout the trial. What a disappointment he had been!

"There's always a chance," he said. "You could have asked for a jury trial," he said, shifting the blame, "but since you agreed to let a judge hear it, I agree with McD. The judge and Mr. Smith are golfing buddies, you know. And Mid-Michigan didn't help your case." *Neither did you,* I thought.

That was a restless night. "It's almost over, poor baby." Dave reached over and patted me. "C'mon, lay your head on my shoulder and try to relax." We were too exhausted to even talk.

The next day, we, the defendants, met with our personal lawyers, Mr. Conley and Mr. B, at the court house. "I have some news from the other side," Mr. B said. "They are willing to concede some points if you will give some too."

"Tell us," I sighed.

"Well, first, they won't give on the position of lots 20 and 21. They insist on that and suggest that lots 18 and 19 each be cut down to 50 feet apiece."

I looked at Dave. "Well, they'd better have a better offer than that," he said heatedly.

"In exchange, Jackie is willing to give up the extra 15 feet of lakefront to your lot 53," he offered.

"That's a start," I replied. "I suppose that Wards are planning to use lot 53 for their boat."

"Perhaps," he said. "They didn't mention that."

"I think you should take their deal," Mr. McDonald put in. "If you let it go to the judge you could lose everything."

Some lawyer he is. Whose side is he on? I thought.

"We need to make a counter offer," said Dave. "Don't take their first offer. What can we counter offer?" he asked.

"Well, I can tell you right now what I want," I interjected. They looked at me in unison. "I want to buy my eldest partner out of the business," I stated flatly.

Everyone was thoughtful. "We could try," offered Mr. B, "but Swains Lake Farms is going to have to buy his shares."

"Not Swains Lake Farms," I said. "We'll buy his shares."

"Make them an offer." I directed Mr. B. *At last, he was being of some use.*

"What should it be?" he asked.

"Two hundred thousand, cash," Dave put in.

"Also, their rear lot lines must be restored to the original description," I added. "No extra lease or footage off our farm."

"Right," Mr. B checked his watch. "I'll be back in five minutes. Be thinking about your top offer," he suggested.

"We'll be in that other room," I pointed.

Mr. B hurried off.

I took Dave's hand and we moved into the empty judge's room where I had found the bathroom. We sat down close together, held hands and bowed our heads. Dave began to pray. "Oh dear Lord, we need you so much. I just pray you will enter Dorothy's heart and give her your peace and your strength. Lord, we need your guidance. This is such an important decision, Lord. We just pray that you will let us know what we should do. Thank you, Jesus."

Dave stood up and reached for me. I stood and leaned into his arms. He encircled me in his comforting embrace and gently patted my back. "It's Ok, honey. We're going to be all right."

"I don't know what to do," I cried.

"We'll get through this," he said gently.

A soft knock came on the door. "Come in," we said and turned toward our lawyer.

"Sorry it took so long," he said. "Your partner isn't too happy about your idea."

"No surprise there," I said.

"I think it might work. The others are putting a lot of pressure on him."

I nodded.

"I'm giving them some time to talk it over. Then I'll go back in," he said as he turned to leave.

"What do you think?" Dave asked me.

"We were supposed to decide how high we could go. We don't have that kind of money," I said.

"I think we can borrow it," Dave said. "I'll phone Steve at the bank. We don't have a mortgage on the Gregory Lake house and our credit is good."

"Yeah, but don't we still owe a couple hundred thousand on the Canadian Lakes house?"

"Something like that," he answered.

When Mr. B returned, he had a smile. "I think we're getting somewhere," he said. "Can you go for $300,000?"

"Oh my goodness!" I exclaimed.

Dave looked thoughtful. "Honey, think about what that's worth."

"Would he take a million dollars?" I quipped.

Dave offered a feeble laugh.

Mr. B. looked at his watch. "We've got 15 minutes," he said.

"Just tell them we can't raise that much money. He'll have to come down," said Dave and shooed him out the door.

Mr. B was back. "The best he can do is $277,500. That's his final offer. He said to tell you take it or leave it."

"Give us a minute," Dave said.

"Don't be long," he warned.

We held each other in silence.

"We need to do this," Dave offered. "I'm willing to pay any price to buy my wife some peace."

"All right," I mumbled into his chest. "I love you."

"Love you back," he said.

Happy to have achieved a settlement, the lawyers and judge sprang into action, practically salivating over the "billing hours" yet to come. We walked through a formal videotaped session before the judge where everyone swore to the terms. Little did I know what a joke that would turn out to be. The judge gave a strong talk to everyone to negotiate the final agreement in good faith, thanked us all and adjourned the trial, awaiting the settlement.

Dave drove us home, while I cried most of the way. "Dave, I can't believe it," I sobbed.

"I know, honey."

I blew my nose. "Nobody will believe this. It's just so crazy." I wiped my eyes and cried some more.

"You're right, baby," Dave said, "But it's over. You won't be bothered anymore."

"Yeah, you're right... if we can get the money."

"I'll get the money," Dave said. "I'll call Steve in the morning. Put your seat back and try to rest, ok?" I put my seat back. Dave turned the interior lights down, dialed in some soft music and handed me the box of tissues.

The judge had accepted the broad outline of the settlement. Now, it was up to a brace of lawyers and one small woman to flesh out the details. After three or four months, the lawyers each drew up their proposed settlement and my ex-partner already started hounding us for his money. I read over the proposals and started rewriting. Back and forth we went.

Slowly, the awful truth dawned on me. The so-called settlement was no settlement at all. It was nothing more than a chance for lawyers to write letters. Lawyers just love to write letters, the purpose of which is to delay a settlement for as long as possible, I suspect. This is a great way to keep that base income flowing in steadily.

The plaintiff's lawyer was the most interested in writing a settlement. He seemed to think that was his privilege and that the rest of us would just cave in. *Hey, wait a minute! Not so fast.*
A big stumbling block was Jackie Douglas. Her attitude hadn't changed a bit. She had her deed and she knew where her lot was and she didn't need anything more.

My own attorney was of little help. Mr. McDonald was happy to talk to me, for as long as I was willing to pay his bill, but that's about as far as that went. I began writing my own version of a settlement and submitting it to the plaintiff's attorney. After about one year of work, we had ironed out most of the words. Now all we needed was everyone's signature, notarized, of course. We all signed off except Jackie. I asked Mr. B to go down to the Jackson courthouse and file an injunction forcing the settlement. He hemmed and hawed a bit on that idea, but promised to consider it.

I had tried praying and calling on Jackie. She just ran her mouth and repeated everything she had said many times already. She didn't hear a word I said.

After months of inactivity, I asked Phil Baldwin what the rules were concerning talking directly to the opposition. "Generally speaking, *I* am not allowed to talk to the opposition party except through their lawyer," he said. "However, there are no rules concerning what *you* can do."

Finally, I called up "Old Bug-Eyes", the opposing lawyer, to make a personal appeal and maybe complain a bit. Instead, I listened to his frustrations. "Dorothy, I've been out there four times. I can't get anywhere with that woman. She's crazy as a fruitcake. I'm just so frustrated that I don't know what to do. What can I do?"

After I picked myself up off the floor, I suggested he get some help. "Has anyone else tried?"

"Yes."

"How about Bev Ward? I asked, "Has she tried?"

"I'm not sure… that might work," he said.

"Okay, try that first, and if that doesn't work, here's what you do…"

"Tell me, please."

I told him.

Before signing off, I gave him a little bargaining chip: "Oh, by the way, my attorney is prepared to file an injunction for a directed order from the court, if that is what it takes."

"I understand," he said.

"Good luck!"

"Thank you. Good-bye."

"Good-bye."

Twelve months after the trial, a settlement was signed and filed with the court. Mid-Michigan Engineering was instructed to re-draw the plat to comply with the court's order and to place new, buried steel corner monuments on the newly designed lots. The Wards and the Mercers drew up a joint easement on the use of their driveway. We, the Mercers, had long since borrowed money and paid off our part of the deal. At this point, Dave and I were paying hefty monthly interest on the loan.

In due course, Dave and I received the 10,000 shares we had purchased and Dave was elected to the Board of Directors of Swains Lake Farms, Inc. Dave assumed the office of Vice President. I looked forward to a new era of peace and cooperation. Now all I had to do was run the company. What a relief!

Except for that minor matter of the assessor's plat…

*   *   *

Chapter Forty-Six

"Golden Wedding Anniversary"

Now that the trial was settled, I had time to do a few other things, like dinner with friends. 2001 was our 50th year of marriage. We needed to do something special and fun. We decided on a year-long celebration.

Dave has always been good about remembering anniversaries, birthdays, Christmas, Valentine's Day and Sweetheart's Day. He never lets an excuse go by to bring me gifts. In fact, he brings me gifts and flowers for no reason. For our 50th wedding anniversary, he was determined to outdo himself. Had my heart been weaker, I would have been done-in by the surprise. Maybe he cashed in his pension plan to buy it. He didn't wait until March 17th to surprise me.

One of the worst early winter snow storms in years nearly blocked the highway as I drove home from Grand Rapids to Canadian Lakes. I had taught lessons at Farrell's Piano World until past seven o'clock that evening. My eyes blurred from staring into the snow for almost two hours, and I hadn't even made it to the freeway exit 131 as yet. The entire trip usually takes an hour and twenty minutes.

My cell phone rang. "Hello?"

"Hi, Babe, just checking. How's it going now?"

"Storm hasn't let up any."

"It's about the same here, too. Have you made it to Eight Mile Road?"

"Not yet. About five more miles."

"Okay. I'm keeping dinner warm for you."

"I had an energy bar when I left the studio," I said.

"That's good. Call me when you leave the expressway."

"Okay. Bye"

The snow plows had been doing a pretty good job of keeping the freeway open, but once I exited, conditions became worse. The road disappeared in a field of white. Shifting my truck into four wheel drive, I turned on the fog lights and low beams. There were no tracks to follow. These next twelve miles were going to be slow going. I picked up my cell phone and punched the redial button.

"Hello," came Dave's welcome voice.

"Hi, it's me."

"Hi, Me."

"I just left the expressway. The road hasn't been plowed, but I'm moving forward, so should be home in half an hour," I said.

"We'll keep a light on for ya'."

"Bye-bye. Love you."

"Love you."

The only way I could stay on the road was to watch the trees alongside and aim my truck halfway between them. There were very few houses on these country roads. I couldn't see them anyway. *I must keep driving and hope for the best.* Both hands had clutched the wheel for so long they were starting to cramp.

I couldn't be sure exactly where I was. I hadn't seen a road sign recently. *Keep going, Dorothy. You've got gas and a cell phone. Turn on the radio.* Click. Static. *Push the 'seek' button.* More static. *Too far from the station. Must be I'm halfway home. There's a dead spot here. Ah, there's a road sign. Flick on the high beams. See if you can read it. 142nd. Jeez. I've missed my turn off. Where am I? Oh, dear... I'm lost... Don't panic... Try Dave again.*

"Hello?'

"Hi Dave, it's me again."

"Hi, me Again. How's it going?"

"I'm not stuck or anything, but I'm not sure where I am."

"Stay there, I'll come after you," he ordered.

"No-no. Don't do that. I can make it, but would you please get out the map and help me?" I asked.

"Sure. Hold on… Okay, I'm ready."

"I'm looking at a sign that says 142nd. I must have missed 155th Avenue. Is it safe to turn left here?" I asked.

"Um, let me find it… No, don't turn there. That is a dead end. You're ok, just go on to the next road at 138th and turn left. That will take you over to Buchanan. Remember there is that big sign on the corner? It says something about saw and knife sharpening services. Watch for that."

"Thanks, honey. I'll keep going. Bye."

"See ya' in a few minutes."

Five minutes later I found the sign and turned left on 138th. *One more mile and right on Buchanan.* Twenty minutes later I pulled into our attached garage, almost too tired to walk into the house.

Dave heard the garage door go up. He was waiting for me and pulled open my door. "Here, let me take your briefcase," he said, helping me out of the car. "Come on, honey, you've had a tough day."

"Thanks, honey, you are a sight for sore eyes." I breathed a sigh of relief. "That warm bath is going to feel good."

"Good idea," he said, "but, look what I've got for you." He gestured toward a candlelit table set for two, a bottle of champagne and two long stemmed glasses, plus a fire glowing in the fireplace. I sighed.

Some delicious food odors assaulted my nose. "Oh, that smells good," I said. "This is lovely. Thanks, Dave."

"Wait until you see the rest." He smiled. "Come with me." He moved away.

"Oh, can't I just sit down?" I headed toward the sofa. "That fire looks so inviting."

"In a minute," he said, "but first, I need you to take care of this one thing in your office." He walked to my office door. "C'mon, honey, please, for just a second."

"Well, if it's important..." I dragged myself up and shuffled the six steps to my office.

Dave smiled and waited patiently. As I met him, he took my hand, turned, threw open the door, reached in and flipped on the light. My upright studio piano was gone. In its place taking up half the room was a shiny, black, brand new Yamaha grand piano with an enormous red bow.

"Happy anniversary, Darling!"

I screamed. "Oh my God!" Suddenly I'm no longer tired. Hands on cheeks, eyes and mouth wide, I screamed again. "Oh my God!" Jumping up and down, waving arms and yelling and crying for ten more minutes.

"It's yours," Dave said.

"Ohhh..."

"Go ahead and play it," Dave suggested.

"Ohhh..." I tentatively reached out one finger.

"Don't be afraid to touch it. It's yours, honey."

"I can't... it's too beautiful... Oh, honey," I placed my arms around his waist and laid my cheek on his chest, "Thank you... Thank you so much... I just love it."

*　　*　　*

Dave doesn't care for big parties. He'd rather be with family or a few friends. So we let our Muskegon family know that the only anniversary party we wanted was a dinner out with them at a fine restaurant. We enjoyed that on a Saturday night.

As a compromise, the next day Shelley and Tom hosted coffee and cake after church at Northland UMC. Then we hoped that they would join us in flying out to Arizona so we could all visit together with the Cormany family. They agreed, so the Watkins family – Tom, Shelley, Amy and Emily – flew out with us to visit with our other daughter's family, the Cormanys: Bill, Ann, Kendal, Alden, Byron and Grant. We had a wonderful time together.

The Cormanys had a beautiful home in the hills overlooking the city of Phoenix. It was enough just to sit on their roof-top balcony and watch the evening sky as lights twinkled on all over the city against the mountains in the background. The kids had a splashing good time in their pool.

There is a lot to do in Arizona. Bill and Ann drove us out through the canyons, the desert areas and the city of Sedona. Tom's treat was to board the special visitor's train in the town of Williams, bound for the Grand Canyon.

Local actors staged a dramatic "shoot-out" in the corral, hijacked the train and faked a "train robbery" along the way. We stayed overnight at the canyon and traveled the tram up and down to gape at the sights. Tom, an avid photographer, took hundreds of pictures. He and I walked as far down as we dared on the canyon trail while the others wimped out on park benches. We knew that the hike back up the trail wouldn't be so easy.

Wonderful as that trip was, Dave and I weren't through celebrating. We had been saving our frequent flyer points for four years, enough for two first-class flights to Australia, returning by way of New Zealand.

Contrasted with a coach experience, the airplane ride was a highlight. Flying first class, before the airlines got into their current cash crunch, was the way it ought to be. I had never encountered treatment like this except in novels. We had our own personal butler; complete with black uniform and white towel draped over one arm. He served us with everything from gourmet four course meals with champagne and two kinds of wine to first run movies, books and every current magazine available. We received our own amenities kit and comfortable knit pajamas with footies. While we were changing, our butler made up our beds, then tucked us in at night and woke us gently in the morning with steaming coffee and a full course breakfast in bed. After breakfast the captain came out to meet us and posed for pictures. *Oh my. Sigh.*

* * *

The world-wide meeting of the International Deacons and Diaconal Ministers is held every four years. I had been scheduled to attend four years earlier when it was held in North America. However, that convocation was canceled because of the Lockerbie, Scotland airliner bombing and subsequent terrorist threats. This was my last chance to attend. The week-long event was held in Brisbane, Australia.

Dave and I had a room at an inn and took a bus into the campus every day. I met other deacons from every continent, in small and large group meetings, heard speakers from many places, and attended worship every day. We could don earphones and listen in our own language, just like the United Nations.

I learned that the difference in the title and ritual that my church had struggled over for so many years actually means very little. The work is the same: service to the Church and the World. Perhaps, just perhaps, this movement can save the world, but the conflict and struggle are far from over.

Leaving the meeting refreshed and reinvigorated, Dave and I rented a car and a cell phone and set out to enjoy the remainder of our two month long celebration. July is winter in Australia, so we headed north into the more tropical areas. We found no shortage of motels and hotels.

Our US dollars had converted into Aussie money at almost a two to one exchange rate, two of theirs for one of ours. What a great time to be an American in Australia!

The host country was more than welcoming and hospitable. Natives could spot us immediately by our manners and accent. We encountered no other Americans. I suppose they would be more likely to vacation here during the Aussie summers when it is warm in the southern half of the country.

Because we toured northward from Brisbane, the weather was perfect for us: sunny with highs in the 80's. We wandered like gypsies, stopping when we felt like it, moving on when we felt like it. A side benefit of winter is that there are no jellyfish in the ocean. Thus, we particularly enjoyed our snorkeling trips out to the Great Barrier Reef.

We had scheduled a two week stopover in New Zealand, planning to tour the country by auto. By now, Dave was quite adept at driving on the left hand side of the road and negotiating traffic circles. We planned to start in the North and fly to the south island for the remainder of our trip, hoping to see whales, penguins and mountains.

Our time here had barely begun when we woke up in a lovely spot on an ocean-side bay on September 11, 2001. The horrible events of that day were being broadcast on every television set in every roadside café. It was a unique experience, being Americans, a half-world away from home, when your beloved homeland is attacked. We were starved for news and stayed up late at night glued to CNN.

The Kiwis[60] treated us like a bereaved part of their own family, with hotels offering us free meals and unlimited access to computers. As in Australia, the natives were able to spot us immediately due to our accents. We seemed to fill a need that they had to express their condolences directly to an American. Unlike the notion of the "Ugly American" being reviled throughout the world, both the Aussies and the Kiwis love Americans and count themselves among our staunchest allies.

The Aussies remember well how the American Navy rescued them during World War II. Their war memorials are prominent landmarks of those battles. Of course, there were New Zealanders killed in the Twin Towers too, so parts of the local broadcasts were spent in counting those losses.

Our New Zealand vacation was curtailed somewhat by events, but we still managed to visit some of the countryside and watch penguins returning from their treks at sea. Except for a one day tour, we bypassed the mountains. That day was somewhat of a bust because the mountain we visited was shrouded in fog.[61]

Airplanes back to America were grounded for most of our remaining time in New Zealand, but were up and running on the day of our scheduled departure. Setting foot on American soil for the first time set our hearts to beating faster. "Do you think we would look too foolish kissing the ground?" I asked.

I would go back to Australia and New Zealand in a heartbeat, but we had other things to do first.

*   *   *

---

[60] Colloquial term for New Zealanders, after the Kiwi bird.

[61] More about our 50th anniversary year can be found in my scrapbooks.

Chapter Forty-Seven

"Miscellaneous Other Careers"

"Gemini persons tend to be restless, intellectual folks...they seem so fickle...great wit...ferocious temper...does not last long...ability to accomplish goals in the face of many obstructions..."[62]

For those of you who dabble in astrology, being born in June meant that I was a "Gemini," the twins. Not that I am a believer in that, but the description of a Gemini does fit me rather remarkably well in some respects.

When I reached retirement age, one of my private jokes was that I was 65 years old before I figured out what I wanted to be. Now, in my 77th year, I wonder if I'll ever figure it out. Not all of my careers have embraced some aspect of music, but those that I loved most certainly did.

Two of my minor careers bear mentioning: piano tuning and playing jazz.

When we moved up to Canadian Lakes, I had to leave my favorite piano tuner behind. He didn't need to roam that far afield to find customers. So, my natural reaction was to teach myself how to tune. Perhaps this harked back to my growing-up years when I learned how to take the keys of our old upright piano apart and put them back together. My mother was astonished, by the way.

Some research led me to "The American School of Piano Tuning", which offered a correspondence course. For some three hundred dollars, I sent away for it. Luckily, it wasn't a sham. Each chapter covered a different aspect of tuning and directions for how to practice on your own instrument. At the end of each chapter, you took a self-administered quiz and mailed it in for grading. After several weeks of learning, I received a graduation certificate and license to purchase supplies.

---

[62] www.astrologyindepth.com/Gemini

After practicing on my own and Shelley's piano a few times, I was ready to put out my shingle. In time, I garnered enough customers to satisfy, in and around Canadian Lakes. It wasn't a way to get rich, but it added to my incomes from teaching, directing, being President of Swains Lake Farm, Inc. and Mercer Publications, Inc., and working for the church.

According to my understanding of the definition of a deacon, I was providing service to the world. Many the beat-up, old upright was rescued and restored to its best possible condition by me. I was fussy about perfection and spent as much as four or five hours tuning and re-tuning until each string was tuned just right. People raved that their piano had never sounded this good before, and it was true. Most owners don't realize how vital a tuning is to the overall sound. When finished, I often sat and played a while, because there is nothing so joyous to a pianist as a freshly tuned piano. It reminds me of a kitty-cat with a new box of litter.

*   *   *

Dave laughed that I had always had a dream of playing in a bar. Well, we didn't quite play in bars, but our jazz group, the "Take Five Trio", got around just the same. We named ourselves after a Dave Brubeck number that was supposed to be our theme song, but after playing it together a few times, Dennis Cox, our resident jazz aficionado, vetoed the number. Dennis is discriminating and very particular about playing things right. Still, the name suited us, so we kept it.

The "Take Five Trio" consisted of three instrumentalists (the trio) and two vocalists, making us five altogether. In addition to Dennis on percussion, Jim Thompson on bass, and me on keyboard, we had Elaine Cox and Tom Shafer as vocalists.

No matter what group I have joined, it seems as if it always fell to me to be the organizer. I've been kidded about that and it is largely accurate. I kept the records for our trio, organizing rehearsals, acting as librarian, obtaining copies of music and making notebooks for each member.

We played in restaurants, clubhouses, open air venues and

an occasional wedding. Our repertoire grew to 150 numbers. It fell to me to rehearse with Jim and with the vocalists separately. It was very little different from my teaching of students.

Once Jim, Elaine and Tom were fairly well along in their progress, we would rehearse with Dennis and with Dave, who served as our sound technician. I loved to perform, but by the time Jim moved away I was growing tired of the organizing and teaching.

"Geminis seek stimulating experiences, and although being somewhat intellectual in nature, they can get bored and lose their interest..."[63] We had stayed together for two or three years. It was a good time to quit.

* * *

---

[63] www.astrologyindepth.com/Gemini

Chapter Forty-Eight

"We Also Serve Who Carry Music Stands"

Accustomed to standing by while his wife greeted her admirers after a particularly fine performance, Dave had a standard reply to the oft repeated query, "Dave, your wife, Dorothy, is so blah, blah, blah; do you sing or play a musical instrument?" In reply he readily quipped, "No, I don't, but we also serve who carry music stands."

Indeed, Dave seemed to have married into a musical family. His wife and daughters, his elder daughter's husband and their two daughters all played wonderfully and sang a bit as well. Dave played the clarinet in high school, but he gave it away after he left school and never picked it up again. Instead, he enjoyed being the "techie", ferrying instruments and sound equipment around to gigs and running everything from sound and lights to cameras, errands, fixit missions and coffee breaks.

Dave claimed to be unable to sing. Just once, I was successful in persuading him to join in one of my choirs. I promised, "If you will sing this once, I will never beg you again", and he did, and I didn't. I praised him, "You worked hard, Honey, and you did Ok, really you did," but one time satisfied me and cured him of ever giving in to that impulse again.

There may have been times when I envied those other couples who had the delight of making music together. But then I would quip, "One temperamental starving musician in a family is enough. Someone has to pay the bills and keep things running smoothly". Many times I counted my lucky stars that I had a wonderful "techie" sidekick like Dave who could and would do anything for me, without whom I could not put on a show.

*   *   *

Chapter Forty-Nine

"Assessor's Plat of Swains Lake"

"Gemini's dualist nature makes them able to find great forgiveness where others seem to hold on to the hurt."[64]

After the trial was settled, work resumed on the assessor's plat at its usual snail's pace. Once again, Kaye, the engineer, and I became telephone buddies. We were beginning to see the light at the end of the tunnel, but there was much left to do.

The six pages of plat maps had to be perfected through draft after draft. Many little legal details had to be corrected such as whether an "out-lot" could be called a "walkway", or whether a drainage easement could be shown on the plat.

A "biggie" was the fact that Swains Lake Drive, the country road through the development, wasn't in the same place as the recorded legal description showed it to be.

After Kaye and I had done all we could, the plat was submitted to the State of Michigan. Several months were required as they discovered minutiae, little things that needed changing in order to fit their statutes. These issues were referred back to Kaye and cleared away, one by one. Sometimes she had to change the simple wording and sometimes she had to consult me. It was important to reach a condition that was as close to perfect as possible, because little mistakes can come back to haunt you years later.

I was not sure we would all live to see the day when the plat would grind its way through all the steps. It was a good thing that our ancestors were long-lived. The youngest of my siblings was just one year from retirement when the plat finally reached the end of the line in June 2003, eleven and one half years after Mother's death. The last one to receive it was the assessor himself, John Hancock. It was a feeling of great accomplishment and relief.

---

[64] www.astrologyindepth.com/Gemini

At last, the Hancock sword no longer hung over my head. We could sell as many lots as our hearts desired.

Mr. Hancock set about issuing new tax numbers and new appraisals for the 76 lots in the plat. His failure to follow the rules made a mess of things that would take me more than six years to straighten out, as I'm still not finished with property tax appeals. That would come later.

*   *   *

SLF, Inc. had been preparing for this day. We had hired a professional licensed property appraiser to appraise our land in great detail. It had been updated eight months before the Assessor's Plat was recorded. Phil Baldwin, our company attorney had worked closely with us in devising a plan for offering the leased lots for sale to the lessees.

We offered the lots for sale to the current lessees at 10% off the appraised price, providing they made a decision to buy within six months. Mr. Baldwin felt that our offer was clear, prudent and fair enough that, should we be sued any judge would be hard-pressed to find fault with our policy. His advice proved to be golden because we were never sued over that policy.

During the first year after the plat was recorded (from July 1, 2003 to early 2004) we closed most of the cases. Only a handful of leases remained, but they were the tough ones.

Anxious to try selling myself, I was looking forward to the day when our contract with our realtor expired. Since then, we have sold one or two pieces every year. A slow pace helps a bit with the taxes as it spreads our income over the years. Just this year, in 2009, we have closed on $83,000 of sales. Anna is celebrating because we just got rid of the very last lease.

Sometimes I wonder what our mom and dad must think of all that has happened. They struggled so long and hard to support us and themselves on an annual income of $2,000. Before she died, I had promised my mother that I would try to preserve and increase her legacy and the wealth of the farm for her descendants. I shall never forget that the money we made on those sales originally came from her legacy, even though my generation has increased it to a nice fortune.

Thus, I have kept an accounting of how the money was spent. After setting aside educational trusts for each of Dave's and my grandchildren and paying off the mortgages, a large portion was carefully invested at interest. I keep careful watch on that, trying to stay up with inflation without losing principle. Managing my investments has become an occupation.

Swains Lake Farms, Inc. has done well. We still own some lake frontage, the farm acreage, which we have placed in the "Farm Preservation Program", sixty acres of wetlands, including seven acres of "Prairie Fen". It pleases me that Phil Railer, a great grandson of Millie Dodes, is working our farm.

SLF, Inc. has a healthy balance in the bank and still has eleven vacant lots left to sell. This year our goal is to finish rehabbing a lakefront house we have taken back. The company is probably still worth roughly one million dollars, not counting the cash.

Dave has done equally well with his profession and has laid aside a nice nest egg. He and I are each millionaires in our own right. When we rid ourselves of the drain on our resources of Swains Lake Farms, Inc. it was like a close cousin of winning the lottery. Now we could enjoy nice vacations and a new car every few years. We don't deprive ourselves, but we live simply on our earned income and Social Security and still shop at Wal-Mart and Penney's. Both of us still work, but we have cut back a lot. I have retired from everything except the ownership of Mercer Publications & Ministries, Inc. and the presidency of Swains Lake Farms, Inc.

There was one more thing that I had pledged myself to do with the money from Mom's legacy. That was to give a portion to the church to which she and Dad had devoted themselves.

*   *   *

Chapter Fifty

"VIM to ZIM[65] in Africa"

"Gemini people... seek stimulating experiences...curious and inquisitive by nature...if the partner is willing to let them have a social life, Gemini will repay them with love and loyalty."[66]

Northland UMC had worn out their carpet some years ago. In my opinion, the church could use a face lift in order to appear more welcoming to guests. The old timers were used to it and were somewhat inured to the appearance, but guests notice those things immediately.

Interestingly, Dave and I had come to separate conclusions on the matter. Without conferring with each other, we had separately offered to make a large gift toward that end, over and above our regular offering, thinking it would help the church to grow, reflecting our care and concern for the Lord's house. My gift was meant to be a share of my inheritance from Mother.

It was about that time that I had my parting of the ways with Northland church. The pastor never accepted the donations. We severed our ties with the United Methodist Church, but as retired clergy, I still received regular mailings from the Conference.

One day I noticed a line about a volunteer mission trip being planned to Zimbabwe, Africa. It was as if one of those light bulbs went off over my head, thinking elephants, giraffes, lions, safaris, herds of wildebeests and hoards of starving Africans in colorful costumes. What a wonderful opportunity for me to spend the tithe portion of my inheritance for good and have a great trip at the same time!

Wasting no time in telling Dave about it, I plied him with details. Ever the willing partner, Dave allowed me to plow ahead.

---

[65] Volunteers In Mission to Zimbabwe

[66] www.astrologyindepth.com/Gemini

We spent the better part of our spare time for the next year preparing. There were forms to fill out, checks to write, physicals and shots to get,[67] clothes to buy, suitcases to select and meetings to attend.

Some thirty of us would be assigned to the Mutare Mission Hartzell Primary School. Dave was to be a handyman and I was to work in the elementary level home economics class in charge of sewing. Dave had to prepare to work entirely with hand tools. He set out to collect as many as he could cram in two large suitcases, along with his clothes. Our allotment was two 70-pound suitcases apiece, plus one backpack or carry-on. Everything had to fit into those pieces.

My first choice was to teach music and my next choice was to tell stories. So when I was first assigned to sewing class, I was alarmed. I hadn't sewn a stitch since my girls were little. In fact, one of the first chores I got rid of when my budget eased was that of making clothes by hand. But no one else would take it, so I gulped and went along with the assignment.

In typical Dorothy fashion, I threw myself into the project. First, I ordered six sewing machines. Five would be shipped over in a container. One I would carry with me, for demonstration purposes. Then I began shopping online through eBay and others to assemble everything required to outfit a sewing classroom. I bought enough so that each child would have three yards of material plus thread of every color, needles, scissors, pins, seam tape, dozens of patterns, tracing paper and wheels, measuring tape, inner lining, etc. – plus two wedding dresses.

I raided my sister's and daughter's caches of supplies and cleaned out my own. It was amazing what I could buy on eBay. It took the classroom teacher a whole day to inventory the stuff I took. Also, I took 8 ½ × 11 photocopies of our home and some of the places we have been, in case I was asked to give a talk.

Ann and Morris Tabor were in charge of our mission. They had enlisted the Reverands Margie and Gordon Schliecher to

---

[67] Immunization shots for the two of us cost $700.

assist. Dave and I were the elders of the group.

The trip and itinerary were all carefully planned. In addition to working in the classroom every day, several nice sightseeing trips were planned up into the beautiful countryside and western mountains of Zimbabwe, to the affiliated high school and hospital, as well as Africa University and to two other elementary schools. We also went on a day trip to a wild animal preserve where we took jeep tours and spotted many of the animals I had come to see.

It turned out that my pre-conceived image of the people was all wrong. This was a country that had been a colony of the British Empire before it was set free. The official language was English and all spoke it in a very refined accent. The students and faculty were highly intelligent, gifted, bilingual, ambitious, extremely well-behaved and courteous. They dressed in a conservative, European style. We women had been advised to wear skirts to the school and that proved to be correct.

Because of the oppressive dictatorial regime in the capital of Harare, the Zimbabwean economy was in shambles, having been reduced from a prosperous, thriving country under British rule to abject poverty under the cruel new government. It was difficult to tell how they managed to scrape out a living. We encountered women selling weavings and men selling carvings made out of native materials. Wherever possible, we bought what we could take home in order to support them with as much dignity as possible.

Dave and I fell into bed, exhausted at night after a day at the school. We had to skip a few events because we simply couldn't keep up. But it was a life-changing experience we figure we are too old to ever repeat.

A favorite place to visit was the orphanage attached to the Mission. Here the pre-school children ran out to see us and were so happy. They were housed in family style homes with a house mother and assorted children of all ages. On this day the older ones were in school. Notice the thumbs-up sign.

After the two weeks at Mutare, Dave and I had scheduled a week's vacation to Victoria Falls on the Zambezi River. We needed a rest after our intense mission week. There we were able to immerse ourselves in another side of African culture. The lavish hotels were made for tourists, so we could bask in some creature comforts.

We planned one trip each day, including going into the town center to shop for gifts, two trips on the river (where we saw hippos and exotic monkeys, animals and birds), two trips to the world's largest waterfalls (where we hiked the National park path along the mile-wide falls), and a hike across the international bridge to Zambia (where we watched bungee jumpers leaping into a huge deep gorge of the river).

Dinner time shows consisted of African dancers and drummers in exotic costumes. One night we took a drumming class ourselves. I loved it.

Two days were spent on safari, walking with wild lions and riding elephants.

Here I was privileged to ride tandem with one of the few women drivers. Like a lazy riding horse, the elephant, Betsy, made frequent stops to nibble on plants and slurp up mud puddles. My driver developed a strong voice and great muscles in her calves digging in her heels and commanding Betsy to move on. Steering the beast was problematical. Besty responded to frequent rewards when and if she felt like it. Mostly she simply moseyed along following the elephant in front.

It didn't do to follow too closely. Whenever the leading animal cut loose with its effluent the waterfall was truly impressive.

A Park Ranger carrying a fierce-looking firearm accompanied us on the trail in case we were attacked by angry water buffalo. We saw two of the animals glaring at us and monitoring our progress from a nearby grove of trees.

*   *   *

After returning, we compiled a slide show of our great experience, hoping to show it around in churches. I wrote letters to the district office and some churches but never received a reply.

We had one successful showing. A friend of mine invited a group into her home to view the pictures and hear the narration that went with them. We displayed some of the crafts we had brought from Africa. Her guests were fascinated and asked many questions. My friend was happy with the evening and thanked me profusely. Later, one of the guests was inspired to make a nice contribution to a Zimbabwe charity.

Much has been made of how dangerous it is in Zimbabwe. Perhaps that is so, but I never felt unsafe. We were well-protected and very careful. As I have reiterated to all my friends, the only time we encountered someone who couldn't speak English and who made us very uneasy was on the way home in a taxicab in Detroit.

* * *

Chapter Fifty-One

"Grandparents at Play"

"Gemini people really need partners who… can keep up with them"[68]

A lthough we both still work, and probably always will, we definitely have more play time now. Couples that marry will learn to adjust to each other along the way, or the marriage probably won't be really happy and successful.

In our case, the task of planning trips and having fun pretty much falls to me. Dave has learned to "go along and keep up". For the most part, he needs to convince me that he is having fun too, if he knows what side his bread is buttered on. After fifty-eight years, he knows. I've found that it is easier to get Dave to take time to swim, play golf, sightsee, read and enjoy entertainment if we are away from home. So, since we enjoy each other's company best of all, I tend to plan lots of trips.

Many of the fun things we do have a connection with our grandchildren, of course. But since this story is for them, except for broad generalities, I will stay away from those tales, lest they catch me in a fib.

We tend to prefer one of two different types of trips. That would be either staying at our time-share properties, or in our motor home. We keep the motor home housed over the winter. Summer seems too short and there is so much other fun to enjoy that it becomes hard to carve out time to do it all; but we try to get away in the motor home at least once per year, even if it is just a short trip to somewhere in Michigan.

Seven years ago, we bought our first timeshare unit, a one week membership that we planned to use at the Mountain Run Resort at Boyne Mountain Ski Area in Boyne City, Michigan. Mountain Run is owned by Bluegreen Vacation Club which specializes in resorts East of the Mississippi, for the most part.

---

[68] www.astrologyindepth.com/Gemini

Every year since, we have spent a winter week or two at Mountain Run. Skiing is mainly for the young, but that didn't sway us. I love to ski and am thrilled by the ride downhill. I've never been good at it, because I didn't start venturing up and down real hills until age 70. In the 1970's and 1980's, I had started learning at the tiny hill at Canadian lakes, but those runs were closed when the equipment wore out. Long after we moved up to C.L. full time, we started going skiing with some friends, first to Crystal Mountain, then to Caberfae Ski Area. Today, we stay at our

Mountain Run time-share villa and ski for free.

Next, we bought a half week at the Marriott Desert Ridge Timeshare resort in Scottsdale, so we could stay there while visiting the Cormanys. Not that they wouldn't have us, but grandparents need to get their rest.

Next, we used our Bluegreen points to stay at The Fountains in Orlando and The Hammocks in Marathon, Florida. On that trip, we added more points to our Bluegreen membership. We spent three October weeks in Hawaii, at the Marriott on Maui

and the Pone Kai on Kauai. On a six-week spring auto tour, we spent one week at each of six resorts, the Mariott in Panama City, The Fountains in Orlando, The World Golf Resort and other places in Florida, Georgia, Williamsburg, and ending up in Washington D.C.

The WWII Memorial on the Mall was incredibly moving. My tears flowed like wine. In this picture, I managed to dry them just in time to smile for the camera.

We happened to hit Washington D.C. on a perfect day. The Japanese cherry trees were in full bloom around the tidal basin.

On many of our Florida trips, we were able to squeeze in a week at Anna's and Duane's mobile home in Palmetto but it wasn't always possible to arrange that. They have done wonders remodeling Mom and Dad's old mobile home into a charming winter getaway.

This past March, we spent nine days in Marathon, one week in Orlando and a third week in Eastern Tennessee. We have ten days scheduled in Scottsdale in May 2009, a fall week in Boyne Mountain and next March at The Hammocks again.

On our second trip to Hawaii, we stayed on Kauai at the Pone Kai and Marriott again. This time, we bought into Shell Vacation Club, because they have a lot of resorts in Hawaii and the West Coast. Finally, we bought another week in Shell and 15,000 more points in Bluegreen. One hopes we are through buying timeshares.

You may surmise that we enjoy timeshares and that is so. The apartments are more private and have more room than motels or hotels. They come with complete kitchens, which suits us because Dave loves to cook and we prefer to eat our own meals. The clientele are all owners, so there is a friendly atmosphere. The well-trained staff tends to add to that.

We discovered that there is a whole world of timeshare facilities out there. One can make an exchange through one of two international exchange clubs to any timeshare resort in the world. Most are located in resort areas and there are not many in the big cities. That suits us fine as we generally avoid big cities, if possible.

The annual maintenance fees and club dues add up to a goodly amount, but once you have invested in the club, it is worth it. We can leave the timeshares to our kids, if they want them. That doesn't cover it all, but you get the idea. I like to travel.

Among my favorite things to do alone around home is to read, walk, work-out, putter around in the yard, take care of my plants, play the piano and e-mail my kids. Favorite things to do with Dave are to watch pro basketball, play cribbage or euchre and square dance.

Dave likes to tell people that I read a book a day and play the piano two hours a day. That is a slight exaggeration, but it is close. There is no question that I have gotten behind on both of those activities since I started this book.

Also, we love to go to our cottage. It is situated on a quiet little lake which is just the right size to canoe around on a still evening as the sun goes down. One of the neat things about that location is that we enjoy both sunrises and sunsets, not necessarily on the same day. Michigan has the most beautiful sunsets in the world.

You could say that, in part, I am a trailblazer. On the farm, we have built a woodland trail and wetlands trails. One of my jobs while at the cottage is to maintain and use the trails. They are so peaceful,[69] with wild grasses and flowers, shrubs and tall, canopied trees. At the risk of repeating a cliché, 'tis said that, "You can take the girl out of the farm, but you can't take the farm out of the girl." In my case, it has certainly proven to be true.

---

[69] Except for the occasional bee sting and poison ivy.

A pair of sand-hill cranesreturns every year to nest in thewetlandss in front of our cottage on Gregory Lake. 'Tis said that only mature pairs can successfully raise two off-spring.

Dave and I enjoy observing them and consider them the next best thing to pets of our own. Here you see the parents proudly parading their two offspring in our yard for us to admire, as if to say, "See what we have done."

Gregory Lake is still and beautiful at any time of day. There is always work to do when you own a cottage. There is no need to overdo, however. A quick dip in the lake is most refreshing after a trail-hike or a few hours of work.

Since we have owned the cottage on Gregory Lake, I have explored most of the farmland owned by SLF, Inc[70]. and much of

---

[70] Swains Lake Farms, Inc.

the wetlands. I have the scratches and bee-stings to show for it; but have never been in serious peril. I can't say the same for my [sometimes] foolhardy husband.

One day, in an attempt to discover where our boundary line lies, we set out together to explore the far western edge of the property. This is an isolated section of wooded wetlands that borders on the lake with a stream along one side. The time was late winter. Dave was wearing hip boots and heavy clothing. A mile from the nearest occupied house, we relied on our own devices since there was no cell phone service.

Walking was difficult in this terrain. I soon fell behind as I took extra time skirting the muddy-mucky areas that Dave plowed right through. A mantle of ice covered the swamp grass alongside the stream. Dave soon discovered that it was much easier to walk on the ice than to stumble over rough terrain and fallen limbs in the woods. My warning to him went unheeded. "Stay off the ice," I cautioned.

"No problem," he shrugged, "I won't fall through. Besides if I break through there is nothing but ground underneath. I'll be fine." (Famous last words.)

No sooner had I turned toward him than he broke through the ice. "Oops, you were right." He grabbed for a limb which broke off. Within seconds he had sunk in to his waist, arms flailing in the air.

My heart stopped. Quickly assessing the danger, I hastened to position myself as close as possible. He was just a few feet from a large tree with sturdy roots. I hung on with one hand and reached out with the other. We grasped hands. I pulled and he pushed. No dice. He merely sunk lower. We tried to pull out one foot at a time. Oops, no dice. The suction of the muck was holding him like quicksand.

Horrible images went through my mind of tales of people slowly sinking out of sight in quicksand. We struggled in this way for a time until we were both gasping for breath.

Why is it that at times like this, the more alarmed I become the more he tries to calm me down?

"No problem," he declared. "I'll be out of here in a jiffy. Not to worry."

I didn't dare to leave him for I knew perfectly well we had to get out of this mess by ourselves as soon as possible before he either went into shock or sank out of sight. I cautioned him to rest a minute while I began gathering as many dead branches as I could from the surrounding forest. I had no tools except for the thermos cup of coffee hanging on my belt. I gave Dave the hot coffee.

I began laying a thick platform of branches from Dave to the edge of the mucky area, ending at the tree. As it built up, the branches gave him something more solid to push against. Finally I leaped up and grabbed hold of a live tree branch. It had to be strong enough to hold us. I pulled it down and used some saplings to tie it into place.

"All right, Dave, we're ready. Here is what you are going to do:" (For once he paid attention.) "You are going to test these branches and see if they will hold up your arms and chest. I want you to stretch out your arms toward me and carefully lay your chest on these branches. Ok?"

"Got it."

"Then we are going to try to lever your feet out of the boots. You want to end up lying level on the surface. I'm going to hold on to this branch while you grab my other hand and pull. Ok?

"Yeah," he grunted. "I hope this works."

"Now which one of your legs feels the most mired in?"

"My right one."

"That's good," I lied. "Now we are going to try to pull out the left one first. Got it?"

"Got it."

"Ok, grab on. Here we go. I'll count three and we'll heave together. One… two… three… heave!"

"Ugh!"

"Ugh!"

"Did it move a little?"

"Maybe a little"

"All right, that's good. Take a half minute break and we'll try again……. One, two, three, heave!"

"Ugh!"

"Ugh!"

"Break… Whew… Are you putting as much weight as you can on the branches?"

"Not enough, maybe."

I gathered some more branches, as large as I could find. "How's that?" I asked.

"Yeah, I think that is better. I'll try laying out on these."

"Good. Here we go again. Ready? One, two, three, heave!"

There was a sucking sound. I groaned. He moaned. Out came a horribly black slimy leg. "Yeah! You're halfway there," I cheered. "Now keep that leg on top. Be careful you don't let it go back in. Let's see if you can scooch a little closer so you can grab onto this limb. We gave a mighty heave. I pulled on the limb and he got hold of it with one hand. I pulled on the other. With all our strength we got the other leg out. He rapidly crawled the rest of the way and collapsed on the bank.

Now bootless and barefoot, he was too cold to shiver. I quickly shed my boots and gave him my socks to put on. He couldn't fit into my boots. I covered him with my coat and stuck his big hands partially into my mittens. "I'm going after the car. You start out if you can." I set off on a dead run through the forest, dodging deadfalls, heading for the trail.

Once on the trail I could go much faster. Still I had up to ¾ of a mile to cover before I got to our house. My lungs were screaming. I quickly threw a couple blankets into the car and sped to the end of the road to the trailhead. Leaving the car running and heater blasting on high, I took off through the woods toward the last place I left him.

We met up about halfway. He leaned on me, sputtering all the while, as we made our way to the car. I wrapped him in a blanket and tucked him in. Arriving at the house, I drove right up on the lawn to the front door, hurried into the house and turned on the shower, before returning to assist him out of the car to the house and into the shower, clothes and all. By now we were both laughing. He looked like a "Creature from the Lost Lagoon", covered with black goo.

We never returned to retrieve Dave's lost boots. Someday in the future an archeologist may uncover them as artifacts of a lost civilization. Maybe they will keep digging and looking for bones.

* * *

Chapter Fifty-Two

"Small Recognitions and Large Blessings"

The years of doing the Memorial Day Service for Canadian Lakes were a time of both blessing and recognition for me. It was an opportunity to speak to the community through my skills, gifts and love. Invariably, the people returned that love with praise, applause and sometimes tears. For once in my life, I knew when to quit – that is, at the top of my game, instead of waiting until I got kicked out, one way or another.

During this year since my retirement from chairing the Memorial Day Service, I've heard many nice compliments from people in the community whenever I go out and about.

t

At the final performance, I was given a standing ovation and a dozen red roses by two of the veterans in the show who had appreciated what I had done. I knew it was symbolic of all their feelings.

Within a couple of weeks the new chair and her committee will take over, which is as it should be. Now that my time is over, it seems right to sit back and write my memoirs.

Another recognition that I have received is to be listed in Who's Who in American Women for six years. In the next edition, I will be listed in Who's Who Finance and Business, Who's Who In America, as well as Who's Who in the World. That is nice, too.

When I was young, I was driven to "be somebody", to accomplish something. At the end of the day, when I took stock of the day's activities, if I hadn't accomplished something, I felt that I had wasted the day. Now, if a *week* goes by when I haven't accomplished something, I merely let it go.

Perhaps that is a blessing, too.

*   *   *

The End of this story.

But there is more... please turn the page...

Postlude

"Gemini people are natural storytellers... [their] memory is less exacting... [they may have a] tendency to alter the original story in a way that makes it more appealing..."[71]

In an attempt to make a better story out of my life, there have been times when I have added dialogue and/or action to make the story come alive. In every case, I have examined my memory, and then checked with Dave. I might say to him, "Honey, I don't remember exactly what was said, but can you believe it would have gone something like this?" or, "Dave, do you think that dialogue sounds like her or him, like something he or she would have said in that situation?" He would give me his opinion. Most of the time he would say, "Oh yes!" If he suggested changes, I heeded his advice.

I tried not to be critical of living persons. If it was essential to the story, I omitted or changed their names or used an initial. If persons have gone on to his-or-her reward, I figured that they didn't care much anymore.

For others who take exception to certain facets of the story, feel free to write your own book. I don't particularly want to know. I did my very best.

Perhaps you might wonder why I chose to write about certain things and omitted others. It wasn't possible to write everything that happened to me unless I filled an entire bookshelf. Who would want to read that? I wrote about happenings that struck me as important to my life, incidents that I remember clearly, that profoundly affected me at the time, and that might be interesting or humorous. It wasn't possible to put them in chronological order, such as a diary, but I did my best to make some sense out of it.

This book has been a revelation to me. I learned that normally I am a person who, first, suffers greatly when hurt or wronged, then forgives, forgets and moves forward without

---

[71] www.astrologyindepth.com/Gemini

looking back. I can't take pride in that, but as you can see, that is the way of Gemini people. I wanted to be somebody and do something lasting and worthwhile with my life. Doesn't everyone? Having muddled through to this point, I can look backward and see a pattern and a purpose to it. Best of all, perhaps someday I can forgive myself for having accomplished so little.

That's pretty darned great!

Dorothy Mercer

May 15, 2009

Epilogue

May 16, 2009

After finishing my memoirs in 35 days, spending one day editing, and sleeping on it for one night, I realize I only mentioned Dave's mother once or twice. Perhaps that may seem like a glaring omission as this book included significant people in my life. Was Altha Mae Mercer, née McDonald, significant? Oh, my yes! The last thing one can say about her is that she was insignificant. By default, she taught me one important characteristic that was totally absent from my upbringing: Altha was an exceedingly strong-willed person. She got things done in her household and in her small town. She tried to micro-manage her family and did quite well at it. When it came to her micro-managing of Dave and me, I grew to resent it.

I was raised by parents who were the direct opposite of Altha in terms of their parenting style. Knowing nothing else, during my first years of marriage, I was dumbfounded by Altha's approach. The more I tried to be polite, courteous, quiet, and accommodating to her directions, the more she took charge. She must have meant well, but it was just her way. She believed that people were either strong or weak: The strong led and the weak followed. I was weak, so it made perfect sense for her to lead her son and give me directions too. It was her calling as a person and as a mother.

After two decades of gnashing my teeth, I grew up. I realized that the way to get along with Altha was to change myself. She wouldn't change. In time, she taught me through experience and observation how to be as strong as she was when I needed to be, without losing touch with my softer side. After that, we got along quite well, all things considered. Oh, she never completely quit sharing her opinions and never stopped trying, but Dave and I learned to take it in stride and laugh about it.

We called her "Mom" or "Mom Mercer". There are a great many intelligent, generous and kind qualities of hers that I could write about Mom Mercer as a person. She made a favorable impact on her town and all who knew her. When I conducted her burial service, I spoke about those things.

From my point of view (married to her son), Mom Mercer was the stereotypical mother-in-law. Enough said for now. But, I can imagine writing her story. Can't you?

* * *

Mother snapped my picture in the back yard of our farm home.
(What do you suppose has happened to my waistline?)

White orchid bouquet.
Newlyweds: Mr. and Mrs. David N. Mercer.
In the background:
The Rev. Chauncy Green, officiating, Allan Rufe, groomsman,
Joe Owens, groomsman.

Wedding cake cost a whopping $35. That included a groom's cake.

Front row: Jessic Donald, née Corey, David's grandmother;
Altha Mae Mercer, née McDonald, David's mother;
Esther Elizabeth Douglas, née Dodes, Dorothy's mother;
Lloyd E Mercer, David's father;
Leon Luther Douglas, Dorothy's father;
Dorothy May Mercer, née Douglas, bride;
David Neal Mercer, groom;
Anna Marie Douglas, bride's sister, maid of honor;
Dorothy Eberly, bride's friend;
Marilyn Ossenheimer, bride's friend;
Back row:
Harry McLeod, best man; George McDonald, David's grandfather

Appendix I

"The United Methodist Church Struggles with Orders"

The United Methodist church went through a long struggle before they ordained women. Perhaps half of the clergy are women now, and women have risen to the highest office, that of Bishop.

The next great struggle came over the question of what to do about professional lay people. For centuries the best route was for them to become ordained elders and simply be Rev. So-and-so, Minister of Music, or Principal of the School or Administrator, or head of the Hospital or Dean of Seminary, or whatever. The only way to receive proper recognition, pay and protection was to be ordained.

The church struggled over the definition of ordination and the difference between Ministries of the Word and Sacraments and Ministries of Service. The debate raged for decades through books, articles, editorials, commentaries, sermons and white papers. The final decision would be made by the highest authority, the General Conference, but it would be thoroughly debated and worked over by the committee system, far and wide, before proposals came before General Conference.

The mother church attempted to define the lay professional church worker by instituting certification in several areas of service, such as music, administration, Christian education and evangelism. Church secretaries had their own organization. Methodists have always been good at organizing. After all, that's the origin of their name.[72]

In time, committees were formed to draw up criteria and design a curriculum. United Methodist schools and seminaries were perfectly equipped to offer the classes. It was a good way to motivate and educate church professionals to a higher level of performance and commitment. Soon brochures and invitations

---

[72] their superior method

landed on desks and bulletin boards in local churches all over. Wasn't it logical for employees who were so much better equipped to expect to be rewarded?

Perhaps in response to the prevailing pattern in corporate America, the mother church began feeling the pressure to change from a hierarchal system to a collegial system. The question became: Is one of the spiritual gifts somehow better than another, or are all spiritual gifts of equal rank in God's kingdom? Or: Are the ministries of Word and Sacrament somehow higher than ministries of Service, or should they be of equal rank?

There were strong proponents on both sides, each trying to exert their influence; each looking for scriptural support for their position. The debate was as old as time. The hierarchal people had history and practice on their side. The system of starting as a deacon and then moving up to elder and bishop had worked well for hundreds of years. The two levels of ordination were deacon and elder. Bishops were at the top of the hierarchy. They were elected from among the elders and consecrated to their task.

Proponents of the collegial system had the example of Jesus Christ on their side. That was difficult to dispute. But the old ways do not die easily and the church changes inch by painful inch. Those with power and prestige are loath to give it up. And the local church is the last to get the message. Some never do – they simply carry on as usual.

If you, dear reader, have waded through the previous information, thank you and please forgive me for boring you. It seemed essential that I try to explain the power struggle going on in the church, to show that I was merely caught up in the fallout.

Indeed, I hope that you have seen, through my story, that I became a trailblazer, working hard and giving much to mentor those coming after me, believing that I was laying the groundwork for the next generation. I hoped that my efforts to promote understanding would pave a much smoother path for those who followed in the ministries of service, whether those ministries were called "Diaconal Ministry" or the "Ministry of the Permanent Deacon".

During my tenure, there was a vast reservoir of resentment and fear of this ancient but upstart form of ministry among some of the powerful bishops, many of the older clergy and some of the laity. Also, there was still a large residue of prejudice against women in any form of ministry. I was getting it from all sides. The better my work the more opposition I gathered. Sadly, much of the laity remains in the dark.

*   *   *

Who's Who Awards:
> In American Women
> In Finance and Business
> In America
> In the World

Other Awards:
> Valedictorian
> Outstanding Achievement in Music
> Associate of Music
> Bachelor of Music – Summa cum Laude
> Pi Kappa Lambda – High Academic Achievement Society
> Certified Director of Music
> Diaconal Minister of Music
> The Order of Deacon

Favorite Charities:

> WWII: World War II Memorial
> National Law Enforcement Memorial
> Paralyzed Veterans of America
> VFW: Veterans of Foreign Wars
> Troops Need You
> Help Hospitalized Veterans
> Paralyzed Veterans of America
> Wounded Warriors Foundation
> USO: United Service Organizations
> United American Patriots Legal Defense Fund
> National Law Enforcement Memorial Fund
> Law Enforcement Legal Defense Fund
> Michigan Police Commanders Association
> Michigan Fraternal Order of Police
> Michigan Fund for Concerns of Police Survivors
> WMU: Western Michigan University School of Music
> Mecosta General Hospital Foundation
> March of Dimes
> Habitat for Humanity

Arbor Day Foundation
The Nature Conservancy
Mid Michigan Land Conservancy
United Methodist – Zimbabwe Volunteers in Mission –
Youth Education & Relief
American Heart Association
Relay for Life – American Cancer Society Foundation
Salvation Army
Thin Blue Line of Michigan

Made in the USA
Charleston, SC
06 August 2015